U.S. Immigration Policy
in an Age of Rights

DATE DUE

U.S. Immigration Policy in an Age of Rights

Debra L. DeLaet

PRAEGER

Westport, Connecticut
London

Library of Congress Cataloging-in-Publication Data

DeLaet, Debra L., 1968–
    U.S. immigration policy in an age of rights / Debra L. DeLaet.
    p. cm.
  Includes bibliographical references and index.
  ISBN 0–275–96733–6 (alk. paper)
  ISBN 0–275–96764–6 (pbk. : alk. paper)
  1. United States—Emigration and immigration—Government policy.
I. Title.
  JV6271 .D45 2000
  325.73—dc21   99–15396

British Library Cataloguing in Publication Data is available.

Library of Congress Catalog Card Number: 99–15396
ISBN: 0–275–96733–6
    0–275–96764–6 (pbk.)

First published in 2000

Praeger Publishers, 88 Post Road West, Westport, CT 06881
An imprint of Greenwood Publishing Group, Inc.
www.praeger.com

Printed in the United States of America

The paper used in this book complies with the
Permanent Paper Standard issued by the National
Information Standards Organization (Z39.48–1984).

10 9 8 7 6 5 4 3 2 1

To my husband, Todd, for always believing in me

Contents

Figures and Tables

Acknowledgments

I owe a great deal of gratitude to many people who helped me along the way with this book. I have had a number of wonderful teachers, during my primary and secondary schooling in the Versailles, Ohio, school system, my undergraduate education at Miami University, and, finally, in graduate school at the University of Notre Dame. So many wonderful teachers have touched my life that I will not try to mention each of you individually out of fear that I might forget someone inadvertently. Just know that you have encouraged me, pushed me to improve, made me believe in my abilities, and helped to shape my moral compass. For all of these things, I will always be grateful. Your example taught me that what teachers do genuinely makes a difference, and so gladly I have joined your ranks!

My advisors and mentors at the University of Notre Dame deserve special thanks for their help on this project. Alan Dowty gave me excellent advice while also allowing me the freedom to develop intellectually on my own. Sharon O'Brien, with warmth and a sense of humor, demonstrated to me that I could pursue my career goals while still keeping a perspective on what is important in life. To all of the faculty in the Department of Government and International Studies and the Kroc Institute for International Peace Studies at the University of Notre Dame, thank you for providing a supportive and stimulating intellectual environment that also challenges students to confront fundamental moral issues in world politics.

I want to give a special thanks to my colleagues in the Department of Politics and International Relations at Drake University. All of you have made my transition from graduate school to the world of college teaching and research a smooth and enjoyable one. You have been incredibly supportive, and I have grown as a teacher-scholar with help from all of you. In particular, I want to thank David Skidmore for his careful reading of earlier versions of this manuscript. His keen insights and suggestions helped to make this a better piece of scholarship. I also want to thank my students at Drake University, who challenge me and make me grateful that I am in this profession.

Finally, I would be remiss if I failed to thank my family and friends who are my anchor in life. My parents, Jack and Sandy DeLaet, have given me unconditional love and encouragement. Along with my parents, my siblings and their significant others and families bring continuous laughter into my life and remind me not to take myself too seriously, either in success or failure. My in-laws also have been a source of joy and support. Last but certainly not least, I want to thank my husband, Todd Knoop, who always has believed in me even when I haven't believed in myself.

Chapter 1

Domestic Politics, Liberal Ideas, and U.S. Immigration Policy

THE POLITICS OF IMMIGRATION POLICY IN AN AGE OF RIGHTS

U.S. immigration policy is being made in an age of rights.[1] Civil rights have been a central part of the discourse shaping the debate over U.S. immigration policy since at least the 1960s. Prior to this time, widespread racism made a restrictive national immigration policy politically viable. However, since the 1960s, the idea that fairness and non-discrimination should fundamentally shape U.S. immigration policy has predominated in the immigration policy debate in this country. As a result, the U.S. government has faced increased difficulty in passing effective restrictions on either illegal or legal immigration.

To say that U.S. immigration policy is being made in an age of rights is not to say that U.S. immigration policy is completely fair, just, or conducive to the protection of immigrant rights. Indeed, immigrant advocacy groups typically criticize U.S. immigration policy for failing to adequately protect the rights of either U.S. citizens who are ethnic minorities or legal residents, illegal immigrants, and potential migrants. The claim being advanced here is not that U.S. immigration policy is perfectly just. In fact, U.S. immigration policy is often unjust, unfair, and discriminatory in its application. Nevertheless, in recent decades, civil rights discourse has been a fundamental factor in determining the policy alternatives available to the U.S. government in its efforts to regulate immigration.

The growing importance of civil rights rhetoric in the debate over U.S. immigration policy has been accompanied by, and has contributed to, rising numbers of both legal and illegal immigrants. Since the 1960s, approximately 150,000 to 200,000 illegal immigrants have entered the United States each year.

Though reliable estimates of illegal immigration prior to this time are not available, most immigration scholars agree that illegal immigration has increased since 1965.[2] Similarly, there has been a steady rise in legal immigration to this country since the 1960s. While only 3.3 million legal immigrants entered the United States in the 1960s, nearly 4.5 million immigrants entered the United States in the 1970s. In the 1980s, this number rose to over 7 million.

Rising numbers of both legal and illegal immigrants since the 1960s have contributed to the widely accepted perception that immigration is "out of control." Politicians frequently speak of "invasion" when they publicly discuss immigration and increasingly treat immigration as a "national security" concern. Proponents of the North American Free Trade Agreement, signed in 1992, argued that this agreement was in the national interest because it would reduce the economic pressures underlying immigration flows from Mexico by stimulating economic growth in that country.[3] Similarly, President Clinton urged Congress early in 1995 to authorize loan guarantees to Mexico as a means of preventing an increase in illegal immigration across the U.S.-Mexican border after the devaluation of the Mexican peso.[4] The bombing of the World Trade Center in New York in 1994 led many politicians to call for stronger border controls. The Clinton administration advocated U.S. involvement in the return of Jean-Bertrand Aristide to office in Haiti as a means of stemming the flow of Haitian refugees to the United States.[5] As demonstrated by these examples, immigration issues have attained growing salience in policy debates in the United States precisely because many politicians have depicted the government's perceived loss of control of the country's borders as a threat to national security. Not surprisingly, public opinion polls indicate that both the scope and intensity of public support for restrictions on both legal and illegal immigration to the United States have increased in recent decades.[6]

The argument that the U.S. government has lost control of its borders typically is predicated on the assumption that the primary challenges to the effective governmental regulation of international migration come from "the outside." Images of masses of individuals fleeing poverty or political violence in the developing world and overwhelming U.S. border controls underlie this assumption. Moreover, the belief that the U.S. government cannot regulate its borders effectively implies that governmental efforts to exert greater control over immigration have failed.

This analysis of U.S. immigration policy challenges the perception that the U.S. government has lost control of the country's borders. Although U.S. immigration policy in recent decades has not provided the government with an effective tool for restricting immigration, it has not been designed to do so.[7] Instead, the fundamental legislative changes to U.S. immigration policy from the 1960s through the 1980s have been comprised of largely liberal measures that have contributed to an increase in immigration to this country.[8]

The Immigration Reform and Control Act of 1986 (IRCA) was ostensibly restrictive legislation designed to reduce illegal immigration to this country by deterring the employment of undocumented workers. This legislation authorized employer sanctions, penalties against employers who knowingly hire undocumented workers, for the first time in U.S. history. However, in order to gain the political support necessary for the passage of employer sanctions legislation, IRCA also included provisions designed to protect the due process rights of employers, to ensure that the labor needs of agricultural employers would continue to be met, to prevent discrimination against ethnic minorities entitled to work in the United States, and to make illegal immigrants who had resided in this country for several years eligible for legalization.

The Immigration Act of 1990 also can be characterized as liberal legislation. This act expanded the number of legal immigration visas available for family reunification and occupational preferences as well as for individuals from countries that have been underrepresented in immigration flows to the United States in recent years. Although Congress introduced the most significant immigration restrictions in years when it passed both illegal immigration reform and welfare reform legislation in 1996, it is not clear that either piece of legislation will enable the government to restrict illegal immigration effectively. Moreover, the system for admitting legal immigrants that was instituted in the Immigration Act of 1990 remains largely intact. In sum, U.S. immigration policy in recent decades has not provided for strong, effective measures to reduce illegal immigration and, at the same time, explicitly authorizes high levels of legal immigration. Thus, high levels of immigration to this country since the 1960s essentially reflect the basic provisions of U.S. immigration policy.

A consideration of domestic political factors is crucial in explaining why the government has adopted liberal immigration policies in spite of widespread public support for a reduction in immigration to this country. Although public opinion favoring immigration restrictions has grown in recent years, in both scope and intensity, Americans still do not view immigration as one of the nation's top policy priorities.[9] In addition, James G. Gimpel and James R. Edwards, Jr. have shown that immigration policy preferences are not a major factor in shaping voters' choices in most congressional elections, except in states in which immigration has particular salience because of large immigrant populations, for example, California. Because immigration policy preferences do not influence election outcomes in most cases, interest groups become particularly influential actors in the immigration policy debate.[10]

In this context, Congress passed generally liberal immigration policies in 1986 and 1990 in spite of widespread public support for restrictive immigration policies because of lobbying by a liberal coalition of ethnic groups, churches, civil rights organizations, and employer associations. Employer associations' demands for access to workers with particular occupational characteristics and for the protection of their due process rights have converged with the civil and human rights concerns of churches, ethnic groups, and civil rights organizations in recent debates over immigration policy reform. Lobbying by these groups has prevented Congress from passing effective, restrictive immigration legislation. Indeed, pro-immigration activists from this informal liberal coalition made explicit efforts to work together in lobbying Congress to promote liberal immigration policy reform and to hinder proposed restrictions. [11]

The growing voice of humanitarian groups in the debate over U.S. immigration policy in the last half of the twentieth century reflects a fundamental shift in prevailing ideas regarding the acceptability of racial discrimination and support for basic civil rights. Whereas broad acceptance of racially-based distinctions shaped U.S. immigration policy in the first half of the twentieth century, growing support for civil rights coupled with increasing opposition to racial discrimination provided the foundation for the liberalization of U.S. immigration policy since the 1960s. Thus, interest group politics, increasingly shaped by liberal norms in recent decades, largely explain why the U.S. government adopted liberal immigration policies in the face of widespread public support for new immigration restrictions in the 1980s. Ultimately, then, domestic politics and liberal ideas have contributed significantly to the increase in immigration to this country in recent decades by leading to the passage of liberal immigration policies. [12]

This analysis of current U.S. immigration policy challenges the argument that "push factors" in immigrant-sending countries, including economic underdevelopment, overpopulation, and political instability, have been the primary constraints on governmental efforts to restrict immigration. According to this argument, these push factors underlie an increase in international migration flows that has overwhelmed existing policy mechanisms for regulating immigration to the U.S. Contradicting this notion, this analysis of U.S. immigration policy indicates that "pull factors," including employers' demands for skilled and unskilled labor, ethnic and social networks, and humanitarian norms favoring relatively open borders, have been extremely important in shaping immigration flows to the United States. These pull factors, representing the demands of a variety of interest groups involved in the immigration policy debate, are acknowledged in the provisions of current U.S. immigration policy and have contributed to the high levels of both legal and illegal immigration to this country in recent decades. In this way, liberal immigration outcomes in the United States reflect the basic provisions of current immigration policies rather than a loss of governmental control.

Although the U.S. government has not fundamentally lost control of its borders, current U.S. immigration policy does not represent a coherent, rational approach for border control based upon well-defined, widely accepted considerations of the national interest. Rather, current U.S. immigration policy reflects a series of legislative compromises designed to address the political demands of well-organized, vocal interest groups. What this means, in essence, is that the capacity of the U.S. government to reduce immigration dramatically in the current period remains unknown because genuinely restrictive measures have not been tested. In sum, though the data on immigration flows does not suggest that the government has lost control of its borders, domestic political considerations have seriously constrained the ability of the U.S. government to regulate international migration flows by preventing the passage of restrictive immigration legislation.

LIBERALISM WITHOUT INSTITUTIONS OR REGIMES: IDEAS AND DOMESTIC POLITICS

This analysis of current U.S. immigration policy has been influenced strongly by the liberal tradition in international relations theory. As clearly described by Moravcsik, a central feature of liberal international relations theory is the "insight that state-society relations—the relationship of states to the domestic and transnational social context in which they are embedded—have a fundamental impact on state behavior in world politics. Societal ideas, interests, and institutions influence state behavior by shaping state preferences, that is, the fundamental social purpose underlying the strategic calculations of governments."[13] This formulation of liberal international relations theory does not deny that states are important actors or that state interests matter; rather, it points out that individuals, non-governmental groups, and groups within government shape state interests and behavior. Similarly, this study indicates that while states remain key actors in understanding the phenomenon of international migration, they do not function as strictly rational, interest-maximizing units operating in an anarchic system where power is the primary force driving state behavior. Rather, transnational ideas shape the policy alternatives considered by states. At the same time, non-governmental groups within states shape the policy responses used by states in their efforts to regulate international migration.

Additionally, this research draws on a growing literature that emphasizes the importance of ideas in shaping foreign policy and international relations.[14] According to Judith Goldstein and Robert O. Keohane, ideas, defined as "beliefs held by individuals," shape people's policy preferences and the political alternatives considered by political actors. This emphasis on the importance of ideas challenges mainstream approaches to the study of international relations, which point to interests, either economic or political, as the driving force of world politics. In challenging prominent rationalistic, interest-based explanations of policy, Goldstein and Keohane do not argue that ideas alone cause policy outcomes or that interests are irrelevant. Rather, they contend that ideas matter; they are not merely "hooks" used by elites to manipulate public opinion. Moreover, they argue that changes in ideas help to account for the ways in which individuals, groups, and states define their interests.[15] Ideas can shape policy, whether or not they are formally set out in international regimes.

International migration should be seen as a multidimensional transnational process that involves not only labor migration but also refugee flows, family reunification, and ethnic and social network migration. While other theoretical perspectives can be used to explain certain types of migration, none of the mainstream perspectives adequately explains international migration in general. However, the liberal framework developed here can be used to explain each category of international migration and, hence, is crucial to understanding the U.S. case. The focus on domestic politics and liberal ideas in this work challenges several other theoretical explanations of international migration.

First, this analysis of the U.S. case, which indicates that politics as well as economics are important in shaping international migration flows, challenges the strict focus of classical economic liberalism and Marxism on economic factors as determinants of international migration. According to classical economic liberalism, individual economic incentives drive international migration. Conversely, a Marxist framework suggests that international migration is determined by structural inequality in the global economic system.[16] Marxist analysis suggests that immigration restrictions are commonly "symbolic laws" designed to appease anti-immigration forces while providing loopholes and weak enforcement mechanisms that meet the interests of the capitalist class.[17] Each of these perspectives offers a plausible explanation of international labor migration, which is driven largely by economic considerations. However, neither classical economic liberalism nor Marxism adequately explains refugee flows, family reunification, or ethnic network migration, which are shaped by political and social forces as well as economics.

Unlike economic liberalism or Marxist analysis, realist interpretations of international migration consider the political as well as the economic determinants of international migration. Realist analysis suggests that the political and economic interests of the state, including military security, foreign relations, territorial integrity, and national integration, drive the regulation of international migration.[18] Realist theory does not predict the levels of immigration that a state will allow. Rather, realism merely suggests that states will allow immigration to the extent that it advances national economic and political interests.[19] Realist analyses emphasize that states retain the sovereign right to determine the criteria for admission into their territory and, as a result, realists discount the importance of international legal norms that purport to protect immigrant rights.[20] Realist interpretations of international migration provide compelling explanations of refugee flows and even labor migration.[21] In the case of labor migration, realists can claim that states will authorize legal labor migration or tolerate levels of illegal immigration that meet employers' needs, thereby contributing to the economic interests of the state.[22] U.S. refugee policy, which has given preference to individuals fleeing from Communist countries and other "unfriendly" regimes, lends credence to the realist claim that the ideological interests of the state determine refugee admissions.[23] However, realism does not adequately explain the emphasis on family reunification in U.S. policy or the increasing ethnic diversity of immigration flows to this country in that it is difficult to support the claim that family or ethnic migration directly advances the national interest in a meaningful way.

Challenging the emphasis of economic liberalism and Marxism on economic factors and realism's focus on state interests, this analysis of U.S. immigration policy, by focusing on domestic politics and liberal ideas, offers a credible explanation of family and ethnic network migration as well as labor migration and refugee flows. A liberal interpretation of U.S. immigration policy, then, points to the importance of ideas as well as interests, of politics as well as economics, and of a variety of non-governmental groups rather than just states or economic classes as key actors.

The liberal analysis of U.S. immigration policy developed here shares much in common with existing "neoliberal" institutionalist analyses of international migration. The neoliberal institutionalist perspective examines constraints on the state stemming from international economic and political interdependence, changes in international norms, and the transformation of international institutions.[24] This perspective focuses to a great extent on international institutions developed by states to deal with collective problems, such as economic stagnation, environmental degradation, or transnational refugee flows. In the absence of formal institutions, neoliberal institutionalists seek to identify international regimes developed by states to address these collective problems.[25]

Applied to the issue of international migration, the neoliberal institutionalist perspective suggests that international migration flows in advanced industrialized countries can be attributed to the confluence of liberal norms in the economic and political spheres in the post-World War II period.[26] Neoliberal institutionalism suggests that states are not able to regulate migration effectively because of the development of liberal international economic regimes and civil rights regimes in advanced industrialized countries. James F. Hollifield, who applies this perspective to the study of international migration, argues that liberal immigration outcomes in advanced industrialized countries, in spite of restrictive immigration policies, reflect not only the "attraction of markets" but also "the protection given to aliens in rights-based regimes."[27] Hollifield does not claim that well-developed international regimes govern the regulation of international migration by states. In this way, his analysis of international migration does not go as far as neoliberal analyses of other international political and economic issues.[28] However, he does argue that convergence around liberal economic and political norms in advanced industrialized countries has led to the emergence of regional migration regimes and has set the stage for the creation of international migration regimes.[29] Likewise, Saskia Sassen argues that "[a]n emerging de facto regime, centered in international agreements and conventions as well as in various rights gained by immigrants, limits the state's role in controlling immigration."[30]

Similarly, in his study of immigration and citizenship in the United States and Western Europe, David Jacobson explores the way in which international human rights norms have constrained state efforts to regulate international migration.[31] Jacobson argues that transnational migrations have contributed to increased support in advanced industrialized countries for universal human rights as opposed to rights based on civic or national identity. Though he considers how domestic factors, including differing political cultures, shape state responses to transnational migration, Jacobson's argument focuses largely on the role of the courts and the influence of international law in shaping immigration policies in advanced industrialized countries. In this way, Jacobson's work can be characterized as neoliberal in that it primarily emphasizes the way in which systemic factors, in this case international human rights law, shape state interests and behavior.

Though its findings are consistent with neoliberal institutionalism, this analysis of current U.S. immigration policy diverges from previous neoliberal analyses in that it is based on a "bottom-up" rather than a "top-down" conception of global politics. This insight is based on Andrew Moravcsik's distinction between a liberal theory of international relations and neoliberal institutionalism. Indeed, Moravcsik does not consider the "neoliberal" perspective an authentic variant of liberal international relations theory. Rather, he labels such theories merely "institutionalism" and reserves the label "liberal" for theories based on a "'bottom-up' view of politics in which the demands of individuals and societal groups are treated as analytically prior to politics."[32] In "neoliberal" or institutional analyses of international migration, a "rights-based politics" is depicted primarily as a feature of liberalism that is embedded in post-World War II developments in the international political and economic *system*.[33] In other words, these analyses argue that normative constraints on states' ability to regulate international migration arise *externally*, from the emergence of a global consensus on the rights of migrants. Conversely, the liberal analysis developed here suggests that the fundamental constraints on states' ability to regulate international migration are *internal*. The focus is primarily on changes in domestic politics rather than changes in the international system. A similar argument is made by both Gary P. Freeman and Christian Joppke who have each suggested that sovereignty in liberal states is internally rather than externally diminished vis-à-vis the control of international migration as a result of what they refer to as "client politics."[34] As Joppke states, "Not globally limited, but self-limited sovereignty explains why states accept unwanted immigrants."[35]

Thus, this analysis of current U.S. immigration policy differs from previous neoliberal institutional analyses in three important respects. First, whereas neoliberals continue to focus on the state as the most important actor, the liberal argument developed here focuses largely on non-governmental groups as the key actors which bring liberal norms to bear in the debate over immigration policy. Second, unlike previous neoliberal analyses of international migration, this analysis does not rely on the identification of emerging formal migration regimes for evidence to support the argument that liberal norms shape state efforts to regulate international migration. Rather, this study points out that liberal ideas can shape state behavior whether or not they are part of a formal international regime. Non-governmental actors can bring liberal ideas to bear in policy debates over immigration in advanced industrialized countries to the extent that they have access to the policy-making process. Finally, neoliberal institutional analyses of immigration policies overstate the level of convergence among advanced industrialized countries. By pointing to the importance of domestic political processes and structures as the means by which liberal norms influence state action in the area of international migration, this study acknowledges that there will be variation across countries and that the influence of liberal norms will not necessarily be permanent.[36] Indeed, considerable differences persist among the immigration policies in advanced industrialized countries. Liberal norms and rights are more firmly embedded in the United States than they are in many other countries, and the liberal framework developed here can be used to explain these differences.

Even though their influence may not be permanent, liberal norms are key to understanding the U.S. immigration policy debate in recent decades. In the U.S. case, a variety of interest groups, including employer associations, ethnic organizations, churches, and civil rights groups, have focused attention on liberal norms in the debate over U.S. immigration policy. Lobbying by these groups has led Congress to adopt generally expansive immigration policies in recent decades, even when these policies have been trumpeted as restrictive. Ultimately, these immigration policies have resulted in large flows of both legal and illegal immigrants to this country. Therefore, liberal immigration outcomes in the United States can be traced to the norms advanced by a liberal coalition of interest groups that has predominated in the debate over U.S. immigration policy since the 1960s. Domestic politics—not formal international migration regimes—provide the link between liberal ideas and liberal immigration outcomes in the U.S. case.[37]

Applying the assumption that ideas are significant in shaping policy outcomes, this research suggests that a transformation in the predominant ideology regarding racial discrimination and civil rights underlies the liberalization of U.S. immigration policy in recent decades. Changes in ideas help to explain why churches, ethnic groups, and civil rights groups aligned with employer associations after World War II in favoring more open immigration policies. This unlikely coalition of humanitarian groups and employers prevented the United States from passing restrictive legislation even in the 1970s when an economic recession and public opinion seemingly would have favored the passage of new immigration restrictions and at a time when other advanced industrialized countries were adopting restrictive policies. As Peter Schuck notes, "Ideas are the glue of a pluralistic politics. Appealing to general ideas is necessary if groups with disparate conceptions of self-interest and public interest are to form coalitions."[38] In this work, a dual focus on ideas and domestic politics is key to explaining the liberalization of U.S. immigration policy and offers insight into the links between domestic and international politics in the regulation of international migration.

IS THE U.S. CASE UNIQUE?

There is no consensus among migration scholars regarding the question of whether advanced industrialized countries have been able to effectively regulate international migration flows. On the one hand, migration scholars relying on the assumptions of the neoliberal institutionalist perspective have argued that the emergence of liberal international economic regimes and civil rights regimes in advanced industrialized countries has hindered their efforts to regulate international migration. On the other hand, migration scholars drawing on the assumptions of neorealist theories of international relations contend that the absence of formal migration regimes and institutions discredits the neoliberal institutionalist analysis of international migration.

In her study of family migration policies in liberal democracies, Gallya Lahav develops a compelling neorealist critique of the notion that a liberal international migration regime is emerging among advanced industrialized countries. Lahav notes that in spite of a variety of international legal norms that promote the desirability of family reunification, states retain the capability to determine the criteria for admission into their territory. Thus, while a variety of international legal instruments, including the Universal Declaration of Human Rights, the International Covenant on Civil and Political Rights, and the International Convention on the Protection of the Rights of All Migrant Workers and Members of Their Families, promote the principle of family reunification, states are not in any way legally obligated to incorporate this principle into their immigration policies. Moreover, states maintain the right to determine who is eligible for family reunification and how the term family will be defined. For instance, no advanced industrialized country makes undocumented immigrants eligible for family reunification.   Also, according to Lahav, advanced industrialized countries commonly define the term *family* according to narrow "Western" standards, typically focusing on the "nuclear" rather than extended family. As a result of the discretion the state maintains in these areas, Lahav contends that the ability of advanced industrialized countries to regulate international migration has not been affected dramatically by liberal norms.[39]

While Lahav's argument is compelling in many respects, her conclusions are influenced by the point of reference she chooses to use when evaluating immigration policies and outcomes in liberal democracies. In essence, she is evaluating the immigration policies of advanced industrialized countries in comparison to an "ideal type" of liberal migration regime in which complete freedom of movement would be allowed. Because it is clear that no advanced industrialized country allows immigration without limitations, Lahav can correctly claim that states maintain a high degree of latitude in regulating international migration flows.

In general, no state allows complete freedom of movement. If this standard is used to evaluate the migration policies of advanced industrialized countries, then the neorealist argument that states' efforts to regulate international migration flows have not been hindered by liberal norms is correct. However, this standard is too rigid and does not allow for a subtle analysis of the changing economic and political circumstances in which advanced industrialized countries are attempting to regulate international migration. While advanced industrialized countries have developed a diverse set of policy tools for regulating international migration, the fact that these policy restrictions exist and that they shape international migration flows to these countries does not mean that liberal norms are irrelevant. Here, the relevant comparative framework is not just across countries but within countries over time. If current policy restrictions in most advanced industrialized countries are compared to historical efforts to restrict international migration, especially those based on racial, ethnic, or nationalistic criteria, rather than to a model based on complete freedom of movement, then it can be seen that liberal norms have impacted the ability of most advanced industrialized countries to regulate international migration. In a recent work published by the Carnegie Endowment for International Peace, Demetrios G. Papademetriou and Kimberly A. Hamilton effectively describe the dilemma faced by advanced industrialized countries:

"[Z]ero immigration," the publicly stated goal of some European states, is not a realistic policy goal. First, immigration systems build their own self-feeding dynamics that encourage even more migration (through family re-unification and the continuing need for more immigrant workers). Second, unless a state buries itself in isolation, all transnational contacts (economic, political, social, and cultural) will have migration consequences. Third, no policy will eliminate illegal immigration; some illegal immigration is in fact a natural by-product of legal immigration, and it will take place no matter how hard a state tries to stop it.[40]

Thus, while neorealists remind us that neither complete freedom of movement nor a formal international migration regime committing states to open borders exists, Papademetriou and Hamilton stress that a significant level of both legal and illegal immigration is inevitable in "open and democratic" societies.

Empirical evidence suggests that immigration policies in advanced industrialized countries have been influenced by liberal norms to varying degrees. A brief comparison of the immigration policies of Canada and France will illustrate this point. The development of Canadian immigration policy since the 1960s in many ways mirrors the changes in U.S. immigration policy during the same period. In regard to policy towards illegal immigration, Canada adopted an employer sanctions law in the 1970s. As in the U.S. case, provisions for legalization accompanied employer sanctions, and employers can only be punished if they "knowingly" hire illegal immigrants.[41]

The development of Canadian policy towards legal immigration also has paralleled the U.S. case. From early in the twentieth century until the 1960s, Canada maintained a "white Canadian" immigration policy that gave preference to the relatives of European immigrants. This policy was abandoned in 1962 as a result of changes in administrative regulations. Immigration legislation was passed in 1967 that officially eliminated immigrant admission preferences based on race or country of origin. Under current Canadian immigration policy, the largest proportion of immigrants is admitted as part of the "family immigrant stream." Canada places very few restrictions on family reunification, which is defined broadly and allows for the immigration not only of "nuclear family" members but also grandparents, grandchildren, and nephews and nieces. "Landed immigrants," the Canadian equivalent of permanent residents in the United States, in most cases have the same right as Canadian citizens to sponsor family migrants. The basic "restrictive" criteria on family reunification involve income requirements for sponsors and a commitment on the part of sponsors to be financially responsible for the family immigrants. Only income requirements are enforced on a regular basis. In recent years, over thirty percent of immigrants to Canada have been in this family immigrant stream.

A second category of immigrant admissions in Canada is the "independent stream." In this category, most immigrants are admitted under a point system that assesses points for admission based on a variety of selection criteria, including education, experience, occupation, age, and knowledge of language. In addition to immigrants admitted under the point system, the independent stream is comprised of immigrants selected for their potential to make significant contributions to the business environment in Canada, including the self-employed, entrepreneurs, and investors. Unlike the family immigrant stream, the number of admissions in the independent stream is adjusted according to economic conditions.[42] In sum, Canada has a quite open immigration policy and, notably, strongly promotes family reunification regardless of economic conditions.

In France, liberal immigration norms have come under greater assault in recent years, and new criteria based on country of origin and at least implicitly on race have been introduced. With their victory in the 1993 parliamentary elections, the rightist alliance of the Rally for the Republic (RPR) and the Union for French Democracy (UDF) almost immediately adopted measures designed to appeal to widespread anti-immigrant sentiment. A series of policies sponsored by Charles Pasqua, head of the Interior Ministry, were put into place. The Pasqua laws give police broad power to detain and deport illegal immigrants *and* legal immigrants whom the police deem to be a threat to public order.[43] Although arrests are not supposed to be made solely on the basis of race, a variety of immigrant groups, churches, and human rights organizations charged that the legislation was racially motivated and would be applied in a discriminatory manner.[44] The Pasqua laws also introduced new restrictions on family reunification and marriage between foreigners and French citizens. Importantly, the Constitutional Council later declared these provisions unconstitutional.[45]

Still, the rightist government in France has persisted in efforts to introduce new immigration restrictions. Based on a 1994 French-Algerian bilateral agreement, new visa restrictions have been placed on Algerians wishing to visit or stay in France for an extended period. The French government also noted in this agreement that it reserved "the right to deport illegal immigrants *presumed* to be Algerians, even in the absence of official documentation of Algerian citizenship."[46]

Preliminary evidence suggests that the Pasqua laws have been effective in restricting the overall flows of immigrants to France. Total immigration to France has declined from 158,493 in 1985, to 99,637 in 1993, to only 79,361 in 1994. Family reunification declined from 32,408 in 1993, a level roughly comparable to average annual family immigration throughout the last decade, to only 20,646 in 1994. However, it should be noted that the most significant proportion of the overall decline in immigration to France can be explained by a decrease in the immigration of seasonal workers. While over 86,000 seasonal workers migrated to France in 1985, only 10,339 seasonal workers were admitted to France in 1994.[47] Also, it should be noted that it is likely that these restrictions on legal immigration have led to higher levels of illegal immigration to France.[48] Because illegal immigration is so difficult to measure precisely, this point is very important. Official statistics on legal immigration give governments the ability to present an image of control whether or not these statistics accurately reflect total immigration flows, both legal and illegal, into a country.

As this brief comparison of Canadian and French immigration policies illustrates, efforts by advanced industrialized countries to regulate international migration vary in significant ways. These differences indicate that no formal international migration regime exists that can compel convergence towards uniform policies for regulating international migration in advanced industrialized countries. Indeed, many European states have been more successful than the United States in restricting international migration. These states have implemented effective bans on the importation of temporary workers and have been successful in reducing levels of permanent labor migration. In regard to illegal immigration, most European states adopted employer sanctions laws in the 1970s, with the notable exception of the United Kingdom.[49] European governments faced fewer political obstacles to the passage of employer sanctions as a result of a general acceptance that they are a legitimate tool for preventing discrimination against native workers and the exploitation of illegal immigrants.[50] The passage of restrictive measures without substantial opposition might be seen as evidence that advanced industrialized countries are able to effectively regulate international migration.

At the same time, it cannot be said that liberal norms are irrelevant to understanding immigration policies in European countries. All member-states of the European Union to some extent promote family reunification in their immigration policies, though the beneficiaries of family reunification vary widely. In France, only spouses and minor children may benefit from family reunification. In contrast, Denmark also allows for family reunification of dependent parents over the age of fifty and other relatives "for special reasons" or in the case of "close ties."[51] Indeed, family reunification, though it is not promoted equally in all European countries, has become "the dominant mode of legal migration flows" in Europe.[52] Moreover, in spite of their success in restricting legal labor migration, the proportion of foreign-born residents as a percentage of total population has either increased slightly or remained steady in many European countries since 1975 when recent efforts to restrict immigration were first initiated.[53] It is also important to note that in many cases, an *increasing* percentage of this foreign-born population is from a non-European Union country.[54] Thus, it cannot be said that increasing numbers of foreign-born residents in European countries merely reflect the process of integration within the European Union. Ironically, this increase in the foreign-born populations in European countries has resulted partially from the bans on foreign labor instituted in many countries in the mid-1970s. After the imposition of these bans, temporary labor migrants increasingly sought permanent residency, to which they often had access under liberal constitutions, and then brought their families to join them. As a result, family ties replaced labor market needs as the primary admissions criteria.[55] Importantly, family migrants also may be serving as a new source of illegal labor in European countries as legal residents without work authorization enter the labor market.[56]

Regarding illegal immigration, some evidence suggests that employer sanctions in Europe also have been accompanied by some of the problems that have marred their effectiveness as a restrictive tool in the United States. In countries like France, the passage of employer sanctions was also accompanied by legalization measures.[57] In his study of employer sanctions in Europe, Mark Miller suggests that they generally have been effective and that, according to employer surveys, most employers comply voluntarily. However, it should be noted that even in the absence of employer sanctions laws, most employers are not hiring undocumented immigrants. Thus, the key in evaluating these laws is to determine how commonly they are enforced and how effective they are in deterring violations. In this regard, Miller concedes that many employers have tried to circumvent the law by turning to subcontracting or taking businesses "underground."[58] Therefore, employer sanctions laws have not been entirely successful.[59]

This brief discussion of immigration policies in advanced industrialized countries suggests that critics of the neoliberal institutionalist analysis of international migration are correct to point out that the efforts of these countries to regulate immigration are not being hindered by a formal international migration regime. However, it is also a mistake by default, then, to conclude that these states are able to regulate international migration exclusively with a view to their "national interests." Though a formal international migration regime does not exist, the debates over immigration policy in advanced industrialized countries are increasingly being framed by a "rights-based" discourse. Although liberal norms do not always prevail in these debates, they, nonetheless, remain a central point of reference. Notably, family reunification, though sometimes defined narrowly, is protected in most advanced industrialized countries in spite of the fact that it does not clearly meet any fundamental national interest. French and German courts have ruled that efforts to suspend family reunification in these countries violate international agreements. Martin Schain is correct to note that "such rulings do not generally represent an expansion of immigrant rights, but rather are attempts to limit or perhaps slow down a contraction of such rights."[60] Nonetheless, it is significant that these rights are protected at all because they reflect a concern with fundamental liberal norms rather than any clearly specified national interest.

Ideas have a pivotal influence in the immigration policy debates in advanced industrialized countries. To the extent that liberal norms remain prominent in advanced industrialized countries, states will have greater difficulty in regulating international migration. On the other hand, if limitations on civil rights and racially discriminatory criteria are more widely acceptable, advanced industrialized countries will be able to regulate international migration more effectively. As noted by Cornelius, Martin, and Hollifield:

Recent efforts by democratic states to regain control of their borders all point to a gradual recognition that effective control of immigration requires a rollback of civil and human rights for noncitizens. Examples include the U.S. policy of interdicting Haitian and Chinese refugees on the high seas (to prevent them from reaching U.S. territory and gaining access to the refugee admissions process), the German decision to radically tighten the provisions of its asylum law (formerly the most liberal in Europe), and new powers to the policy in France and Spain to carry out random identity checks on any suspicious (or foreign-looking!) individual.[61]

Thus, in recent years, France has had some success in restricting international migration as a result of a head-on assault on liberal norms by the governing coalition of the right. Similarly, Britain has had greater success than other countries in limiting immigration by utilizing country of origin and ethnic criteria in its immigration policy. Notably, Japan's immigration policy remains very restrictive in comparative terms; this fact can be attributed, at least in part, to the more widely accepted validity of ethnic distinctions in the domestic political culture in Japan. In contrast, liberal norms have been far more influential in the immigration policies of the United States and Canada, and, accordingly, immigration outcomes to these countries have been more liberal.

Although immigration policies in the advanced industrialized countries are not converging in the formation of a formal liberal international migration regime, they also are not converging towards a uniform and comprehensive model of restriction. What, then, explains the divergent influence of liberal norms across advanced industrialized countries? Domestic politics provide the key to understanding this divergence. Similarly, the degree to which various interest groups have access to the policy-making process will partially determine the impact of liberal norms on immigration policy. In corporate models of government, parliamentary systems, or in centralized as opposed to federal states, churches, immigration organizations, and civil rights groups are likely to have less influence in the immigration policy debate as there are fewer points of political access in these models. Thus, it might be expected that liberal norms will be less central to the immigration policy debates in these political systems. In these cases, advocates of liberal immigration may have fewer opportunities to influence the content of immigration policies and, consequently, immigration outcomes. Furthermore, the strength of political support for liberal norms varies across countries. Variations in the strength of liberal norms and in the access of liberal interest groups to the policy-making process help to explain why some states have been more effective in restricting immigration than others. In the U.S. case, strong liberal norms and a system in which interest groups play a significant role in policy-making have contributed to the liberalization of U.S. immigration policy since the 1960s.

FREEDOM OF MOVEMENT OR SOVEREIGNTY?

According to Article 12 of the International Covenant on Civil and Political Rights, all human beings have a right to leave any country, including their native lands. However, this right to freedom of movement does not imply that states are obligated to accept individuals who wish to immigrate to their countries. To the contrary, sovereign states under international law have a right to control their borders and to decide who may legally enter their territory. In practice, then, individuals' right to freedom of movement is limited by states' willingness to allow immigration and emigration.[62] The right of sovereign states to regulate immigration remains largely intact today.

A few international legal norms limit the right of sovereign states to regulate immigration to some extent. Under the 1951 Convention on Refugees and the 1967 Protocol to this convention, contracting states may not legally expel or forcibly return any refugee to his or her country of origin. However, states determine which individuals meet the criteria to be defined as refugees and typically make these decisions based on ideological or foreign policy concerns rather than humanitarian considerations.[63] Hence, states' ability to control immigration has not been constricted significantly by international obligations to accept refugees. In terms of general migration flows, the Helsinki Accords direct signatory states to promote family reunification. However, the principle of family reunification can be characterized at best as a non-binding promotional guideline rather than a binding legal norm backed up by strong enforcement mechanisms. Thus, the right of states to restrict immigration remains an important obstacle to freedom of movement, and the few international legal norms designed to promote freer movement of people in the modern global system do not constitute a strong, liberal international migration regime. Moreover, there is not a serious movement among states to deregulate state control in the area of international migration, which differs significantly from the development of international legal norms in other issue areas, such as international trade or international financial markets.[64]

Although a well-developed liberal international migration regime does not exist, current U.S. immigration policy suggests that international legal norms can still indirectly shape state efforts to regulate immigration. As Saskia Sassen points out, individuals and non-state actors can make claims on states based on basic human rights norms codified in international law.[65] For example, the Helsinki Accord's guideline that states should promote family reunification has bolstered the support of churches, ethnic groups, and civil rights associations in the United States for this principle. Similarly, an evolving international human rights regime has lent support to rights-based arguments for liberal immigration policies in the United States. In sum, international legal norms have shaped the beliefs and ideas of key actors in the debate over U.S. immigration policy. As noted by Goldstein and Keohane, ideas alone do not cause policy outcomes. Nevertheless, ideas shape the way in which individuals, groups, and states define their interests.[66] It is in this respect that ideas have shaped U.S. immigration policy. Ultimately, changes in normative beliefs have had significant effects on the types of immigration policies adopted by the U.S. government. The transformation from a system of immigrant selection based primarily on national and racial criteria to one fundamentally resting on non-discrimination and emphasizing family reunification reflects a significant transformation in the American political context in the ideas regarding the acceptability of racial discrimination and the need for civil rights. The argument is not that U.S. immigration policy always prohibits or prevents discrimination or that it always effectively promotes and protects human rights. Instead, the argument is that to the extent that U.S. immigration policy has incorporated non-discrimination and basic civil rights as values, these changes can be attributed to the influence of interest groups promoting these norms in the immigration policy debate in this country.

In the final analysis, then, what does this examination of current U.S. immigration policy suggest about the ability of states to regulate international migration in the modern global system? Fundamentally, this study indicates that the U.S. government has not lost control of its borders in that relatively liberal immigration outcomes generally reflect the provisions of current U.S. immigration policy. However, current immigration policy represents political compromises designed to address the demands of a variety of interest groups rather than a rational approach intended to advance well-defined national interests. The U.S. government has been able to regulate immigration into this country in the sense that the movement of people across U.S. borders does not occur freely. Only a certain number of immigrants can enter the United States legally each year. Moreover, although current policy does not allow for a harsh crackdown on illegal immigration, some illegal immigrants have been deterred by border controls and interior enforcement. Yet, while the government has been able to regulate immigration, it has not been able to dramatically restrict immigration in recent years as a result of strong opposition to more rigid restrictions on freedom of movement among large segments of the American population. In other words, the policy options available to the U.S. government have been limited by domestic opposition to immigration restrictions which, in turn, has been based largely on support for the liberal norms of non-discrimination in admissions criteria for legal immigration and basic immigrant rights.

Even though the sovereign right of states to regulate international migration remains essentially intact, the U.S. case suggests that international interdependence has influenced the way in which states exercise this right. Domestic politics do not occur in isolation from global politics. In the United States, international norms and ideas regarding basic human rights have been incorporated into the immigration policy debate in this country by a variety of civil rights organizations. Ultimately, the influence of these ideas has limited the acceptable immigration policy alternatives available to the government. Similarly, the growing exposure of the domestic economy to global competition has transformed the interests of key economic actors involved in the debate over U.S. immigration policy. The globalization of economic relations, in particular, has reinforced employers' traditional support for liberal immigration policies by contributing to their need for highly-skilled workers.[67] International migration flows themselves have altered the political, social, and economic composition of U.S. society and, subsequently, have transformed the debate over U.S. immigration policy. The historical migration of various ethnic groups to this country ultimately resulted in the creation of a variety of immigrant organizations. By the 1960s, many of these organizations had achieved significant political power and joined civil rights groups in demanding the liberalization of U.S. immigration policy.

In this way, the United States has become vulnerable and sensitive to the economic and political factors that underlie international migration flows as a result of interaction between domestic politics and transnational processes. International migration has had an important impact on the economic, political, and social composition of the populations in industrial democracies. In this way, international migration has an effect on domestic politics in these countries. At the same time, domestic politics influence international migration flows by shaping the types of immigration policies adopted by states. As illustrated by the U.S. case, it is crucial to consider the links between domestic politics and transnational political and economic processes in examinations of the ability of states to regulate international migration in the modern global system.

In sum, the domestic political debate over immigration has not been immune to the influence of external factors but, rather, takes place in an interdependent world. Though the sovereign right of states to regulate their borders remains fundamentally intact, states in an increasingly interdependent world cannot prevent the transnational flow of ideas. The growth in transnational support for basic civil rights and for family reunification as a humanitarian norm has altered the political discourse that shapes immigration policy debates in most liberal democracies. Whether liberal norms will survive the assault from a new wave of anti-immigrant and restrictionist sentiment in most advanced industrialized countries remains to be seen.

NOTES

1. The title of this book borrows from Louis Henkin's *The Age of Rights* (New York: Columbia University Press, 1990).

2. Frank D. Bean, Barry Edmonston, and Jeffrey S. Passel, eds., *Undocumented Migration to the United States: IRCA and the Experience of the 1980s* (Washington, D.C.: The Urban Institute; Santa Monica: The RAND Corporation, 1990): 1–2.

3. Philip L. Martin, *Trade and Migration: NAFTA and Agriculture* (Washington, D.C.: Institute for International Economics, October 1993).

4. David E. Sanger, "U.S. Seeks Mexican Steps in Bid to Aid Bailout Plan," *The New York Times*, 26 January 1995, A14.

5. Larry Rohter, "Foreign Policy: Florida Has One," *The New York Times*, 22 May 1994, 1 (Section 4).

6. Kenneth K. Lee, *Huddled Masses, Muddled Laws* (Westport, CT: Praeger, 1998): 22–28.

7. Freeman defines migration policy as "state efforts to regulate and control entry into the national territory and to stipulate conditions of residence of persons seeking permanent settlement, temporary work or political asylum." Gary P. Freeman, "Migration Policy and Politics in the Receiving States," *International Migration Review* 26:4 (Winter 1992): 1145. Unlike Freeman's definition, the definition used in this examination of U.S. immigration policy explicitly distinguishes between legislative rules and their enforcement. In this way, this definition was influenced by Weiner's discussion of the access rules regarding international migration. According to Weiner, access rules include not only legal norms but "the administrative capacity and the willingness of states to enforce legal norms; they also include the expectations states have of one another, their reputations for behaving in a particular manner." Myron Weiner, "On International Migration and International Relations," *Population and Development Review* 11:3 (September 1985): 449. Thus, the definition used in this work assumes that current U.S. immigration policy reflects a series of legislative compromises designed to meet the demands of a variety of interest groups rather than a coherent, rational approach for the regulation of immigration into this country.

8. The characterization of immigration policies as "liberal" is intended to signal that these policies reflect changes facilitating relatively open immigration to this country and/or that these policies include provisions designed to protect basic civil rights.

9. Lee: 27–28.

10. James G. Gimpel and James R. Edwards, Jr., *The Congressional Politics of Immigration Reform* (Boston: Allyn and Bacon, 1999): 41–45.

11. For an overview of specific congressional lobbying efforts by this informal "left-right alliance" in the 1980s and 1990s, see Lee: 101–114.

12. Leah Haus offers an alternative explanation for the liberalization of U.S. immigration policy in the 1980s. Haus contends that organized labor, becoming convinced that governmental efforts to control illegal immigration would be ineffective as a result of the growing transnationalization of the labor market, came to favor open immigration policies that would facilitate the organization of foreign-born workers and contribute to the strength of the labor movement. As a result, she argues that "cultural conservatives" became isolated in their support for restrictive immigration policies. Leah Haus, "Openings in the Wall: Transnational Migrants, Labor Unions, and U.S. Immigration Policy," *International Organization* 49:2 (Spring 1995): 285–313. Haus' description of the interests of organized labor is compelling, and the changes in the preferences of trade unions likely were a contributing factor to the liberalization of U.S. immigration policy in the 1980s. However, Haus does not provide a thorough explanation of immigration policy reform in the 1980s. In addition to organized labor, other actors, including churches and civil rights groups, were integrally involved in the debate over immigration reform in the 1980s. Moreover, testimony in congressional subcommittee hearings on proposed immigration reform indicates that liberal ideas favoring non-discrimination, family reunification, and civil rights were key elements in the immigration policy debate, a marked change from the debates over immigration policy prior to the 1960s.

13. Andrew Moravcsik, "Taking Preferences Seriously: A Liberal Theory of International Politics," *International Organization* 51:4 (Autumn 1997): 513.

14. Judith Goldstein and Robert O. Keohane, "Ideas and Foreign Policy: An Analytical Framework," in Goldstein and Keohane, eds., *Ideas & Foreign Policy: Beliefs, Institutions, and Political Change* (Ithaca, NY: Cornell University Press, 1993); Kathryn Sikkink, *Ideas and Institutions: Developmentalism in Brazil and Argentina* (Ithaca, NY: Cornell University Press, 1991).

15. Goldstein and Keohane: 3–11.

16. Stephen Castles and Godula Kosack, *Immigrant Workers and Class Structure in Western Europe*, 2d ed. (Oxford: Oxford University Press, 1985); M.J. Piore, *Birds of Passage: Migrant Labor and Industrial Societies* (Cambridge: Cambridge University Press, 1979).

17. Kitty Calavita, *Inside the State: The Bracero Program, Immigration, and the I.N.S.* (New York: Routledge, 1992); Calavita, *U.S. Immigration Law and the Control of Labor: 1820–1924* (London: Academic Press, Inc., 1984); Alejandro Portes, "Of Borders and States: A Skeptical Note on the Legislative Control of Immigration," in Wayne A. Cornelius and Ricardo Anzaldúa Montoya, eds., *America's New Immigration Law: Origins, Rationales, and Potential Consequences* (San Diego: University of California, Center for U.S.-Mexican Studies, 1983): 24–28; Jorge A. Bustamente, "Undocumented Immigration: Research Findings and Policy Options," in Riordan A. Roett, ed., *Mexico and the United States, Managing the Relationship* (Boulder: Westview Press, 1988): 109–131.

18. Aristide Zolberg, "International Migrations in Political Perspective," in Mary M. Kritz, Charles B. Keely, and Silvano M. Tomasi, eds., *Global Trends in Migration* (New York: The Center for Migration Studies, 1981): 3–27; Zolberg, "The Next Waves: Migration Theory for a Changing World," *International Migration Review* 23:3 (Fall 1989): 403–430.

19. In contrast to Marxist analysis, realists do not see state actions in the area of immigration policy as unique to capitalist economies. Non-capitalist states also will adopt immigration and emigration policies that contribute to regime maintenance. See Zolberg, "Contemporary Transnational Migrations in Historical Perspective: Patterns and Dilemmas," in Mary M. Kritz, ed., *U.S. Immigration and Refugee Policy* (Lexington, MA: Lexington Books, 1983): 15–51.

20. Gallya Lahav, "Migration Norms and Constraints in Liberal Democracies: Towards an International Family Reunification Regime," Paper presented at the annual meeting of the International Studies Association, April 16–20, 1996, San Diego: 5.

21. Alan Dowty also analyzes international migration within a realist framework, though he focuses primarily on policies designed to limit emigration and/or to forcibly expel individuals or groups. He concludes that these policies are largely driven by the state's political and ideological interests and, like Zolberg, that states have been "relatively" effective in controlling emigration and immigration in the twentieth century. Alan Dowty, *Closed Borders: The Contemporary Assault on Freedom of Movement* (New Haven: Yale University Press, 1987).

22. Aristide Zolberg, "Labour Migration and International Economic Regimes: Bretton Woods and After," in Mary M. Kritz, Lin Lean Lim, and Hania Zlotnik, eds., *International Migration Systems: A Global Approach* (Oxford: Clarendon Press, 1992): 315–334.

23. Dowty: 107–109.

24. Robert O. Keohane and Joseph S. Nye, Jr., *Power and Interdependence* (Boston: Little, Brown, 1977); Joseph Nye, "Neorealism and Neoliberalism," *World Politics* 40:2 (1988): 235–251.

25. Elsewhere, regimes have been defined as "sets of implicit or explicit principles, norms, rules, and decision-making procedures around which actors' expectations converge in a given area of international relations." See Stephen D. Krasner, "Structural Causes and Regime Consequences: Regimes as Intervening Variables," *International Organization* 36 (Spring 1982): 186.

26. James F. Hollifield, *Immigrants, Markets, and States* (Cambridge: Harvard University Press, 1992): 28.

27. Ibid.: 216.

28. See, for example, Keohane and Nye.

29. Hollifield, *Immigrants, Markets, and States*: 28. The classification of Hollifield's work as "neoliberal" here does not imply that he entirely neglects differences across cases or that he disregards the importance of domestic politics. In fact, in his work on the French case, he focuses on the importance of the French "republican identity" as a determinant of French immigration policy. In his general analysis of immigration policy in advanced industrialized countries, he stresses the importance of "rights-based politics" within immigrant-receiving countries. However, his emphasis is on systemic convergence among advanced industrialized countries. See, for example, James F. Hollifield, "Immigration and Republicanism in France: The Hidden Consensus," in Cornelius, Martin, and Hollifield, eds., *Controlling Immigration: A Global Perspective* (Stanford, CA: Stanford University Press, 1994): 143–175.

30. Saskia Sassen, *Losing Control? Sovereignty in an Age of Globalization* (New York: Columbia University Press, 1996): 67.

31. David Jacobson, *Rights Across Borders: Immigration and the Decline of Citizenship* (Baltimore: The Johns Hopkins University Press, 1996).

32. Moravcsik: 517.

33. Cornelius, Martin, and Hollifield: 31.

34. Gary P. Freeman, "Can Liberal States Control Unwanted Migration?" *The Annals of the American Academy of Political and Social Science* 534 (July 1994): 17–30; Christian Joppke, "Why Liberal States Accept Unwanted Immigration," *World Politics* 50 (January 1998): 266–93.

35. Joppke: 270.

36. The argument that differences in domestic structure are key in determining the impact of transnational relations is developed in great detail in Thomas Risse-Kappen, ed., *Bringing Transnational Relations Back In* (Cambridge: Cambridge University Press, 1995). The 1994 book edited by Cornelius, Martin, and Hollifield, *Controlling Immigration: A Global Perspective*, provides a recent exception to the general neglect of domestic politics in the literature on international migration. This volume includes a variety of country case studies that explore the ability of industrial democracies to control international migration and that consider the domestic sources of immigration policies, though none of the case studies explores in detail the role of interest groups in the immigration policy-making process.

37. The decision to focus on the role of domestic politics and ideas in this study was influenced by Martin O. Heisler's insight that neoliberal research commonly neglects the links between domestic politics and international relations. According to Heisler, it is important to consider the way in which domestic regimes as well as international regimes affect international relations and international migration. See Martin Heisler, "Migration, International Relations and the New Europe: Theoretical Perspectives from Institutional Political Sociology," *International Migration Review* 26:2 (Summer 1992): 598–601.

38. Peter H. Schuck, "The Politics of Rapid Legal Change: Immigration Policy in the 1980s," *Studies in American Political Development* 6 (Spring 1992): 81.

39. Lahav: 15–30.

40. Demetrios G. Papademetriou and Kimberly A. Hamilton, *Managing Uncertainty: Regulating Immigration Flows in Advanced Industrialized Countries* (Washington, D.C.: Carnegie Endowment for International Peace, 1995): 27.

41. Manuel García y Griego, "Canada: Flexibility and Control in Immigration and Refugee Policy," in Cornelius, Martin, and Hollifield, eds., *Controlling Immigration: A Global Perspective* (Stanford, CA: Stanford University Press, 1994): 131–135.

42. Demetrios G. Papademetriou, "International Migration in North America: Issues, Policies, Implications," in Miroslav Macura and David Coleman, eds., *International*

Migration: Regional Processes and Responses (New York and Geneva: United Nations Economic Commission for Europe and United Nations Population Fund, Economic Studies No. 7, 1994): 89–99.

43. Hollifield, "Immigration and Republicanism": 168–171.

44. Demetrios G. Papademetriou and Kimberly A. Hamilton, *Converging Paths to Restriction: French, Italian, and British Responses to Immigration* (Washington, D.C.: Carnegie Endowment for International Peace, 1996): 33.

45. Hollifield, "Immigration and Republicanism": 170; Sassen: 67.

46. Papademetriou and Hamilton, *Converging Paths to Restriction*: 30.

47. Ibid.: 12–13.

48. Martin A. Schain, "Policy Effectiveness and the Regulation of Immigration in Europe," Paper presented at the annual meeting of the International Studies Association, February 21–25, 1995, Chicago: 4, 8.

49. Mark J. Miller, *Employer Sanctions in Western Europe: A Report Submitted to the German Marshall Fund of the United States* (New York: Center for Migration Studies, 1987): 1, 46.

50. Ibid.: 3.

51. Lahav: 41.

52. Ibid.: 3.

53. Demetrios G. Papademetriou, *Coming Together or Pulling Apart? The European Union's Struggle with Immigration and Asylum* (Washington, D.C.: Carnegie Endowment for International Peace, 1996): 14–15.

54. Schain: 3.

55. Ibid.: 7.

56. Miller, *Employer Sanctions*: 14.

57. Ibid.: 36.

58. Ibid.: 38, 48–49.

59. Cornelius, Martin, and Hollifield: 20.

60. Schain: 9.

61. Cornelius, Martin, and Hollifield: 10.

62. Dowty: 7–11.

63. Ibid.: 107–109.

64. Sassen: 66.

65. Ibid.: 94–95.

66. Goldstein and Keohane: 3, 11.

67. Mark J. Miller, "Never Ending Story: The U.S. Debate over Illegal Immigration," in Gary P. Freeman and James Jupp, eds., *Nations of Immigrants: Australia, the United States, and International Migration* (Oxford: Oxford University Press, 1992): 69; Elizabeth S. Rolph, *Immigration Policies: Legacy from the 1980s and Issues for the 1990s* (Santa Monica, CA: The RAND Corporation, 1992): 12.

Chapter 2

From Nativism to Non-Discrimination: U.S. Immigration Policy in Historical Perspective

CHANGING IDEAS AND THE POLITICS OF BORDER CONTROL

In an address to the U.S. Congress in 1903, President Theodore Roosevelt articulated a simple vision of the basic goals of U.S. immigration policy: "We can not have too much immigration of the right kind, and we should have none at all of the wrong kind. The need is to devise some system by which undesirable immigrants shall be kept out entirely, while desirable immigrants are properly distributed throughout the country."[1] These words illustrate a fundamental, general objective that has guided efforts to regulate immigration throughout U.S. history—the goal of keeping out "undesirable" immigrants while facilitating the migration of "desirable" immigrants.

While this objective has integrally shaped the national debate over immigration policy, the prevailing ideas regarding which immigrants have been considered desirable or undesirable has shifted dramatically in the twentieth century. In early federal regulations, "undesirable immigrants" were typically categorized in racial terms. Commonly viewed as racially inferior and unassimilable, ethnic minorities became the targets of early federal efforts to restrict immigration. In the 1880s, strong exclusionary measures were taken against Asians in the form of the Chinese Exclusion Acts of 1882 and 1884. Racial exclusion was taken to a new level in the 1920s with the quota and national origins legislation, which was designed to limit immigration of the "inferior races" of southern and eastern Europe. In the last half of the twentieth century, explicit racial restrictions have been removed from U.S. immigration policy. In an era in which opposition to racial discrimination is widespread, the new method of regulating immigration is based on non-discriminatory national quotas within an annual immigration ceiling. Every country receives an equal number of quota allowances, and preference within these allowances is given to relatives of citizens and legal residents as well as individuals with certain personal qualifications. (See Appendix A for an overview of the major developments in U.S. immigration policy.)

A significant shift in public attitudes from widespread acceptance of racist policies to growing support for civil rights has altered the immigration policy debate dramatically. The change from an immigration policy based on racial exclusion to one founded on non-discrimination is to a great extent the product of this shift in public attitudes. A dramatic change in the prevailing public ideology regarding race has modified interest groups' positions on immigration and, ultimately, has contributed to the liberalization of U.S. immigration policy since the 1960s. As this chapter will show, the policies of racial exclusion in the late nineteenth and early twentieth centuries provide historical evidence of relatively successful governmental regulation of immigration to the United States. The shift from racial exclusion to non-discrimination in U.S. immigration policy beginning in the 1960s has contributed to the growing number of illegal and legal immigrants to this country in recent decades.

THE DEFEAT OF NATIVISM IN THE GOLDEN DOOR ERA

The predominant ideology that shaped U.S. immigration policy for most of this country's history was that of nativism, which has been defined as "intense opposition to an internal minority on the ground of its foreign . . . connections."[2] Nativist opposition to foreigners is predicated on a fervent nationalism—foreigners are viewed as a threat to the survival of the nation in which they reside. Defined in this manner, nativism has underlain calls for immigration restriction throughout American history. In fact, the desire for religious, racial, and ideological homogeneity can be traced back to colonial regulations that were designed to deter the immigration of Catholics, Quakers, Germans, and other foreigners as well as paupers and criminals.[3]

Nativist opposition to foreigners influenced the earliest federal legislation addressing the treatment of immigrants in this country. The 1798 Aliens Act and Alien Enemy Act, commonly known as the Alien and Sedition Acts, were adopted in response to the French Revolution and Napoleonic Wars, which had heightened nativist concerns regarding the immigration of radical democrats from Europe.[4] These acts authorized the president to deport aliens who threatened U.S. peace and security and to deport or detain male aliens from enemy countries during wartime. While nativism contributed significantly to the passage of the Alien and Sedition Acts, political activism on the part of immigrant groups led to their ineffectiveness. Public opposition to this legislation was immediate and strong, and immigrant groups were vocal in their criticism. Because the Federalists had been strong advocates of the Alien and Sedition Acts, many newly naturalized citizens were reluctant to join the

Federalist Party while the Democratic-Republicans continued to receive a majority of immigrant support. In a clear demonstration of the political influence of immigrant groups in early U.S. history, the Alien and Sedition Acts were not enforced rigorously while in effect.[5]

Aside from the unpopular and ineffective Alien and Sedition Acts, there were few developments in federal immigration policy in early U.S. history. In a 1793 executive statement, President George Washington had announced an open-door immigration policy.[6] In the first half of the nineteenth century, several groups articulated opposition to this open-door policy, including charitable organizations, which were burdened with the provision of welfare to impoverished immigrants, labor groups, and several nativist organizations, among them the Know-Nothing Party, the American Protective Association, the Native American Party, and the Order of United Americans. In spite of significant opposition to immigration, no major federal immigration restrictions were adopted.[7]

With a seemingly endless frontier and economic expansion, the golden door to immigration was held open by pro-immigration forces, including industrialists, shipping companies that transported immigrants, land developers in the expanding Western frontier, and urban "political machines," which thrived on the support and dependency of immigrants.[8] In the first half of the nineteenth century, the absence of federal inducements to immigration as well as a lack of restrictive legislation characterized the open-door policy. This situation changed during the Civil War when worker shortages, a significant decline in immigration, and industrial expansion led to active federal encouragement of immigration. The Homestead Act of 1862 was designed to attract settlers to sparsely populated Western states and served as an inducement to immigration with its provision of free land. The 1864 Contract Labor Act legalized binding contracts for labor immigration. Advocating the adoption of this act at the opening session of the Thirty-eighth Congress, President Lincoln argued that immigrants contributed to national economic well-being and pointed to the growing need for labor, especially in agriculture and mining.[9]

Although the 1864 Contract Labor Act was repealed in 1868, largely at the urging of labor unions, private agencies continued to arrange contract labor agreements. Moreover, U.S. consuls encouraged immigration, and employers, trade associations, and states actively recruited labor in the post-Civil War era.[10] Additionally, the federal government's foreign policy during this period was characterized by a liberal attitude towards immigration. For example, U.S. efforts in the nineteenth century to gain access to China for trade and commerce culminated in the 1868 Burlingame Treaty with China, which called for freedom of migration between the two countries for travel, trade, and residence, though not necessarily citizenship.[11]

Active federal encouragement of labor immigration was possible not only because of economic conditions before and after the war but also because of the decline of nativism. The Know-Nothing Party already had fallen apart in the 1850s as a result of disagreement on the issue of slavery.[12] Additionally, the military participation of individuals from various immigrant groups in the Civil War contributed to the decline of nativism, which was replaced by an optimistic intellectual outlook emphasizing tolerance and the potential for an American "melting pot."[13]

In sum, the period from the founding of the United States through much of the nineteenth century was a golden age for immigration. In spite of nativist demands for restriction, no significant federal immigration regulations were adopted in the early 1800s. In fact, when it became evident that immigration flows were not sufficient to meet the needs of an expanding industrial economy during the Civil War, federal legislation designed to encourage immigration was adopted. In early U.S. history, then, proponents of an open immigration policy triumphed over advocates of restriction in the immigration policy debate. During the "golden door" era, liberal attitudes towards immigration predominated over latent nativism.

RECESSION, RACISM, AND SELECTIVE RESTRICTION IN THE LATE 1800s

A sharp increase in annual immigration levels and sporadic economic growth after the Civil War rejuvenated efforts to restrict immigration. In the early 1800s, only approximately 25,000 immigrants annually arrived in the United States. By the end of the 1840s, average annual immigration was greater than 100,000.[14] After the Civil War, these annual figures almost doubled.[15] Due to business cycle fluctuations in the 1870s, annual immigration levels began to decline. In fact, net immigration was negative in 1874 as a result of the economic recession.[16] However, anti-immigration forces were not content to rely on the mechanisms of the international labor market. New restrictionist movements emerged, frequently organized around nativist principles.[17]

Congress responded to new demands for restriction by adopting the first major federal immigration regulations. The Immigration Act of 1875 marks the beginning of direct federal regulation of immigration. This legislation defined prostitutes and convicts as excludable aliens. In addition, the law specified that no Asians could be brought into the country without their consent in an effort to suppress the "coolie trade," which some critics of the practice likened to slavery. This provision also addressed the anti-Chinese sentiment of labor organizations, especially on the West Coast, which saw the Chinese as competitors for jobs during a period of economic decline.[18] In the 1882 Immigration Act, the mentally ill and destitute individuals were added to the list of excludable aliens.[19] Though federal regulations were opposed by many business and manufacturing associations, steamship lines, and western and midwestern states, the anti-immigrant forces prevailed in this period of economic uncertainty.[20]

These early efforts at federal regulation were not considered sufficient by the anti-immigration forces, which began to target Chinese immigrants in their demands for restriction. Labor organizations, driven by fears of job displacement and the belief that Chinese workers increasingly were being used to break strikes, were at the forefront of efforts to restrict Chinese immigration.[21] Nativist organizations also actively lobbied for restrictions against Chinese immigrants because of their perceived racial and cultural unassimilability and the nativist fear that the Chinese eventually would outnumber the white population.[22] In a period of economic decline, the identifiable differences of Chinese immigrants had made them easy scapegoats for economic and social ills.

Early congressional efforts to adopt legislation restricting Chinese immigration were hindered by resistance in the executive branch, which was more concerned with foreign policy objectives.[23] However, Chinese exclusion efforts eventually triumphed. The first Chinese Exclusion Act of 1882 suspended the immigration of Chinese laborers for ten years, though merchants, tourists, state officials, and skilled workers in "new industries" for which adequate domestic labor was unavailable were exempt from this suspension of immigration. The act also allowed for the deportation of Chinese illegally residing in the United States and specified that Chinese immigrants were not to be admitted for citizenship.[24] Clearly incorporating a racial element into immigration policy, the Chinese Exclusion Act of 1884 clarified the previous legislation by explicitly providing that all Chinese, whether or not they were subjects of the Chinese government, were covered by the 1882 act. The 1888 Chinese Exclusion Act prohibited the entry of any Chinese person into the United States except government officials, teachers, students, merchants, or tourists, and the 1892 Chinese Exclusion Act extended the previous Chinese exclusion laws for ten years.[25]

The Chinese Exclusion Acts did not totally prevent the immigration of Chinese laborers. As in the case of other attempts at exclusion, some Chinese laborers were able to enter illegally, generally by using fraudulent documents.[26] Nevertheless, a drastic reduction in the number of legal Chinese immigrants followed the adoption of the Chinese exclusion laws. While in 1881 almost 12,000 Chinese individuals legally immigrated to the United States, this number was only 23 in 1885.[27] As these figures demonstrate, racial restrictions provided an effective method for restricting legal Chinese immigration to the United States.

In addition to the Chinese exclusion laws, Congress acknowledged nativist demands for restriction by adopting the Alien Contract Labor Act of 1885. The Federation of Organized Trades and Labor Unions as well as the Teamsters Union and other labor groups were instrumental in gaining the passage of this act and were opposed to contract labor for two basic reasons. First, the labor groups believed that employer reliance on cheap immigrant labor displaced domestic workers and kept wages low. Second, labor groups focused their attention on contract labor because employers regularly used contract laborers to break strikes and weaken unions.[28]

In an apparent response to labor concerns, the 1885 Alien Contract Labor Act made it illegal to contract to import workers or in any way to encourage immigration to the United States for labor or service. However, the legislation included several important loopholes that have been attributed to employer interests, including exemptions for skilled workers in new industries and relatives of legal residents, which weakened the restrictive objectives of labor groups.[29] The Alien Contract Labor Act was ineffective not only because of the loopholes in the legislation but also because the act did not affect the private labor exchanges that contracted the labor of immigrants who had already arrived in the country.[30] Moreover, contract labor inspectors did not ask immigrants if they had a contract unless they looked "suspicious," and, even if asked, immigrants were instructed by their contractors not to admit that they had a contract.[31] As a result of these obstacles to enforcement, the 1901 House Industrial Commission estimated that only approximately 8,000 immigrants were excluded under the legislation. Unlike the Chinese exclusion laws, based explicitly on racial criteria, the Alien Contract Labor Act essentially was ineffective.

Average annual immigration had nearly doubled from 1870 to 1890 and remained high throughout the 1890s. At the same time, an increasing proportion of overall immigration was from southern and eastern Europe.[32] While immigration levels rose, economic growth continued to be sporadic, and unemployment was high during most of this decade. Economic uncertainty coupled with the increasing proportion of largely unskilled workers from southern and eastern Europe generated growing support for immigration restrictions.

In spite of pressure for stronger regulation of immigration, few restrictions were passed during this decade. Nevertheless, nativist forces persisted in their demands for new restrictive legislation. In the 1890s, nativist groups embraced the literacy test as a means of restricting immigration because they assumed it would deter the immigration of "undesirable races" from southern and eastern Europe.[33] Nativist concerns also converged with the interests of labor because the literacy test was viewed as a means of excluding unskilled labor.[34] This literacy test bill was passed by both the House and the Senate but was vetoed by President Cleveland. The congressional effort to override the veto was unsuccessful primarily because of opposition from urban congressional districts with large immigrant voting blocs.[35] As a result of continued opposition to a literacy test on the part of immigrant organizations and some employers, the House voted not to consider an 1898 Senate bill calling for a literacy test.[36] Though these early literacy test bills were defeated, the racial emphasis in restrictive efforts was growing and would provide the foundation of U.S. immigration legislation in the first half of the twentieth century.

THE RACIAL FOUNDATIONS OF U.S. IMMIGRATION POLICY IN THE TWENTIETH CENTURY

In the early part of the twentieth century, support for immigration regulations based on racial criteria continued to grow. One of the most important factors driving the calls for racial exclusion was the increasing proportion of immigrants from southern and eastern Europe at a time when overall immigration was increasing. From 1882 to 1896, overall immigration from Europe into the United States was 6,575,039 with approximately seventy-one percent of this number coming from the "old immigrant" countries of northwestern Europe. From 1897 to 1914, there were 13,041,124 European immigrants to the United States, and over seventy-five percent were "new immigrants" from southern and eastern Europe.[37] (See Figure 2.1.)[38]

Calls for racial exclusion were based not only on the view that these new immigrants were culturally different and more difficult to assimilate but also on the perception that they were racially inferior. Many social scientists in the early part of the twentieth century were developing theories that emphasized racial differences, especially eugenics researchers who adopted racial categories to explain the inheritance of cultural and personal traits like intelligence, morality, and poverty. Psychologists, in turn, reinforced racial distinctions through their development of intelligence tests that were said to support the theory that demonstrable racial differences in intelligence existed. Many social scientists and academics disputed the racial theories of this period and, in particular, rejected the way in which they were interpreted and advanced by nativist organizations. However, a significant number of scientists, doctors, professionals, and perhaps most importantly, the general public, accepted racial theories; "scientific racism" thus provided the basis for arguments against immigration in the early part of the twentieth century.[39]

In 1904, a new Chinese exclusion act authorized the continuation of all previous Chinese exclusion acts. Unlike the previous act, this legislation included no time limits on Chinese exclusions. Although no legislation designed to exclude Asians from Japan was adopted, the Roosevelt administration successfully negotiated the 1907 Gentleman's Agreement with Japan, in which Japan agreed to restrict the migration of Japanese workers, with exceptions for legal residents returning to the United States and family members of legal residents.

In addition to the exclusion of Asians, the restrictionist movement continued to exert pressure for the passage of a literacy test designed to deter immigrants from southern and eastern Europe. The American Legion, the Immigration Restriction League, the "100-Percenters," organized labor, and some law enforcement agencies and charitable groups were united in support of a literacy test. However, pro-immigration forces, including a large number of employer associations and ethnic organizations, again were able to obstruct efforts to adopt a literacy test in the early 1900s.[40] Amendments providing for a literacy test were deleted from the 1903 and 1907 immigration legislation so that these acts could garner enough support for passage.[41] However, the restrictionist forces would not relent in their pursuit of the literacy test or other anti-immigration measures. The Dillingham Commission, created in 1907 to study immigration problems, submitted its report in 1911. Racial concerns were prevalent in this report, and a literacy test and other restrictions were advocated.[42]

World War I proved to be the turning point that swayed the debate over restriction in favor of the anti-immigration forces. Nationalism during the war

Figure 2.1
Immigration from Europe to the United States by Region of Origin: 1871–1920

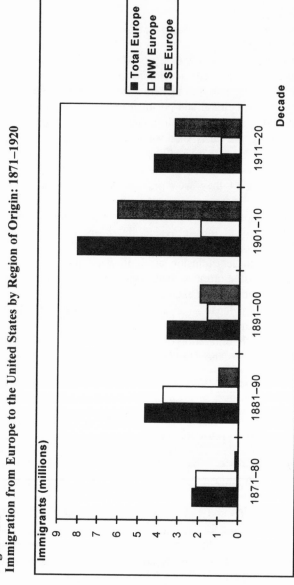

Source: U.S. Immigration and Naturalization Service, *Statistical Yearbook of the Immigration and Naturalization Service, 1992:* 26–29.

converged with racial thinking and strengthened the restrictionists' distrust of "unassimilable" immigrants from distinct ethnic groups. Economic conditions were beginning to decline by 1915 and reinforced the desire for racial exclusion.[43] Even though immigration levels dropped significantly during the war without legislative restrictions, postwar isolationism in the United States bolstered the desire for restrictive legislation.[44] In addition, the fear of radicalism, aggravated by the Russian Revolution in 1917, reinforced nativism both during and after the war and diminished the opposition of many industrialists to immigration restrictions. As a result of these developments, anti-immigration forces gained advantage in the immigration policy debate.

The racism, nationalism, and fear of radicalism that were prevalent during and after World War I, as well as uncertain economic conditions, set the stage for major changes in U.S. immigration policy. Passed over President Wilson's veto, the 1917 Immigration Act contained several restrictive provisions. This legislation replaced previous exclusions on Asian immigration with a provision creating an Asiatic barred zone from which immigration for permanent residence was prohibited. In another provision aimed at racial restriction, Congress finally adopted a literacy test intended to reduce immigration from southern and eastern Europe. For the first time, the 1917 act also made it a misdemeanor to bring in or knowingly harbor illegal immigrants, though the legislation did not specifically define employment as harboring.[45]

Long a major goal of restrictionist forces, the literacy test authorized in the 1917 legislation did not prove to be effective either in deterring southern and eastern European immigrants or in reducing overall immigration levels. Contradicting racist expectations, large numbers of southern and eastern European immigrants passed the literacy test and gained entry. Moreover, Mexican workers typically were exempted from the literacy test, and Mexican immigration increased rapidly in the ensuing years.[46] In 1920, despite a brief economic recession, immigration levels began to rise.[47] Though the literacy test had not proven effective, the public desire for racial restrictions remained extremely strong.

Thus, anti-immigrant forces began to advocate national quotas as a new approach for limiting immigration from southern and eastern Europe. National quotas differed from the literacy test in that the objective of excluding immigrants from certain racial or ethnic groups was made explicit. "Scientific racism" was gaining widespread acceptance and was crucial in securing sufficient support for the passage of quota legislation in that it shifted the traditional alignments in the immigration policy debate. Immigrant organizations had been significant opponents of immigration restriction in the past. However, while many immigrant groups spoke out against the proposed racial exclusions, including the Vasa Order of America, the German-American Citizens League, the Sons of Norway, and the American Jewish Committee, some of the more powerful organizations of "old immigrants" accepted and, in some cases, even advocated restrictions against the racially distinct "new immigrants."[48]

Racial concerns also were an important factor in the increased acceptance of quota legislation among employers, another group that had traditionally opposed immigration restrictions.   For example, Henry Ford, whose *Dearborn Independent* publication was renowned for its anti-Jewish themes, supported the quota laws as a way of excluding undesirable races.[49] Though the National Association of Manufacturers and other employer groups represented at the hearings on the 1921 quota legislation were opposed to the law because they feared labor shortages, the mood of employers outside of the hearings varied. The *Commercial and Financial Chronicle*, the *Mining and Scientific Press*, and other industry journals pointed to the need to exclude undesirable immigrants, including radicals and the "unassimilable." Hence, various employers accepted the need for some restrictions largely because of nativist concerns.[50]

Though a 1921 bill to limit annual immigration to three percent of the foreign-born population in the United States had been vetoed by President Wilson, the Emergency Immigration Restriction Act was passed in 1921 without the veto of the new Republican president, Warren G. Harding. This legislation established annual immigration quotas based on national origin. Annual quotas for each nation were set at three percent of that nationality in the U.S. population according to the 1910 census. Because immigration from southern and eastern Europe had only begun to increase significantly by the end of the 1800s, immigrants from this region still represented a small percentage of the overall U.S. population in 1910. Therefore, the future immigration of these nationalities would be significantly limited by the quota legislation. The Asiatic barred zone created by the 1917 Immigration Act was maintained in the 1921 legislation. Exemptions from the quotas, largely a concession to economic and foreign policy interests, were granted to government officials, tourists, businesspersons, and individuals who had resided in the Western Hemisphere for at least one year.[51] First adopted for one year, this act was extended for two years in 1922 until permanent quota legislation could be put into place. Under this temporary quota legislation, overall legal immigration declined from 805,228 to 309,556 during fiscal year 1921–1922, including non-quota immigration.[52]

Almost immediately after the temporary quota legislation was passed, the debate over the creation of a permanent quota system began. This debate was initiated as signs of economic prosperity were returning and as many employers were beginning to experience labor shortages, especially of unskilled labor. Nevertheless, continuing technological progress in mechanization and enduring racial thinking on the part of many employers again ensured the relative acquiescence of the business community in regard to quota legislation.[53] Similarly, immigrant organizations were divided over the question of permanent quota legislation.   While widespread acceptance of racism weakened the traditional opponents of immigration restriction, it strengthened restrictionist forces that easily prevailed in gaining passage of the permanent national origins system during a period of general economic prosperity. The debate over this policy, which was passed by a wide majority, cut across class and party lines.

While critics of racism voiced opposition to this legislation, their voices basically were silenced by the majority, which endorsed racial exclusions.

The Immigration Act of 1924 provided for the creation of a permanent quota system even more restrictive than the 1921 temporary quota legislation. The 1924 quota legislation incorporated two methods for racial exclusion. The first method was a temporary measure to be used until the permanent national origins system could be put into place. This temporary measure reduced national quotas to two percent of a nationality's population in the 1890 U.S. census. Under this system, the overall annual ceiling derived from the quotas was reduced from approximately 356,000 to less than 165,000. Moreover, racial restrictions against southern and eastern Europeans were made more stringent because even fewer immigrants from that region resided in the United States in 1890. The second method was the national origins system, which provided for an overall ceiling of 150,000. National quotas under this ceiling were based on the proportion of each nationality's population in the overall white population in 1920. Each method for determining quota allowances under the 1924 Immigration Act was more restrictive than the 1921 temporary quota legislation, both in terms of overall immigration and racial exclusion.[54]

The 1924 Immigration Act firmly established the principle of racial exclusion in U.S. immigration policy. Supporters of the more restrictive quota systems created under this legislation disputed charges that quota restrictions were discriminatory by arguing that the maintenance of the racial status quo was the fairest way to represent the interests of the current population. Sections of the House Committee report on the 1924 legislation explaining why 1890 was selected as the base year for quotas illustrate the way in which the racial restrictions were viewed as both necessary and fair:

If immigration from southern and eastern Europe may enter the United States on a basis of substantial equality with that admitted from the older sources of supply, it is clear that if any appreciable number of immigrants are to be allowed to land upon our shores the balance of racial preponderance must in time pass to those elements of the population who reproduce more rapidly on a lower standard of living than those possessing other ideals. . . . The use of the 1890 census is not discriminatory. It is used in an effort to preserve, as nearly as possible, the racial status quo in the United States. It is hoped to guarantee, as best we can at this late date, racial homogeneity in the United States.[55]

Thus, the majority of the House Committee members in this case believed that racial restrictions provided a fair method for regulating immigration that would foster economic, political, and social stability.

Though racial considerations were crucial in shaping the 1924 immigration legislation, other factors came into play. A number of exemptions were included in the legislation that can be attributed to a variety of factors. Natives of the Western Hemisphere and their families were exempted from the national quota basically for two reasons. First, agricultural industries in the southwestern United States were particularly reliant on cheap labor from Mexico. Second, foreign policy was important as Secretary of State Kellogg was attempting to improve U.S.-Mexican relations in the 1920s. Hence, economic interests and foreign policy prevailed in the case of Western Hemisphere immigration.[56] In addition to the exemption for natives of the Western Hemisphere, wives and unmarried minor children of citizens were able to immigrate outside of quota allowances. Relatives also were given preference within the quota system, with up to fifty percent of each country's quota reserved for unmarried minor children, parents, and spouses of citizens. This emphasis on family reunification in the 1924 legislation can be attributed, in part, to humanitarian concerns, though the interests of immigrant organizations were likely also a factor.[57] In spite of provisions allowing for family reunification, the quota legislation adopted in the 1920s was highly restrictive and clearly made discrimination a central element of U.S. immigration policy.

The figures on immigration suggest that the quota legislation of the 1920s was effective in restricting immigration from Europe. Average annual immigration declined from 800,000 from 1900 to 1910, to 600,000 from 1910 to 1920, to an annual average of only 400,000 from 1920 to 1930. In 1921, there were more than 800,000 immigrants from Europe but less than 150,000 by 1930. The effects on southern and eastern European immigrants were especially strong; only 24,002 immigrants from southern and eastern Europe were admitted under quotas in 1930 compared to 116,062 from northwestern Europe.[58] (See Figure 2.2.)[59] During the 1930s, average annual immigration was well under 100,000, and net migration was negative as annual emigration exceeded annual immigration for the only decade in U.S. history, with the poor economy of the Depression converging with the restrictive effects of the quota legislation. In fact, immigration for every region was well below the quota allowances throughout the 1930s.[60] (See Table 2.1.)[61]

Though nativism continued to shape U.S. policy after the 1920s, as evidenced by public opposition to congressional legislation that would have relaxed the national origins quotas to allow the entrance of refugees from Europe during the 1930s, the national origins system represents the peak of nativist influence. The restrictive tide began to turn during World War II. Several wartime bills to suspend immigration during the war failed.[62] Furthermore, in spite of strong opposition to Western Hemisphere immigration among restrictionist forces, the Roosevelt administration initiated the wartime Bracero Program in 1942 through bilateral treaties with various Western Hemisphere countries, including Mexico, in order to meet foreign policy and economic needs.[63] Giving the state a direct role in recruiting temporary workers, especially for agricultural labor in the Southwest, this program strengthened an economic and social network that had generated migration from Mexico to the United States since the mid-1800s.[64]

In another liberalizing development, the Naturalization Act of 1943 gave the right of naturalization to Chinese immigrants. As a result, China was given an annual quota under the national origins system. Congress removed additional racial restrictions in our naturalization law in the 1946 Naturalization Act, which authorized the naturalization of individuals from the Philippines and India and which again made them eligible for immigration under the quota laws.[65]

Figure 2.2
Immigration from Europe to the United States by Region of Origin: 1901–1950

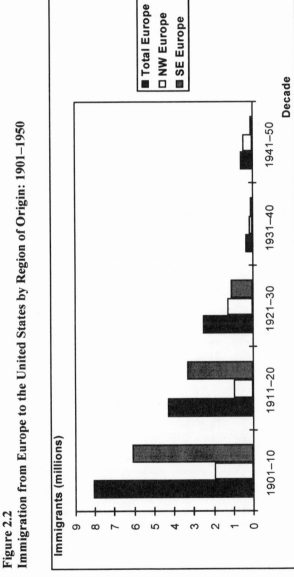

Source: U.S. Immigration and Naturalization Service, *Statistical Yearbook of the Immigration and Naturalization Service, 1992: 26–29.*

Table 2.1
Immigration to the United States by Region of Origin: 1881–1950

	TOTAL	Europe	Americas	Asia	Africa	Oceania
1881–90	5,246,613	4,735,484	426,967	69,942	857	12,574
1891–00	3,687,684	3,555,352	38,972	74,862	350	3,965
1901–10	8,795,386	8,056,040	361,888	323,543	7,368	13,024
1911–20	5,735,811	4,321,887	1,143,671	274,236	8,443	13,427
1921–30	4,107,209	2,463,194	1,516,716	112,059	6,286	8,726
1931–40	528,431	347,566	160,037	16,595	1,750	2,483
1941–50	1,035,039	621,147	354,804	37,028	7,387	14,551

Source: U.S. Immigration and Naturalization Service, *Statistical Yearbook of the Immigration and Naturalization Service, 1992: 26–29.*

However, quotas of only approximately 100 visas were established for these Asian countries, and, hence, our immigration policy remained extremely discriminatory towards Asians.[66]

Nativism, largely in the form of racial discrimination, provided the foundation of U.S. immigration policy in the first half of the twentieth century. The national origins system developed in the 1920s was the first comprehensive system of immigrant selection in immigration policy and was influenced significantly by nativist ideas, which had gained widespread acceptance during this period. During World War II, foreign policy concerns and economic interests were beginning to strengthen pro-immigration forces. In the decades after World War II, these factors would converge with the growing civil rights movement and, ultimately, would result in monumental changes to U.S. immigration policy.

U.S. IMMIGRATION POLICY AFTER WORLD WAR II

Soon after World War II, two basic developments led to demands for the liberalization of U.S. immigration policy. First, growing public awareness of Nazi atrocities during World War II created unprecedented support for human rights. In the debate over U.S. immigration policy, this support for the idea of human rights was translated into demands for the admission of refugees and the elimination of the discriminatory national origins system. Second, the emerging Cold War with the Soviet Union also resulted in calls for the admission of refugees from Communist countries and the liberalization of the quota system, which discriminated against several European allies.[67]

In spite of new pressures for liberalization, one of the earliest policy developments in the post–World War II period, the 1952 Immigration and Nationality Act, can be characterized as restrictive. Commonly known as the McCarran-Walter Act, this legislation retained the majority of the provisions of the racially discriminatory national origins system. However, initial steps were taken to reduce racial discrimination in U.S. immigration policy. The act removed racial barriers to naturalization, thus making individuals of all races eligible for immigration and permanent residence. Quotas for independent, self-governing, and UN trustee areas within the former Asiatic barred zone, now called the Asia-Pacific Triangle, were established. Nevertheless, the McCarran-Walter legislation remained essentially discriminatory. Immigrants with one-half or more Asian ancestry were charged to the Asian quota regardless of their country of origin. Moreover, the system for determining national quotas based on the proportion of that nationality in the United States in 1920 resulted in very small Asian quotas and continued the small quotas for immigrants from southern and eastern Europe.[68]

The interest group dynamics shaping the debate over the bill were similar to previous policy debates. Many ethnic organizations opposed the continuation of the discriminatory national origins system. Though opponents of the bill criticized the retention of the national origins system as racist, continued discrimination was advocated by nativist groups. The Senate Committee report, defending the national origins system, reflects the persistent influence that nativist views exerted in U.S. immigration policy:

[T]he peoples who had made the greatest contribution to the development of this nation were fully justified in determining that the country was no longer a field for further colonization, and henceforth further immigration would not only be restricted but directed to admit immigrants considered to be more readily assimilable because of the similarity of their cultural background to those of the principle components of our population.[69]

As in the 1920s, Congress viewed the maintenance of the racial status quo as both necessary and fair. However, unlike the debate over the 1920 quota legislation, arguments supporting the retention of the quota system in the 1952 McCarran-Walter Act were based largely on concerns about cultural assimilation rather than *explicit* references to the notion of racial superiority.[70]

President Truman vetoed this legislation because he opposed the discriminatory national origins system. In his veto message, President Truman justified his opposition to continued racial exclusions on both foreign policy and humanitarian grounds:

In one respect this bill recognizes the great international significance of our immigration and naturalization policy, and takes a step to improving existing laws. All racial bars to naturalization would be removed, and at least some minimum immigration quota would be afforded to each of the free nations of Asia. . . . But now this most desirable provision comes before me embedded in a mass of legislation which would perpetuate injustices of long standing against many other nations of the world, hamper the efforts we are making to rally the men of East and West alike to the cause of freedom, and intensify the repressive and inhumane aspects of our immigration procedures. The price is too high, and in good conscience I cannot agree to pay it.[71]

In spite of Truman's appeal to foreign policy and humanitarian concerns, Congress overrode his veto with bipartisan support.[72]

As indicated by Truman's speech, foreign policy objectives and humanitarian concerns after World War II underlay new demands for the liberalization of immigration policy. These concerns also were prominent in the report of the President's Commission on Immigration and Naturalization, created by President Truman under an executive order in September 1952. The commission's report concluded that the national origins system was discriminatory and should be eliminated. In addition to criticizing the national origins system as discriminatory, the report stated that existing immigration policy did not meet labor needs and hindered U.S. foreign policy, especially given the ideological conflict between the United States and the Soviet Union.[73] However, the persistence of nativist opposition to liberalization prevented stronger modifications of immigration policy during the 1950s.

Largely because of the exceptions to the national origins system made for various refugee groups and non-quota immigration from the Western

Hemisphere, immigration levels from the end of World War II to the mid-1960s doubled the allowances under the quota system. An estimated 1 million Western Hemisphere immigrants, over one-half of whom were Canadian, entered legally during this period,[74] and almost two-thirds of legal immigrants entered outside of quota restrictions from 1952 to 1965.[75]

Though anti-immigration forces opposed the policy allowances that resulted in these large numbers, the economic and political environment increasingly favored advocates of liberalization in immigration policy.   Inflation and unemployment were extremely low while growth rates were high throughout most of the 1960s.   U.S. investments in Europe after World War II, intended to further economic interests as well as political advantage in the ideological struggle with the Soviet Union, were paying off in the form of economic expansion in Europe and the United States.   The civil rights movement also shifted the immigration policy debate in favor of pro-immigration forces. Academic research which disputed earlier racist theories was becoming more widely accepted.   Individuals with immigrant backgrounds were reaching positions of political leadership in greater numbers. Ethnic consciousness was on the rise. All of these factors contributed to the growth of the civil rights movement.   In turn, one of the early objectives of this movement was to eliminate racial discrimination in U.S. immigration policy.

The statement on immigration in the 1960 Democratic Party platform, which called for the elimination of the national origins system, indicates the way in which foreign policy concerns, economic interests, and civil rights demands were converging in favor of a liberalized immigration policy:

The revision of immigration and nationality laws we seek will implement our belief that enlightened immigration, naturalization, and refugee policies and humane administration of them are important aspects of our foreign policy. . . .   These laws will bring greater skills to our land, reunite families, permit the United States to meet its fair share of world programs of rescue and rehabilitation, and take advantage of immigration as an important factor in the growth of the American economy.[76]

The Republican Party platform only advocated a slight moderation of the discriminatory national origins system through the use of 1960 as the base year for determining proportional quotas.[77]

The Democrats won the 1960 election, and pro-immigration forces won the debate over the liberalization of immigration policy.   President Kennedy presented a bill to Congress in 1963 that called for the elimination of the national origins system.   This bill provided the impetus for immigration reform that culminated in the 1965 amendments to the Immigration and Nationality Act.[78]

Just as widespread racism weakened the traditional coalition of pro-immigration forces in the 1920s, growing acceptance of civil rights tempered the opposition of the conventional opponents of liberal immigration in the 1960s. In the congressional hearings on the 1965 amendments to the Immigration and Nationality Act, only a few interest groups, including the Daughters of the American Revolution and the American Coalition of Patriotic Societies, testified in opposition to the proposed amendments to U.S. immigration policy. The majority of individuals and groups testifying before Congress registered their support for the removal of ethnic discrimination in U.S. immigration policy. Representatives of religious organizations, ethnic groups, and the American Civil Liberties Union provided testimony supporting the elimination of the national origins system. Importantly, the AFL-CIO and the American Veterans Committee also added their endorsement of the proposed change to U.S. immigration policy.[79] The breadth of support for the removal of racial exclusions ensured passage of the 1965 legislation.

The 1965 amendments to the Immigration and Nationality Act eliminated the national origins system and its underlying racial criteria from U.S. immigration policy. An immigration ceiling of 170,000, with per-country limits of 20,000 visas, was established for the Eastern Hemisphere. Within the Eastern hemispheric limit, visas were allotted according to a seven-category system that gave preference to relatives of citizens and legal residents and individuals with special occupational skills. The immediate relatives of U.S. citizens were exempted from the quotas. Though criticized as detrimental to foreign relations with Latin America, an immigration ceiling for the Western Hemisphere was established for the first time to address concerns regarding growing population pressure in Latin America and to meet restrictionist sentiment in an effort to assure the passage of this act.[80] Initially, the country limits and preference system were not applicable in the Western Hemisphere, and Western Hemisphere applicants for visas had to obtain labor market certification for entry. A 1976 amendment to the Immigration and Nationality Act extended the 20,000 per-country limit and the preference system to the Western Hemisphere. A 1978 amendment combined the hemispheric allowances into an overall global ceiling of 290,000 with a retention of the per-country limits and preference system within this overall limit.[81]

At Ellis Island, in a statement on the 1965 policy, President Johnson commented on the importance of non-discrimination in U.S. immigration policy:

Now under the monument which has welcomed so many to our shores, the American nation returns to the finest of its traditions today. The days of unlimited immigration are past. But those who do come will come because of what they are, and not because of the land from which they sprang. . . . Over my shoulder here you can see Ellis Island, whose vacant corridors echo today the joyous sounds of long-ago voices. . . . And today we can all believe that the lamp of this grand old lady is brighter today—and the golden door that she guards gleams more brilliantly in the light of an increased liberty for the peoples from all the countries of the globe.[82]

Though his rhetoric hearkens back to the 1889 Emma Lazarus poem inscribed on the Statue of Liberty, President Johnson was not celebrating a return of U.S. policy to the open-door immigration policy that characterized most of nineteenth century immigration policy. The United States would continue to regulate immigration, but it would do so without explicitly discriminating on the basis of national origin.

The system of immigrant selection embodied in the 1965 legislation remains the basic foundation of U.S. immigration policy today. Racial exclusions have been removed. Instead, the regulation of legal immigration is now accomplished through the use of a non-discriminatory quota system by which each nation is allotted an equal number of quotas within an overall immigration ceiling. Rather than race, eligibility for immigration is based on family reunification, personal qualifications, and order of application.[83]

The effects of the 1965 legislation have been dramatic. In the decade after the 1965 amendments were implemented in 1968, immigration increased by approximately sixty percent.[84] This increase can be attributed, in part, to the elimination of the national origins system. Even though the 1965 legislation raised the annual immigration ceiling for the Eastern Hemisphere by only 20,000 visas to 170,000, the elimination of the national origins system increased the likelihood that annual immigration levels would reach this ceiling. While the large quotas granted to northwestern European countries under the national origins system often were not filled, the demand for visas under the new system typically has outweighed quota allowances, especially in the less-developed countries of southern and eastern Europe and Asia.[85]

In addition to an increase in overall legal immigration, a clear change in the ethnic composition of immigrants has resulted from the elimination of the national origins system. In the 1950s, over fifty percent of legal immigrants were from Europe; since 1970, that proportion has declined to fifteen percent. Conversely, the proportion of immigrants from Latin America has increased from twenty-five percent to forty percent, and the proportion of immigrants from Asia also has risen significantly.[86] In fact, Asians and Latin Americans comprised approximately seventy-five percent of legal immigration flows in the 1970s.[87] (See Table 2.2.)[88]

In spite of the dramatic consequences of the 1965 amendments to the Immigration and Nationality Act, critics have argued that this legislation remains discriminatory in its effects. Civil rights advocates contend that the per-country limits under the 1965 legislation hinder family reunification, as well as immigration in general, for individuals from countries where the demand for visas is high. While quotas are underutilized in some countries, especially in Europe, demand for visas exceeds quota allowances in many developing countries. Hence, family members of legal residents in countries where demand exceeds visa allowances frequently have to wait much longer to obtain visas than applicants within a lower preference category, such as skilled workers, from a European country with underutilized quotas. Therefore, many civil rights advocates have continued to demand additional changes to U.S. immigration policy, including the elimination of per-country limits.[89]

In fact, civil rights considerations have been one of the most important factors shaping U.S. immigration policy since 1965. The changes to U.S. refugee policy in 1980 were shaped, in part, by demands for equitable treatment of refugees from all countries. In accordance with the 1951 Convention on Refugees and the 1967 Protocol to this convention, the 1980 Refugee Act changed the definition

Table 2.2
Immigration to the United States by Region of Origin: 1900–1990

	TOTAL	Europe	Americas	Asia	Africa	Oceania
1901–10	8,795,386	8,056,040	361,888	323,543	7,368	13,024
1911–20	5,736,811	4,321,887	1,143,671	274,236	8,443	13,427
1921–30	4,107,209	2,463,194	1,516,716	112,059	6,286	8,726
1931–40	528,431	347,566	160,037	16,595	1,750	2,483
1941–50	1,035,039	621,147	354,804	37,028	7,387	14,551
1951–60	2,515,479	1,325,727	996,944	153,249	14,092	12,976
1961–70	3,321,677	1,123,492	1,716,374	427,642	28,954	25,122
1971–80	4,493,314	800,368	1,982,735	1,588,178	80,779	41,242
1981–90	7,338,062	761,550	3,615,225	2,738,157	176,893	45,205

Source: U.S. Immigration and Naturalization Service, *Statistical Yearbook of the Immigration and Naturalization Service, 1992: 26–29.*

of refugee so that it covered all refugees fleeing from persecution based on race, religion, or nationality rather than only refugees from Communist or Middle Eastern countries.[90] Passage of the 1986 Immigration Reform and Control Act, designed to reduce illegal immigration through the use of employer sanctions, would not have been possible without a provision, advocated by civil rights groups as well as ethnic organizations, legalizing residents who had been in the United States for a specified period of time. In spite of widespread public support for a reduction in both legal and illegal immigration, the 1990 Immigration Act increased annual allowances for legal immigration partly to facilitate family reunification and to promote diversity in immigration flows to this country. As the most recent developments in immigration policy demonstrate, the trend in the post–World War II period has been away from the nativist policies of earlier years towards an immigration policy based on non–discrimination.

IMMIGRATION CONTROL IN AN ERA OF NON-DISCRIMINATION

One distinct change clearly distinguishes between the immigration policy debates in the early twentieth century and the post–World War II period. The racial theories during the first part of the twentieth century garnered enough support from workers, employers, powerful immigrant groups, and even governmental leaders concerned with foreign policy to gain passage of the restrictive and discriminatory national origins system. Conversely, the civil rights movement in the postwar period converged with employer interests in access to labor migrants as well as the interest of various immigrant groups in a liberalized immigration policy. Labor opposition to a more liberal immigration policy was mitigated by a growing belief that racial discrimination was unacceptable, and nativist organizations increasingly were isolated in their unwavering support for restrictive immigration policies. Nativist arguments are still a fundamental part of the immigration policy debate in the United States, as are concerns about the state of the economy, the labor needs of employers, and foreign policy and national security. However, the idea that racial discrimination is invalid and unacceptable had displaced the predominance of "scientific racism" by the 1960s. As a result, growth in support for civil rights has dramatically changed the framework in which the immigration policy debate takes place and has altered significantly the range of policy alternatives that are considered legitimate by the main actors involved in this debate.

The growing importance of civil rights in the post–World War II period has serious implications for the legislative regulation of international migration. Historically, legislative restrictions based on race, including Asian exclusions and the national origins system, were effective in reducing both the overall quantity of immigration and the ethnic composition of immigrant flows. The post–World War II modifications of U.S. immigration policy have removed this method of regulating immigration.

The elimination of discriminatory national origins quotas and an emphasis on family reunification in U.S. immigration policy have resulted in an increase in the annual legal ceiling on immigration. Moreover, civil rights considerations affect the way in which immigration officials can enforce immigration policy. The implementation of U.S. immigration policy continues to be marred by racial discrimination and civil rights violations.[91]   Nevertheless, Congress and the courts have expanded the due process rights of immigrants to a limited extent since World War II.[92]   Furthermore, provisions designed to prevent discrimination in hiring decisions by employers have diluted the potential strength of employer sanctions. In sum, prohibitions against discrimination have resulted not only in the liberalization of the criteria for admission but also in more cautious enforcement of immigration law.

The growing emphasis on civil rights indicates that the government has not lost control over its ability to regulate immigration to external forces. Instead, increased attention to civil rights suggests that non-discrimination and fairness have become important values among large segments of the population and that these values affect *how* and *to what extent* immigration can be controlled. Since the 1960s, the immigration policy debate in the United States has been shaped by support for civil rights and non-discrimination. The liberalization of U.S. immigration policy in recent decades can be attributed, in large part, to these ideas and is reflected in the increase in illegal and legal immigration to this country in recent decades. The way in which a system of selective restriction based on non-discrimination has affected the government's ability to regulate immigration is explored in great detail in the following chapters on the 1986 Immigration Reform and Control Act and the 1990 Immigration Act.

NOTES

1. *Congressional Record* 38:3 cited in E.P. Hutchinson, *Legislative History of American Immigration Policy: 1798–1965* (Philadelphia: University of Pennsylvania Press, 1981): 134.

2. John Higham, *Strangers in the Land: Patterns of American Nativism: 1860–1925*, 2d ed. (New Brunswick: Rutgers University Press, 1988): 4.

3. Emberson Edward Proper, A.M., *Colonial Immigration Laws* (New York: Columbia University Press, The MacMillan Company, Agents, 1900): 17–20.

4. Hutchinson: 12–16.

5. Hutchinson: 16;   Milton R. Konvitz, *Civil Rights in Immigration* (Ithaca, NY: Cornell University Press, 1953): 94–96.

6. Michael C. LeMay, *From Open Door to Dutch Door: An Analysis of U.S. Immigration Policy Since 1820* (New York: Praeger, 1987): 17. The only exception to this open-door policy was legislation passed by Congress in 1807 prohibiting the importation of slaves after January 1, 1808. Due to a lack of funding and political support, this legislation was never enforced effectively. Therefore, America's "golden door" stood open for the slave trade, which resulted in involuntary migration, as well as immigration in general. Vernon M. Briggs, Jr., *Immigration Policy and the American Labor Force* (Baltimore: The Johns Hopkins University Press, 1984): 17.

7. Thomas J. Curran, *Xenophobia and Immigration, 1820–1930* (Boston: Twayne Publishers, 1975).

8. Aristide Zolberg, "Contemporary Transnational Migrations in Historical Perspective: Patterns and Dilemmas," in Mary M. Kritz, ed., *U.S. Immigration and Refugee Policy* (Lexington, MA: Lexington Books, 1983): 23

9. *Congressional Globe*, 38th Cong., 1st sess., Appendix, pp. 1–2 cited in Hutchinson: 48.

10. Kitty Calavita, *U.S. Immigration Law and the Control of Labor: 1820–1924* (London: Academic Press, Inc., 1984): 46.

11. Roy L. Garis, *Immigration Restriction* (New York: The MacMillan Company, 1927): 288–289.

12. Briggs, *Immigration Policy*: 22; LeMay, *Open Door to Dutch Door*: 33.

13. Higham: 12–23.

14. Zolberg, "Contemporary Transnational Migrations": 22.

15. LeMay, *Open Door to Dutch Door*: 22.

16. Calavita, *U.S. Immigration Law*: 20.

17. Lawrence H. Fuchs, "Immigration, Pluralism, and Public Policy: The Challenge of the *Pluribus* to the *Unum*," in Mary M. Kritz, ed., *U.S. Immigration and Refugee Policy* (Lexington, MA: Lexington Books, 1983): 297.

18. Briggs, *Immigration Policy*: 26–27.

19. Hutchinson: 65–66, 80.

20. LeMay, *Open Door to Dutch Door*: 54.

21. Curran: 78–92.

22. Lawrence H. Fuchs, *The American Kaleidoscope: Race, Ethnicity, and the Civic Culture* (Hanover, NH: University Press of New England, 1990): 112–115.

23. Fearing that Chinese exclusions would hinder economic and political interests in Asia and recognizing that such exclusions would violate the 1868 Burlingame Treaty, President Hayes vetoed the 1879 Chinese Exclusion Act. In the place of legislative restrictions, President Hayes negotiated voluntary restrictions in an 1880 treaty with China in which China agreed to limit the emigration of "coolie workers," criminals, prostitutes, and the sick. Garis: 292–294. In spite of the successful negotiation of voluntary limits on emigration from China, Congress passed another Chinese Exclusion Act in 1881. This act would have suspended immigration of both unskilled and skilled laborers from China for twenty years but again received a presidential veto, this time from President Arthur.

24. Hutchinson: 494–495.

25. Ibid.: 92–97, 109–110. Well-established in legislation by the end of the 1880s, Chinese exclusion laws generally were upheld by the courts. Stephen H. Legomsky, *Immigration and the Judiciary: Law and Politics in Britain and America* (Oxford: Clarendon Press, 1987): 247–248.

26. Hutchinson: 439–441.

27. The number of Chinese immigrants rose to 40,000 in 1882 as many individuals immigrated before the law went into effect but had already declined to 8,031 by 1883. Michael C. LeMay, *The Struggle for Influence* (Lanham, MD: University Press of America, 1985): 185–186.

28. Calavita, *U.S. Immigration Law*: 47–51.

29. Ibid.: 47–54.

30. Ibid.: 44–46.

31. Ibid.: 62.

32. LeMay, *Open Door to Dutch Door*: 4–6, 38.

33. Curran: 119–128.

34. Hutchinson: 465.

35. Claudia Goldin, "The Political Economy of Immigration Restriction in the United States, 1890 to 1921," *National Bureau of Economic Research Working Paper Series, Working Paper No. 4345* (Cambridge, MA: National Bureau of Economic Research, April 1993): 6–9.

36. Hutchinson: 121–124.

37. Garis: 205.

38. While the Immigration and Naturalization Service provides information on total immigration from Europe as well as immigration from individual European countries, it does not categorize European immigrants by region. However, in Figure 2.1, I have separated the immigration figures for countries in northwestern and southeastern Europe in order to examine the effects of U.S. immigration policies on the ethnic composition of immigration flows. The northwestern European countries include Belgium, Denmark, France, Germany, Ireland, the Netherlands, Norway, Sweden, Switzerland, and the United Kingdom. The southeastern European countries include Austria, Hungary, Czechoslovakia, Greece, Italy, Poland, Portugal, Romania, Russia/the Soviet Union, Spain, and Yugoslavia.

39. Curran: 129–144; Higham: 270–277.

40. Higham: 186–193; LeMay, *Open Door to Dutch Door*: 12, 59–69.

41. Hutchinson: 133, 138–143.

42. Briggs, *Immigration Policy*: 36–38.

43. Goldin: 11.

44. LeMay, *Open Door to Dutch Door*: 70–77.

45. Hutchinson: 166–168, 600–601.

46. Calavita, *U.S. Immigration Law*: 133–136.

47. Higham: 308.

48. LeMay, *Open Door to Dutch Door*: 81.

49. Curran: 132–134; LeMay, *Open Door to Dutch Door*: 12, 33–37, 74.

50. Though racism was a key factor, economic developments also proved important in gaining the acquiescence of enough employers to ensure the passage of quota legislation. Increased use of Western Hemisphere labor, blacks, and women during World War I had reduced employers' reliance on cheap immigrant labor from Europe. Also, many employers were beginning to recognize the benefits of increased mechanization as an alternative to cheap labor. Calavita, *U.S. Immigration Law*: 151–157.

51. Hutchinson: 176–181.

52. Calavita, *U.S. Immigration Law*: 150.

53. Higham: 315–318; LeMay, *Open Door to Dutch Door*: 79–83.

54. Originally supposed to go into effect in July 1927, the national origins provision was not in operation until July 1929. LeMay, *Open Door to Dutch Door*: 91.

55. House Report 350 (68–I), pp. 13–14 cited in Hutchinson: 484–485.

56. LeMay, *Open Door to Dutch Door*: 90.

57. Hutchinson: 505–520.

58. A.W. Carlson, "One Century of Foreign Immigration to the United States: 1880–1979," *International Migration* 23:3 (September 1985): 77.

59. As in the case of Figure 2.1, I have separated the immigration figures for countries in northwestern and southeastern Europe for the purpose of analysis even though the Immigration and Naturalization Service does not categorize European immigration by region. See note 38.

60. LeMay, *Open Door to Dutch Door*: 75–93.

61. Figures cover immigrants admitted for permanent legal residence. Figures on total immigration also include small numbers of immigrants whose region of origin was not specified in immigration records. The Oceania category covers immigration from Australia and New Zealand.

62. Ibid.: 251–268.

63. Jorge I. Domínguez, "Immigration as Foreign Policy in U.S.-Latin American Relations," in Robert W. Tucker, Charles B. Keely, and Linda Wrigley, eds., *Immigration and U.S. Foreign Policy* (Boulder: Westview Press, 1990): 151–152.

64. Rodolfo O. de la Garza, "Immigration Reforms: A Mexican-American Perspective," in Gillian Peele, Christopher J. Bailey, and Bruce Cain, eds., *Developments in American Politics* (New York: St. Martin's Press, 1992): 312–313.

65. Hutchinson: 264–265, 272–273.

66. David M. Reimers, *Still the Golden Door: The Third World Comes to America*, 2d ed. (New York: Columbia University Press, 1992): 11–36.

67. Gil Loescher and John A. Scanlan, *Calculated Kindness: Refugees and America's Half-Open Door, 1945 to the Present* (New York: The Free Press, A Division of MacMillan, Inc., 1986): 1–24.

68. Within the quotas, preferences were given, in the following order, to immigrants with high technical qualifications, parents of citizens, and spouses and children of legal residents. Hutchinson: 303–311.

69. U.S. Congress, Senate, Committee on the Judiciary, *The Immigration and Naturalization Systems of the United States*, 81st Cong., 2d sess., 1950, Senate Report 1515: 455 cited in LeMay, *Open Door to Dutch Door*: 104.

70. U.S. Congress, Congressional Research Service, *U.S. Immigration Law and Policy: 1952–1979*, 96th Cong., 1st sess. (Washington: U.S. Government Printing Office, 1979): 8.

71. Cited in full in Konvitz: 159–171.

72. Konvitz: 18.

73. President's Commission on Immigration and Naturalization, *Whom We Shall Welcome*, Report of the President's Commission on Immigration and Naturalization (Washington, D.C.: U.S. Government Printing Office, 1953).

74. Zolberg, "Contemporary Transnational Migrations": 30–31.

75. Carlson: 312.

76. Cited in Hutchinson: 641.

77. Ibid.: 641–642.

78. U.S. Congress, Congressional Research Service, *U.S. Immigration Law*: 48–50.

79. U.S. Congress, House Subcommittee on Immigration and Nationality, *Hearings on H.R. 2580: To Amend the Immigration and Nationality Act*, 89th Cong., 1st sess. (Washington, D.C.: U.S. Government Printing Office, 1965); U.S. Congress, Senate Subcommittee on Immigration and Naturalization, *Hearings on S. 500: To Amend the Immigration and Nationality Act*, 89th Cong., 1st sess., Parts 1 and 2 (Washington, D.C.: U.S. Government Printing Office, 1965).

80. Robert L. Bach, "Immigration and U.S. Foreign Policy in Latin America and the Caribbean," in Tucker, Keely, and Wrigley, eds., *Immigration and U.S. Foreign Policy* (Boulder: Westview Press, 1990): 144–145.

81. Hutchinson: 377–378.

82. Lyndon B. Johnson, "Remarks on Immigration Law," *Congressional Quarterly*, October 1965: 2063–2064 cited in LeMay, *Open Door to Dutch Door*: 113.

83. Hutchinson: 377–378.

84. LeMay, *Open Door to Dutch Door*: 114.

85. U.S. Commission on Civil Rights, *The Tarnished Door: Civil Rights Issues in Immigration* (Washington, D.C.: U.S. Government Printing Office, 1980): 13–19.

86. Frank D. Bean, Jurgen Schmandt, and Sidney Weintraub, eds., *Mexican and Central American Population and U.S. Immigration Policy* (The Center for Mexican American Studies, the University of Texas at Austin, 1989): 1.

87. Carlson: 315–316.

88. Figures cover immigrants admitted for permanent legal residence. Figures on total immigration also include small numbers of immigrants whose region of origin was not specified in immigration records. The Oceania category covers immigration from Australia to New Zealand.

89. U.S. Commission on Civil Rights: 13–19.

90. Because it removed explicitly ideological criteria from U.S. refugee policy, the 1980 Refugee Act can be seen as a liberal development. However, it also can be seen as a restrictive measure in that it called for numerical limits on annual refugee admissions. Furthermore, though this act eliminated the explicitly ideological content of earlier policies, it is still administered in a manner that places higher priority on perceived foreign policy interests than humanitarian concerns, as demonstrated by the differential treatment of asylum-seekers from various countries. Loescher and Scanlan: 170–208.

91. Elizabeth Hull, *Without Justice for All: The Constitutional Rights of Aliens* (Westport, CT: Greenwood Press, 1985); John Crewdson, *The Tarnished Door* (New York: Times Books, 1983).

92. Edwin Harwood, *In Liberty's Shadow: Illegal Aliens and Immigration Law Enforcement* (Stanford, CA: Hoover Institution Press, 1986): 20–23;   "Immigration Policy and the Rights of Aliens," *Harvard Law Review* 96 (April 1983): 1286–1465; Peter H. Schuck, "The Transformation of Immigration Law," *Columbia Law Review* 84: 1 (January 1984): 1–90.

Chapter 3

Domestic Politics, Liberal Ideas, and the Immigration Reform and Control Act of 1986

ILLEGAL IMMIGRATION, EMPLOYER SANCTIONS, AND U.S. IMMIGRATION POLICY

The primary focus of the immigration policy debate in the United States has shifted in recent decades from the selection criteria for legal immigration to the control of illegal immigration. This shift has resulted from the rising numbers of illegal immigrants and the widely-held perception that they generate net social and economic costs. In spite of significant disagreement over exact figures, most immigration scholars agree that illegal immigration to the United States has increased since 1965.[1] Public concern over rising numbers of illegal immigrants has been exacerbated by the widely-held belief that these immigrants displace U.S. workers and drain social welfare programs, even though immigration scholarship does not clearly support this perception. While the debate over U.S. immigration policy historically has been centered primarily on a consideration of the system of legal immigration, illegal immigration became central to this policy debate by the 1970s as a result of growing public concern regarding this issue.

By the 1970s, an increasingly common assessment of the problem had come to dominate public debate: economic incentives were viewed as the root cause of illegal immigration. As a result, employer sanctions, penalties on employers who hire undocumented workers, emerged as the most prominent policy proposal to reduce illegal immigration.[2] At the same time, the growing influence of civil rights norms in the immigration policy debate, in general, ensured that considerations of fairness and non-discrimination would fundamentally shape any national policy discussion of illegal immigration.

Proposals for employer sanctions were not new to the debate over U.S. immigration policy. Several bills were proposed in the 1930s that would have prohibited the employment of illegal immigrants but were unsuccessful.[3] The Mexican government, to no avail, introduced the concept of employer sanctions into negotiations over the Bracero Program early in the 1950s as a means of protecting Mexican workers from exploitation and preventing migration outside of the government-sanctioned labor program.[4] Amendments to the Immigration and Nationality Act in 1952 made it a felony to bring in or harbor illegal aliens, but the so-called "Texas Proviso," necessary to ensure passage of the amendments, stated that employment was not to be considered harboring.[5] A bill introduced in both 1954 and 1955 that would have made it illegal to knowingly hire illegal immigrants or to accept illegal immigrants in labor unions similarly was unsuccessful.[6]

The debate over employer sanctions in the 1970s and 1980s reflected continuing conflict among various interest groups regarding the question of how to regulate immigration both effectively and fairly. Organized labor typically favored employer sanctions as an appropriate tool for preventing the job displacement and wage depression believed to result from undocumented workers. At the same time, labor organizations generally urged that liberal legalization programs be adopted along with employer sanctions. In contrast, anti-immigrant organizations and population control groups generally supported sanctions but argued for less generous amnesty programs.

Two basic groups led opposition to employer sanctions. First, employer associations commonly argued that employer sanctions would unfairly make employers responsible for the enforcement of U.S. immigration law and would render them incapable of meeting labor needs. As an alternative to sanctions, employer associations often advocated an expanded temporary foreign worker program to ensure that they had access to a sufficient supply of legal workers. Second, ethnic groups, civil rights associations, and church organizations generally opposed sanctions primarily because of a belief that they would lead to discrimination against ethnic minorities. These opponents of sanctions typically advocated liberal legalization programs as a means of reducing the illegal immigrant population in the United States.

After a contentious and extended debate, employer sanctions finally were adopted in the 1986 Immigration Reform and Control Act (IRCA). Passage of this legislation would have been impossible without compromise measures that addressed the concerns of sanctions opponents. Thus, this legislation authorized legalization for undocumented immigrants who had resided in the United States since before 1982 and included anti-discrimination measures in an effort to address the concerns of ethnic groups, churches, and civil rights organizations. Additionally, this legislation expanded the H-2 Temporary Foreign Worker Program and created a new temporary worker program for seasonal agricultural workers, provisions included to meet the political demands of powerful employer associations. While these compromise provisions were necessary to ensure the passage of this legislation, they significantly weakened the potential effectiveness of employer sanctions as a policy tool for controlling illegal immigration. Although the Immigration Reform and Control Act of 1986 was touted as a restrictive measure, a close analysis of its provisions and the debate leading to its passage indicates that it reflects a continuation of the liberalizing trend in U.S. immigration policy since World War II.

THE POLICY DEBATE OVER ILLEGAL IMMIGRATION IN THE 1970s

The origins of the Immigration Reform and Control Act can be traced back to the early 1970s. In 1971 and 1972, the House Subcommittee on Immigration and Nationality held a series of hearings on "illegal aliens" in Los Angeles, New York, Denver, Detroit, Chicago, and El Paso. The purpose of these hearings was to address the general problem of illegal immigration as well as to obtain specific feedback on proposed House legislation, H.R. 14831, which would have raised penalties for immigrants illegally residing in the United States and would have instituted civil and criminal penalties for employers who knowingly hired illegal immigrants.[7]

An examination of these hearings reveals the extent to which non-discrimination had displaced nativism as the dominant ideology in the U.S. immigration policy debate by the 1970s. In contrast to the legislative debates over the restrictive legislation of the 1920s, nativist organizations were not represented at the 1971 and 1972 House hearings on illegal immigrants. In fact, testimony consistently emphasized sympathy with the motives and experience of individual migrants, and even many strong supporters of a crackdown on illegal immigration seemed reluctant to penalize individual illegal immigrants harshly. Representative Peter W. Rodino, then Chairman of the House Subcommittee on Immigration and Nationality, demonstrated this attitude as he questioned one of the individuals testifying before the committee:

You would make some distinction though—wouldn't you—between the penalties that are imposed on the employer and on the illegal alien; one is looking to improve his lot in life, while the other is trying to put someone in human bondage, you might say? Knowing the illegal alien is looking for an opportunity to improve his economic circumstances, the employee takes advantage of him, and by so doing sets in consequence a chain of events whereby he not only misuses this individual, but he deprives other American citizens of a job. He is doing it for his own personal gain—if you will—and nothing more.[8]

As indicated by this quotation, the debate over illegal immigration in the 1970s focused primarily on the economic incentives for illegal immigration and the economic impact of illegal immigrants. For many supporters of employer sanctions, the employers, and not undocumented immigrants, were the "villains" in the problem of illegal immigration.

The interest alignments and policy positions that emerged in these House hearings would come to characterize the debate over illegal immigration throughout the 1970s and 1980s. Support for employer sanctions came from a variety of interest groups. Most representatives of organized labor recorded their support for employer sanctions; interestingly, they commonly adopted the language of civil rights in their testimony. For example, several labor groups contended that employers were depriving legal migrants of their civil rights by hindering union organization, depressing wages, and displacing workers. The National Association for the Advancement of Colored People testified in support of employer sanctions, especially because of high unemployment among blacks and legal migrants.[9]

Ethnic organizations, churches, civil rights organizations, immigration lawyers, and employer associations led opposition to employer sanctions. Ethnic organizations, including the Mexican-American Political Association and the League of United Latin American Citizens (LULAC), the American Civil Liberties Union, and a number of church groups cautioned that employer sanctions might result in discrimination against legal migrants. These groups typically advocated widespread legalization for the illegal immigrant population in the United States as an alternative to sanctions. Employer associations consistently testified in opposition to employer sanctions, arguing that the "burden of enforcement" was being placed on them and that often they could not fill positions in spite of high unemployment rates. In the place of sanctions, employer associations commonly urged a renewal of the Bracero Program as a means of reducing illegal immigration. Reinforcing the concerns of churches, civil rights groups, and ethnic organizations, employers also warned that they might be forced to discriminate if employer sanctions were adopted.[10] In support of the employers' arguments, a number of immigration lawyers testified and consistently emphasized the legal difficulties in establishing "knowing employment" and the potential discriminatory effects of sanctions.

These hearings provided the foundation for H.R. 16188, passed on September 12, 1972, which provided a three-step system of administrative, civil, and criminal penalties for employers who knowingly hired illegal immigrants. An amendment requiring the Attorney General to give due process in administrative hearings to an employer accused of employing illegal immigrants also passed and was an acknowledgment of employers' concerns expressed during the hearings. However, neither legalization nor an expanded foreign worker program was included in this bill. In spite of strong criticism, this bill passed the House with a strong majority, but the Senate failed to act on the legislation. Opponents of the bill in the Senate argued that sanctions would place a burden on employers and might result in discrimination against ethnic minorities.[11]

Ineffectual legislative action on this issue continued throughout the 1970s as a number of bills designed to meet the demands of various interest groups died in Congress. Several bills were introduced that provided for legalization as well as employer sanctions but received no further action. At least one bill, introduced in the Senate, would have expanded employers access to temporary foreign labor, but it, too, was unsuccessful.[12] In spite of economic stagnation in the United States in the mid-1970s and the efforts of various congressional leaders to present these bills as partial solutions to the nation's economic woes, employer sanctions legislation stagnated in both houses.

The various legislative proposals stagnated in Congress as they were unable to balance the competing demands of various interest groups.[13] Proposals for employer sanctions with only moderate civil penalties typically were unacceptable to organized labor. Anti-immigrant organizations, like Zero Population Growth, favored proposals for strong sanctions but would support only limited amnesty proposals. Church groups, ethnic associations, and civil liberties associations like the American Civil Liberties Union persisted in their opposition to strong sanctions which, they argued, might result in discrimination and advocated a liberal legalization program as an alternative. Yet, a number of congressional leaders continued to oppose liberal amnesty programs because of widely-held public opinion that legalization would reward lawbreakers and contribute to future streams of illegal immigrants.[14]   Business groups insisted that they should not be unfairly burdened with the enforcement of the government's immigration laws. Although employers expressed a desire for fairness in legislation addressing illegal immigration, they did not unanimously oppose employer sanctions.[15]

In sum, the policy debate over illegal immigration in the 1970s stagnated because of the difficulties in achieving a legislative compromise acceptable to all concerned interest groups.   Contradicting the common expectation that restrictive immigration policies will be adopted during periods of economic stagnation, Congress was unable to pass employer sanctions during the mid-1970s when economic conditions declined as a result of the OPEC oil embargo. Congress's failure to pass employer sanctions legislation is even more striking given the fact that public opinion reflected overwhelming support for new restrictions on illegal immigration by at least the late 1970s.[16] Congressional gridlock on this issue can be attributed not only to employer interests but also to the concerns of ethnic associations, churches, and civil rights organizations. In this way, the failure of employer sanctions legislation in the 1970s reflects the importance of the liberal forces shaping the immigration policy debate in the United States in the postwar period.

THE SELECT COMMISSION ON IMMIGRATION AND REFUGEE POLICY

Unable to negotiate a compromise on comprehensive immigration policy reform in the 1970s, Congress authorized the creation of the Select Commission on Immigration and Refugee Policy in a provision of the 1978 amendments to the Immigration and Nationality Act. The mandate of this commission was to evaluate and recommend changes to existing U.S. immigration policies pertaining to undocumented migration and the admission of immigrants and refugees. The Select Commission submitted its final report to Congress and the president on March 1, 1981, and identified illegal immigration as the "first order of priority" for U.S. immigration policy.[17] The commission's findings, which took into consideration the competing demands of a variety of interest groups,

marked the beginning of an end to the impasse in the debate over illegal immigration.

The Select Commission's recommendations to reduce illegal immigration included stronger border and interior controls, more rigid enforcement of wage and occupational safety standards, employer sanctions, and legalization. In this way, these recommendations parallel many of the policy proposals advocated by interest groups in the debate over immigration policy in the 1970s. The concerns of organized labor and anti-immigrant groups were addressed by the recommendation for employer sanctions. The commission voted, 14–2, to recommend that Congress adopt employer sanctions. In spite of general agreement on the principle of employer sanctions, significant disagreement within the commission was manifested on specifics. Some commissioners argued that only civil penalties should be adopted because of the high costs of criminal prosecution. These commissioners conceded that criminal sanctions might be necessary for "extended and flagrant violations." Other commissioners argued that a more definite series of graduated penalties should be adopted. In the end, the commission, reflecting disagreement among competing interest groups, was unable to agree on the specific types of penalties that should be adopted.

The concerns of church, ethnic, and civil rights organizations were reflected in the commission's recommendation for a liberal amnesty program. The commission rejected mass deportation as a means of reducing the illegal population residing in the United States because of the potential for civil rights violations, as in Operation Wetback in 1954 when many legal Mexican-Americans were deported along with illegal immigrants. In support of a liberal amnesty program, the commission argued that legal immigrants are less likely to be exploited and, thereby, depress wages. The commission also argued that legal immigrants are more likely to participate in the legal system and to seek health care for illnesses that otherwise might constitute a public health threat. Moreover, since Congress had not adopted strong penalties against employers, some commissioners advocated legalization because of their view that the government had some responsibility for the presence of illegal immigrants in the country. Specifically, the Select Commission recommended that legalization should be offered to illegal immigrants who were in illegal status before January 1, 1980, and had been in continuous residence for a time period to be specified by Congress.[18]

Although addressing the concerns of organized labor, churches, ethnic groups, and civil rights organizations, the commission rejected employer demands for an expansion in the temporary labor program. The commission concluded that it should not recommend a large-scale temporary worker program, similar to the Bracero Program, in spite of the fact that employers, especially in agriculture, urged that it would be necessary in order to meet labor shortages resulting from the tightening of U.S. borders.[19] Moreover, though it proposed that the Department of Labor should streamline the application process for H-2 workers in order to facilitate their admission when labor shortages exist, the commission did not recommend a major liberalization of the H-2 Temporary

Foreign Worker Program and concluded that dependence on temporary labor should be reduced. To this end, the commission concluded that employers should be required to pay federal insurance contributions and unemployment insurance for H-2 workers to minimize their incentive to hire these workers.[20]

In the view of the commission, the proposals for employer sanctions, legalization, and stronger border controls needed to be part of a coherent approach to illegal immigration. This coherent approach would allow the government to address the problem of illegal immigration with due concern for rights that illegal immigrants may have earned in U.S. society. According to the commission, legalization without sanctions might encourage more individuals to enter or stay in the country illegally in the hopes of receiving amnesty in the future. Sanctions without legalization would leave too many undocumented immigrants in second-class status and vulnerable to exploitation and deportation, in spite of ties to U.S. society that they may have established.

The Select Commission on Immigration and Refugee Policy reported at a time when a contentious debate over illegal immigration had been in progress for nearly a decade. The commission's recommendations reflect a compromise among the proposals and concerns advanced by a variety of interest groups throughout the previous decade. Additionally, the recommendations of the Select Commission represent an intentional strategy to eliminate the racial dimension of the immigration policy debate that had been central to discussions of immigration policy in the first half of the twentieth century. Though the Select Commission did not settle the debate over illegal immigration, its report laid the groundwork for the legislative compromise that would emerge in the 1980s.

THE POLICY DEBATE OVER ILLEGAL IMMIGRATION IN THE 1980s

In 1982, Senator Alan Simpson, a Republican from Wyoming, and Representative Romano Mazzoli, a Democrat from Kentucky, introduced joint legislation, H.R. 5872 and S. 2222, which incorporated the recommendations of the Select Commission on Immigration and Refugee Policy regarding illegal immigration. As also recommended by the Select Commission, this legislation would have increased legal immigration by raising the annual immigration ceiling to 425,000, though immediate relatives would have been included within this ceiling. The Simpson-Mazzoli bill called for a graduated schedule of civil and criminal penalties for employers who knowingly hired undocumented immigrants and authorized permanent legal status for illegal immigrants who could show continuous residence since January 1, 1978.[21] However, reflecting the recommendations of the Select Commission on Immigration and Refugee Policy, the Simpson-Mazzoli legislation did not provide for a new temporary foreign worker program. In spite of significant opposition, the Senate passed the bill by a vote of 80 to 19 in August 1982. However, the bill died in the House, buried under a plethora of amendments. The Simpson-Mazzoli legislation, providing for both employer sanctions and legalization, was reintroduced in both houses in 1983. After hearings on the 1983 legislation, the Simpson-Mazzoli bill was modified in an effort to meet the demands of critics. One amendment authorized a three-year transitional period for agricultural employers during which they could hire temporary workers without H-2 certification. Another amendment added measures to reduce discrimination. The bill passed the Senate by a vote of 76 to 18 but again failed in the House.[22]

Even though it incorporated the recommendations of the Select Commission on Immigration and Refugee Policy, the Simpson-Mazzoli legislation failed in both 1982 and 1983 because Congress was unable to negotiate a compromise acceptable to all of the actors who were integrally involved in the immigration policy debate. Disagreement over the Simpson-Mazzoli legislation was manifested on each of the three basic policy considerations that had dominated the debate over illegal immigration since early in the 1970s: employer sanctions, legalization, and an expanded temporary foreign worker program. As in the 1970s, interest alignments shifted in each case.[23]

In the debate over the Simpson-Mazzoli legislation, support for employer sanctions came primarily from organized labor, environmental groups, and anti-immigrant organizations. The AFL-CIO, the International Ladies' Garment Workers Union, and the NAACP were among the most vocal supporters of employer sanctions.[24] The United Farm Workers of America testified in support of employer sanctions and urged that sanctions be accompanied by effective enforcement mechanisms, including the creation of a counterfeit-proof social security card and a large budget and staff for the enforcement of sanctions.[25] Zero Population Growth, which had testified in support of sanctions in the 1970s, was joined by the Environmental Fund as a major proponent of employer sanctions. The Federation for American Immigration Reform (FAIR) also joined the debate over illegal immigration in the 1980s and emerged as one of the driving forces behind the Simpson-Mazzoli legislation.[26]

Ethnic organizations, civil rights associations, churches, and representatives of the business community led opposition to sanctions. The American Civil Liberties Union, the American Immigration Lawyers Association, the National Conference of Catholic Bishops, the Mexican-American Legal Defense and Education Fund, the League of United Latin American Citizens, TransAfrica, the Organization of Chinese Americans, and the Anti-Defamation League of the B'nai B'rith were among the groups testifying against sanctions because of the possibility that they would result in discrimination against ethnic minorities. Most employers associations testified against sanctions. The Chamber of Commerce persisted in its strong opposition to sanctions and argued that an affirmative defense clause would be necessary to protect the rights of employers but would enable unscrupulous employers to evade the law. Similarly, agricultural associations, including the National Council of Agricultural Employers, the National Cattlemen's Association, the United Fresh Fruit and Vegetable Association, and several state-level associations, maintained that they would continue to oppose sanctions unless a temporary worker program was also adopted.[27]

Interest coalitions shifted in the debate over the legalization provisions in the Simpson-Mazzoli legislation. The AFL-CIO, the International Ladies' Garment Workers Union, Zero Population Growth, and the NAACP, all supporters of sanctions, joined churches, ethnic associations, and civil rights organizations in support of legalization. Church organizations, including the National Conference of Catholic Bishops, the Church World Service, American Baptist Churches, Church of the Brethren, the United Church of Christ, and the American Jewish Committee testified in support of legalization and commonly argued that a more generous amnesty program should be adopted. The American Immigration and Nationality Lawyers and the American Bar Association testified in support of the legalization provisions in the Simpson-Mazzoli legislation while the American Civil Liberties Union argued that amnesty should be expanded to cover undocumented immigrants who had entered the United States prior to January 1, 1982. Ethnic organizations consistently testified in support of legalization and generally argued that the cutoff date for eligibility should be more generous. The primary opponents of legalization included the Federation for American Immigration Reform, the American Legion, Conservatives for Immigration Reform, and Americans for the Rights of Citizens. The basic argument of these critics of legalization was that it rewarded lawbreakers and might increase illegal immigration as new immigrants attempted to enter illegally in expectation of future amnesty. Employer associations generally were silent on the issue of legalization.

Interest coalitions shifted yet again in the debate over temporary workers. Although the Simpson-Mazzoli legislation in 1982 and 1983 did not include any provisions authorizing a new, government-sponsored temporary worker program similar to the Bracero Program, many interest groups discussed this policy alternative in their testimony. The AFL-CIO, United Farm Workers of America, the NAACP, and Zero Population Growth testified that they would oppose any legislation that provided for a new temporary worker program. Although most ethnic organizations did not discuss this issue in their testimony, the Mexican-American Legal Defense and Education Fund testified in opposition to a new guest worker program. Like most ethnic organizations, churches and civil rights groups generally were silent on this issue. Support for the addition of a temporary work provision to the Simpson-Mazzoli legislation came primarily from agricultural employer associations, for example, the Farm Labor Alliance, which insisted that employer sanctions would be unacceptable without expanded access to temporary workers.[28]

As indicated by the above discussion, employer sanctions legislation continued to stagnate in the early 1980s because Congress was unable to negotiate a compromise acceptable to competing and shifting interest coalitions. In 1984, two important amendments were added to the Simpson-Mazzoli legislation in an effort to mitigate the opposition of critics of sanctions. One amendment provided for a new guest worker program, and another amendment called for the creation of a U.S. immigration board to deal with charges of discrimination. In spite of these amendments, opposition to the legislation remained strong.[29] Nevertheless, the bill again passed in the Senate and, for the first time, passed the House by a narrow vote of 216–211. The House and Senate versions of the bill died in the conference committee because conferees could not reach a compromise on the amount of federal reimbursement to states for the costs of the legalization program.[30]

In 1985, Senator Simpson submitted a new version of the legislation with the same provisions as the 1984 bill with the exception that, under the new bill, legalization would begin only after sanctions were put into place and found by an independent commission to be reducing illegal immigration. Senator Pete Wilson, a Republican from California, submitted an amendment providing for the creation of a new temporary worker program that was added to the Senate version of the legislation. Additionally, an amendment to allow for phasing out of sanctions if the General Accounting Office found discrimination resulting from sanctions after three years also was passed. As amended, the bill passed the Senate in September 1985 by a 69–30 majority. In the House, Representative Rodino submitted a new bill, co-sponsored by Representative Mazzoli, which provided for more liberal legalization, stricter sanctions, the creation of a new Justice Department agency to protect against discrimination, and easing of existing H-2 procedures rather than a new guest worker program.[31]

In 1986, negotiators in the House tried to resolve the difference between the Simpson bill and the Rodino-Mazzoli bill. Disagreement primarily focused on the Senate proposal for a new guest worker program, which was strongly opposed by organized labor, versus the House H-2 expansion, which was opposed by agricultural interests as insufficient to meet their labor needs. In June 1986, the House Judiciary Committee reached a compromise. Undocumented immigrants employed in agriculture for at least sixty days in the year before May 1, 1986 were given permanent legal status. Additionally, beginning in 1989, a provision allowing for the entry of foreign agricultural workers to replace legalized immigrants who left agricultural work would take effect.[32] In September 1986, the bill was in danger of dying in the House again largely because of opposition among Republicans, who favored the Senate approach. As a result, House leaders of immigration reform and Senator Simpson devised another behind-the-scenes compromise. The new compromise continued to provide temporary legal status for agricultural workers but placed more restrictions on their legalization. House debate over the compromise bill took place in October, and several amendments were adopted, including language specifying that it was not discrimination to "hire an equally qualified citizen over a legal resident and a requirement that the Immigration and Naturalization Service must have warrant to conduct searches in open, agricultural fields. Another amendment to remove the legalization provision of the legislation narrowly failed, and the Simpson proposal that legalization be delayed until sanctions were working was dropped from the final legislation.[33]

Significant opposition to the Simpson-Mazzoli legislation remained, but the last-minute legislative compromises garnered sufficient support among various interest groups and their supporters in Congress to ensure passage of the legislation.[34] Moreover, according to many lobbyists and members of Congress, sanctions opponents were willing to support the legislation in 1986 because of the Reagan administration's packaging of the bill as a means to fight drug smuggling and fears that the political environment was becoming more conducive to the passage of restrictive legislation.[35] A strong, bipartisan majority in both the House and the Senate passed the bill in the middle of October.[36] After a long and contentious struggle, the Immigration Reform and Control Act was signed into law by President Reagan on November 6, 1986.

The final provisions of the Simpson-Mazzoli legislation reflect the competing demands of the various interest groups that had been involved in the debate over illegal immigration since early in the 1970s. In an effort to meet the demands of organized labor, anti-immigrant groups, and public opinion, Congress adopted employer sanctions for the first time in U.S. history. However, acknowledging the concerns of ethnic groups, churches, and civil rights organizations, IRCA stated that employment discrimination against citizens, permanent residents, refugees, or legalized immigrants was illegal and provided for civil fines against employers who violate this provision. Additionally, the legislation provided Congress with the option of repealing the legislation under expedited procedures if the General Accounting Office found that sanctions had led to a widespread pattern of discrimination after the legislation had been in effect for three years. IRCA also provided for a generous amnesty program, making illegal immigrants who had resided continuously in the United States since before January 1, 1982, eligible for temporary legal status and eventual permanent legal status. Though not as liberal as many supporters of legalization would have liked, this provision clearly was designed to meet their demands and was far more generous than opponents of legalization wanted. Finally, IRCA included two concessions to agricultural employers. First, the H-2 program was modified, creating a new H-2A category for agriculture; while employers seeking workers under this provision still need Department of Labor certification, the Secretary of Agriculture also has input into certification decisions. Second, under the Special Agricultural Workers Provision, immigrants who had worked in seasonal agriculture for at least ninety days in each of the last three years became eligible for temporary legal status; these SAW workers could adjust to permanent status after two years. IRCA also provided that replenishment workers (RAWs) could be brought in from 1990 to 1993 if the Departments of Labor and Agriculture jointly determined that a legitimate demand for seasonal workers existed.[37] (See Appendix B for a detailed overview of the major provisions of IRCA.)

Although it included provisions that acknowledged the interests of most interest groups concerned about the issue of illegal immigration, no one considered the Immigration Reform and Control Act the ideal solution to the problem of illegal immigration. After over a decade of debate, Congress had finally passed legislation ostensibly designed to reduce illegal immigration. However, few analysts or politicians were extremely confident about the prospects for IRCA's success. Compromise made the passage of sanctions legislation possible, but it did not generate a perception that strengthened governmental control over illegal immigration was probable. Though it is considered landmark legislation in the history of U.S. immigration policy, the

Immigration Reform and Control Act of 1986 clearly did not resolve the policy debate over illegal immigration.

THE EFFECTS OF IRCA ON ILLEGAL IMMIGRATION TO THE UNITED STATES

Soon after the passage of IRCA, an editorial in *The New York Times* praised the compromise legislation:

To undo the Texas proviso is to do justice. To legalize aliens already here is to undo hypocrisy. To close the back door against the illegal tide that so tries public patience is to offer fairness to millions waiting around the world for legal entry. Doing all this, the Immigration Reform and Control Act of 1986 does honor to America.[38]

Less optimistic assessments of IRCA's potential effectiveness appeared elsewhere in the editorial pages of major newspapers. An opinion piece in the *Chicago Tribune* criticized the legislation, saying "the new policy is likely to be about as ineffective at solving the nation's illegal alien problem as Prohibition was in dealing with alcohol."[39] Similarly, an opinion piece in *The New York Times* predicted IRCA's failure: "If laws could really alter market forces or curb the ups and downs of labor supply and demand, then the Immigration Reform and Control Act of 1986 . . . might have worked. In reality, those flows cannot be easily toyed with, and the legislation will not be effective."[40]

Politicians were reserved in their statements on the potential effectiveness of the legislation. After IRCA was passed, Representative Charles E. Schumer, a Democrat from New York who was highly involved in negotiating the compromise legislation, stated, "The bill is a gamble, a riverboat gamble. There is no guarantee that employer sanctions will work or that amnesty will work. We are headed into uncharted waters." Also cautious in his assessment of IRCA's potential effectiveness, Senator Simpson emphasized his confidence that employers would comply voluntarily with the legislation but conceded, "I don't know what the impact will be, but this is the humane approach to immigration reform."[41]

The available evidence regarding the effectiveness of the legislation has affirmed cautious assessments of IRCA's potential impact on illegal immigration to the United States. Research findings on the post-IRCA flows of illegal immigrants are ambiguous. Immigration and Naturalization Service (I.N.S.) apprehensions declined from 1,767,400 in 1986 to 1,190,488 in 1987 despite an increase in funding for the Border Patrol.[42] In 1988, apprehensions declined slightly, to 1,008,145, and in 1989, I.N.S. apprehensions again declined to 954,243.[43] The average number of Border Patrol apprehensions per hour also declined after IRCA.[44] This decrease in apprehensions suggests that the flow of undocumented immigrants may have declined somewhat in the years immediately following IRCA's passage.

Additional evidence supports the apprehensions data. Applications and waiting lists for permanent immigration visas increased in several major sending countries; a possible explanation for this increase is that more potential immigrants sought legal access to this country as a result of the deterrent effects of employer sanctions.[45] A statistical model comparing flows of illegal immigrants after IRCA with estimates of what the flows would have been in the absence of IRCA also indicates that illegal immigration to the United States declined after the legislation was passed.[46]

However, the apprehensions data has been challenged by other studies. The residual analysis of population data gathered in surveys conducted by the Census Bureau suggests that the annual flow of undocumented immigrants in the two years following IRCA was 246,000, an estimate that does not differ statistically from the annual estimates of illegal immigration in the years preceding IRCA.[47] Moreover, surveys conducted in various Mexican communities that have served as a major source of emigrants to the United States indicate that IRCA has not decreased the propensity of individuals to migrate illegally to the United States. These surveys also suggest that neither the probability of apprehension nor the costs of illegal entry increased significantly as a result of IRCA.[48] In addition, there are other possible explanations for the decrease in I.N.S. apprehensions after IRCA, including the effects of legalization, evidence that the use of smugglers increased after IRCA,[49] and the possibility that illegal immigrants may have foregone return visits to their country of origin out of fear that they would have more difficulty attempting to enter the United States illegally as a result of the new policy.[50] In short, though no consensus exists regarding IRCA's precise effects on the flow of undocumented immigrants to the United States,[51] even the most favorable assessments of the legislation indicate only a modest reduction in the flows of illegal immigrants in the years immediately following the IRCA's passage. Moreover, in 1990, I.N.S. apprehensions climbed to 1,169,939 and have been rising steadily in recent years.[52] The return of I.N.S. apprehensions to pre-IRCA levels suggests that IRCA's long-term impact on the flows of undocumented immigrants has been minimal. (See Figure 3.1.)

Research on the stock of illegal immigrants residing in the United States clearly demonstrates that IRCA has not had a dramatic impact on illegal immigration.[53] Although the residual analysis of census data indicates that the stock of illegal immigrants declined in the years immediately following the passage of IRCA, this decline cannot be attributed to a strong deterrent effect of employer sanctions in the labor market. Rather, IRCA's legalization provisions are primarily responsible for the decline in the number of undocumented immigrants residing in the United States.[54] By the end of the legalization period, over 1.7 million immigrants had been legalized under IRCA's general amnesty provision. An additional 1.3 million immigrants applied for legalization under the Seasonal Agricultural Worker provision, though only approximately 1.1 million of these applications ultimately were successful.[55] These numbers indicate that the legalization programs clearly resulted in a short-term reduction in the stock of undocumented immigrants residing in the United States. However, the I.N.S. estimated that by 1989 the illegal population remained at a level of 2 to 3 million.[56] By 1994, the I.N.S. estimate of the illegal immigrant

Figure 3.1
I.N.S. Apprehensions Before and After IRCA: 1980–1992

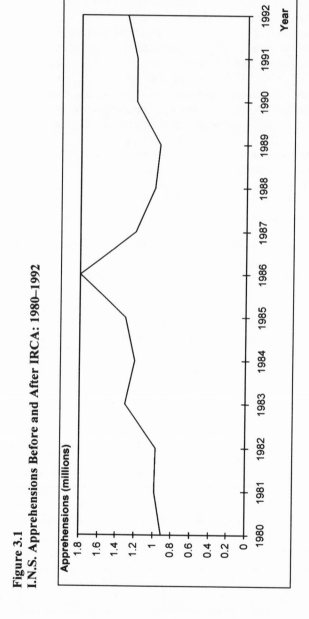

Source: U.S. Immigration and Naturalization Service, *Statistical Yearbook of the Immigration and Naturalization Service, 1992:* 156.

population in the United States had climbed slightly to 3.2 million.[57] In part, the stock of illegal immigrants residing in the United States remains high because undocumented immigrants, even if they are unable to find a job, commonly do not leave the United States as proponents of employer sanctions might have hoped.[58] Furthermore, because the flow of illegal immigrants has not declined significantly, the stock of illegal immigrants residing in this country likely has and will continue to rise.[59]

Labor market evidence suggests that employer sanctions have not been effective in reducing the employment of undocumented workers. Interviews conducted by Kitty Calavita in 1987 and 1988 indicate that many employers did not alter their hiring practices in response to IRCA. Calavita interviewed employers in Southern California in industries that have traditionally relied on immigrant workers. Forty-eight percent of the employers she interviewed said that they thought they had undocumented workers on their payrolls, and eighty percent of the employers interviewed said that the Immigration Reform and Control Act had not altered their hiring practices. In fact, at least one employer suggested that the legislation would protect them by enabling them to comply with the law by examining the appropriate documents even if they knew they were hiring illegal immigrants.[60]

An analysis of the wage effects of IRCA also indicates that the legislation has not altered employers' hiring practices. If employer sanctions have served as a deterrent to the use of cheap, illegal labor, then increases in wage rates should have accrued for legal workers. However, IRCA has not resulted in significant changes in the wages or wage rates of legal workers.[61] In the case of native-born workers, IRCA has had neither positive nor negative effects on wages. Conversely, some evidence exists that the legislation may have resulted in a decline in the wage rates for both legal and illegal immigrants. For example, while the wages of native-born Mexican workers have not changed as a result of IRCA, the wages of undocumented Mexican workers and even legal Mexican immigrants who have resided in this country for several years have declined since employer sanctions were instituted. This decline in the wages of undocumented Mexican workers and legal Mexican immigrants can be attributed, in part, to IRCA's legalization provisions. By increasing the supply of legal yet still relatively cheap labor, legalization may have resulted in downward pressure on the wages of legal immigrants.[62] Similarly, the expansion in the supply of cheap, legal workers resulting from legalization may have exerted downward pressure on the wage rates of undocumented workers. According to Donato and Massey, rather than reducing employer reliance on undocumented workers, "IRCA may simply have pushed undocumented migration further underground."[63]

An examination of the implementation of employer sanctions provides key insights into the limited impact of the Immigration Reform and Control Act. By January 1989, the I.N.S. had conducted 70,000 investigations and had issued 3,683 citations or warnings. Only 1,387 intents to fine had been issued by the I.N.S. Ultimately, only 610 fines were ordered while the rest of the cases either were negotiated or were pending hearings.[64] Employer sanctions have not had a more substantial impact for three basic reasons. First, fraudulent documents proliferated after IRCA's passage, and some evidence indicates that the price of such documents dropped as well. Easy access to these documents facilitated the entry of illegal immigrants and their ability to obtain jobs in spite of employer sanctions.[65] The widespread use of fraudulent documents serves as an explanation for the low number of fines for violations of IRCA because employers are only required to examine appropriate documents and not to ascertain their authenticity.

Second, consistent with IRCA's provisions, which authorized a six-month education period and an additional year in which only warning citations would be given, the I.N.S. adopted implementation guidelines which emphasized cooperation with the business community and the encouragement of voluntary compliance with employer sanctions regulations.[66] In part, the I.N.S. pursued this strategy out of fear that a more aggressive approach to enforcement would lead employers to discriminate and, ultimately, would result in the repeal of sanctions.[67] Even after the six-month education period had expired, the I.N.S. emphasized education in its enforcement efforts.[68] For example, guidelines issued by former I.N.S. Commissioner Alan Nelson mandated that employers were to be warned rather than fined if they had not received an education visit prior to a violation. Another enforcement guideline required the I.N.S. to give employers three days' notice before their records were inspected. Instead of widespread fining, the I.N.S. central office under Commissioner Nelson urged investigations officers to negotiate settlements with employers who admit their violations and to limit fines to "egregious" cases.[69]

This emphasis on voluntary compliance and employer education has not been completely successful. Department of Labor (D.O.L.) audits suggest that sixty-two percent of employers were complying partially or fully with employer sanctions requirements by the beginning of fiscal year 1989. Similarly, I.N.S. investigations indicate that sixty-eight percent of employers were in compliance with the law by February 1989.[70] Although a majority of employers are in compliance with the law, the widespread use of fraudulent documents makes it possible even for unscrupulous employers to comply with the letter of the law when they may be aware they are hiring illegal immigrants.[71] Moreover, while a majority of employers were not hiring undocumented workers by 1989, the D.O.L. and I.N.S. estimates demonstrate that a significant number of employers were not in compliance with IRCA's requirements at this time. It is difficult to interpret this information without knowing how many employers used undocumented workers prior to IRCA. Nevertheless, estimates that significant flows of illegal immigration have persisted after IRCA suggest that many undocumented workers continue to be employed in spite of employer sanctions.

Finally, a fundamental reason that employer sanctions have not had a more substantial impact is that both the I.N.S. and Congress have given the investigation of sanctions violations low budgetary priority, largely because of insufficient political support for the strong enforcement of sanctions.[72] Provisions in IRCA authorized the appropriation of an additional $422 million in fiscal year 1987 and $419 million in fiscal year 1988. Actual appropriations were significantly lower than the promised supplemental funds. In 1987, the I.N.S. received only $123 million in supplemental appropriations, and in 1988, supplemental funds totaled $169.5 million.[73] Congress also had specified in IRCA that a sufficient amount of supplemental funds was to be used to expand the Border Patrol by fifty percent, and the I.N.S. division of the supplemental funds reflects this priority. In 1987, the I.N.S. used $70.5 million of the supplemental appropriations for border enforcement while only $33.7 million was used for the implementation of employer sanctions. In 1988, the funding gap narrowed with $67.2 million budgeted for border enforcement and $59.7 million budgeted for the investigation of sanctions violations.[74] The I.N.S. overall budget for enforcement did grow from $366 million in 1986 to $694 million in 1990, but the I.N.S. also had increased responsibilities in implementing employer sanctions legislation. In spite of the fact that employer sanctions had been touted as a central element in the policy effort to bring illegal immigration under control, the Border Patrol continued to receive the largest share of the I.N.S. budget.[75] By the end of the 1980s, budget deficits impeded the enforcement efforts of an already overburdened I.N.S.[76] In sum, the I.N.S. budgets after the passage of IRCA do not reflect a strong congressional or administrative commitment to employer sanctions.

In terms of giving legal status to a large number of undocumented immigrants residing in the United States, IRCA's legalization provisions generally have been successful. Approximately two-thirds of eligible illegal immigrants applied for legalization.[77] As noted previously, over 1.7 million immigrants were legalized under the general amnesty program, and over a million individuals attained legal status under the SAW provisions.[78] In the short term, then, the legalization programs significantly reduced the number of illegal immigrants residing in the United States, one of IRCA's primary objectives.

However, the available evidence suggests that the impact of IRCA's legalization provisions will be minimal in the long term. Reliable estimates of the number of illegal immigrants residing in the United States prior to IRCA range from 2 to 4 million. These estimates have not declined since IRCA. Thus, although a very high number of undocumented immigrants obtained legal status under IRCA, significant numbers of illegal immigrants continue to reside in the United States. In part, the large number of illegal immigrants who continue to reside in the United States reflects the limitations of the legalization program as written by Congress, which specified that immigrants who arrived in the United States after 1982 were ineligible. This language may have excluded up to 2 million illegal immigrants from amnesty.[79] Furthermore, the continuing flow of illegal immigrants after the passage of IRCA has contributed to a resurgence in the number of undocumented immigrants residing in the United States.

The initial implementation of the amnesty programs was characterized by several problems that reduced the number of immigrants who applied for legalization. Early in the implementation of legalization, the I.N.S. was criticized for not making stronger efforts to reach out to eligible immigrants, for being too restrictive in its implementation of legalization, and for not providing adequate documentation to support its denial of amnesty in certain cases.[80] For example, the I.N.S. did not make significant efforts to find out if deportable immigrants were eligible for amnesty or to educate them regarding their potential rights. Additionally, the I.N.S. initially denied legalization to immigrants who had used public assistance in the past rather than assessing their current ability to support themselves. Moreover, the I.N.S. also initially denied derivative legal status to ineligible family members of legalization applicants.[81] Finally, critics have suggested that legalization was marred by "implementation bias," which favored some groups, such as Mexicans, but made it harder for other groups, including women, to obtain amnesty.[82]

Though initially restrictive, the implementation of IRCA's legalization programs was liberalized both by court challenges and administrative revisions in I.N.S. regulations. Reflecting the influence of civil rights on immigration policy in the current period, the courts argued that the I.N.S. had the burden of proof in making a decision to reject a legalization application. Moreover, the courts frequently overturned restrictive I.N.S. practices, though the I.N.S. has been slow to implement court decisions.[83] As the implementation of amnesty proceeded, the I.N.S. improved its outreach efforts in at least two important ways. First, the I.N.S. revised its administrative regulations on IRCA and began to give derivative legal status to the spouses and minor children of immigrants who had been granted amnesty.[84] Second, the I.N.S. expanded its efforts to reach eligible immigrants through ethnic newspapers, radio and television, and other efforts targeted at immigrant communities.[85] In fact, by the time the legalization program was concluded, a strong majority of legalization applications had been filed directly with the I.N.S. rather than through the qualified designated entities, which it was assumed illegal immigrants would be more likely to trust.[86]

In addition to administrative problems with implementation, there is evidence that IRCA's legalization programs, especially the SAW Program, were marred by significant fraud. The SAW applications greatly exceeded estimates of the number of foreign agricultural workers in the United States prior to the program's implementation.[87] Surveys of potential Mexican immigrants indicate that many Mexican migrants who did not qualify were legalized under IRCA; even some migrants who had not previously resided in the United States at all were induced to migrate to the United States in the hopes of obtaining amnesty.[88] Ineligible immigrants who wanted to apply for amnesty under IRCA's Seasonal Agricultural Worker provision may have purchased fraudulent employment histories from unscrupulous employers or farm labor contractors.[89] In sum, evidence suggests that legalization under the SAW Program exceeded the expectations of Congress and, in the case of fraudulent applications, circumvented congressional intentions. Ironically, legalization also may have facilitated future flows of illegal immigrants by bolstering social networks of immigrants residing in this country and expanding the availability of fraudulent documents for new pools of agricultural labor in Mexico and Central America.[90]

The primary objective of IRCA's legalization provisions was to reduce the number of illegal immigrants residing in the United States, and the high participation in the amnesty programs demonstrates that this basic objective was reached in the short term. However, large numbers of illegal immigrants who were eligible for amnesty did not apply. Conversely, many legalized immigrants may have obtained amnesty through fraud. Moreover, IRCA may have facilitated the permanent settlement of undocumented immigrants who previously had seen their stay in this country as temporary, an outcome that does not reflect the basic intent of the framers of the legislation.[91] These results reflect the competing pressures on the I.N.S. both to be flexible in their approach to legalization but to guard against fraudulent applications and abuse of the program.[92] As indicated by the above discussion, the I.N.S. has had mixed success in balancing these competing pressures.

While the effects of IRCA have not fulfilled the restrictionist objectives of many of its proponents, it has confirmed the fears of some of the legislation's critics. As required under IRCA, the General Accounting Office (GAO) submitted its report on the effects of employer sanctions on employment discrimination in March of 1990. The GAO concluded that a "serious pattern" of discrimination existed in the labor market, much of it attributable to employer sanctions.[93] In a random sample of employers, nineteen percent of the employers surveyed indicated that they had adopted discriminatory practices in response to the legislation, either by refusing to hire individuals with a foreign appearance or accent or by basing hiring decisions on citizenship status.[94] Discriminatory practices adopted by employers after IRCA largely resulted from employers' lack of knowledge about the legislation's requirements or a fear of penalties rather than malicious disregard for the law.[95] Regardless of employers' intent, the law did contribute to widespread discrimination in the labor market according to the GAO report.

The way in which employer sanctions were implemented by the I.N.S. can be blamed for much of the discrimination resulting from sanctions. Though the I.N.S. emphasized education and voluntary compliance in its implementation of employer sanctions, the agency neglected to educate employers sufficiently about the non-discrimination provisions in IRCA.[96] Because much of the employment discrimination after IRCA appeared to result from a lack of employer knowledge about the legislation's provisions, the General Accounting Office advocated an expansion in I.N.S. efforts to educate employers about IRCA's non-discrimination provisions.[97] In the Immigration Act of 1990, Congress responded to the GAO's recommendation by authorizing the appropriation of an additional $10 million for employer and community education on sanctions and IRCA's non-discrimination requirements.[98] In spite of continuing efforts at employer education, the GAO finding that employer sanctions have contributed to widespread discrimination in the labor market has confirmed the fears of sanctions opponents. At the same time, heightened concerns regarding employer sanctions and discrimination may frustrate the objectives of proponents of employer sanctions by reinforcing the tendency of

I.N.S. officials to de-emphasize sanctions in the enforcement of U.S. immigration law.[99]

IRCA's modest impact on the flow and stock of undocumented immigrants clearly did not meet the goals of restrictionists. The relative success of legalization generally met the objectives of supporters of amnesty, including churches, ethnic groups, and civil rights organizations. However, these groups also had warned that employer sanctions would lead to discrimination, and, thus far, their fears have been confirmed. As a result, many of these groups have urged Congress to repeal employer sanctions. Several business groups also have advocated the repeal of employer sanctions. However, perhaps because their due process rights have been guaranteed and cooperation has been emphasized in the implementation of employer sanctions, the opposition of the business community has been mitigated to some extent.[100] Although several bills advocating the repeal of employer sanctions have been submitted in Congress, none has received major action.[101] At the same time, a perennial complaint of proponents of sanctions is that the I.N.S. does not emphasize sanctions sufficiently in its enforcement efforts. Though the Immigration Reform and Control Act of 1986 is commonly considered landmark immigration legislation, the debate over employer sanctions remains at an impasse almost a decade after its passage.

DOMESTIC IMPEDIMENTS TO THE REGULATION OF ILLEGAL IMMIGRATION

After well over a decade of contentious public debate over employer sanctions, they were finally adopted in the Immigration Reform and Control Act of 1986. However, though often described as a restrictive immigration policy, IRCA has not altered the liberalizing trend in U.S. immigration policy since World War II. In response to employers' demands for access to cheap labor, IRCA included provisions that expanded employer access to temporary foreign workers. Lobbying by representatives of the business community also ensured that IRCA provided for an affirmative defense under which employers would only be responsible for examining documents and not identifying fraud. Critics argue that this affirmative defense clause has provided employers with a convenient loophole for evading the law, but proponents of this clause argue that it is necessary to protect the due process rights of employers. Lobbying by ethnic groups, churches, and civil rights organizations led to IRCA's legalization and non-discrimination provisions. These compromise measures, necessary to ensure IRCA's passage, weakened the potential effectiveness of employer sanctions from the beginning.

IRCA's implementation also clearly reflected the influence of liberal pressures on current U.S. immigration policy. In accordance with congressional intent, the I.N.S. emphasized cooperation with the business community and voluntary compliance in the implementation of employer sanctions. Both Congress and the I.N.S. have given employer sanctions low budgetary priority and, instead, have continued to emphasize the more visible activities of the

Border Patrol in the government's efforts to reduce illegal immigration. The 1990 GAO report that employer sanctions had led to significant discrimination likely has reinforced the I.N.S. practice of giving employer sanctions lower priority than border enforcement. Though the I.N.S. initially was criticized for being too restrictive in its implementation of IRCA's legalization provisions, the courts frequently overturned restrictive I.N.S. practices in cases brought to court by immigrant advocacy groups. As a result of these various liberal pressures, IRCA has not resulted in a significant decline in either the annual flow of illegal immigrants to the United States or the number of illegal immigrants residing and working in the United States. Conversely, it has led to a substantial increase in the size of the legal immigrant population in the United States, an outcome that likely pleased liberal critics of employer sanctions but clearly was not the intent of many of the restrictionists who strongly supported IRCA.

The key role of liberal ideas and interest group politics in shaping the Immigration Reform and Control Act of 1986 challenges strictly economic explanations of U.S. immigration policy as well as analyses which suggest that national security will be the key determinant of policy. Economic conditions and foreign policy considerations, which historically have played a role in shaping U.S. immigration policy, had minimal impact on the content and implementation of the Immigration Reform and Control Act. While economic conditions certainly influenced the terms of the debate over illegal immigration, they were not crucial in shaping IRCA's provisions. In fact, contradicting the common expectation that restrictive immigration policies will be adopted during periods of economic decline, Congress failed in its attempts to pass employer sanctions even when economic conditions declined during the mid-1970s. Foreign policy was mentioned rarely in the debate leading to IRCA's passage, though the State Department expressed concern about the legislation's effects on U.S.-Mexican relations and unsuccessfully tried to initiate consultations with the Mexican government. The relative unimportance of economic conditions and foreign policy considerations in shaping the specific provisions of IRCA and its ultimate passage in 1986 contradict Marxist analyses, which suggest that structural economic factors and class are the key determinants of policy, and realist interpretations, which contend that national security concerns drive policy making.[102]

In conclusion, domestic politics and liberal ideas have strongly impacted the government's ability to regulate international migration. In the case of the Immigration Reform and Control Act of 1986, domestic opposition, framed primarily in terms of liberal norms, has hindered the ability of the U.S. government to control illegal immigration. In this way, the inability of the U.S. government reflects insufficient political will more than a lack of capability. Intense and well-organized opposition to stronger restrictions has been led by a liberal coalition of ethnic groups, churches, civil rights organizations, and representatives of the business community. Employers' demands for access to cheap labor and due process rights coupled with the opposition of churches, ethnic groups, and civil rights advocates to policy proposals that might result in discrimination or the infringement of civil liberties have moderated U.S. policy towards illegal immigration. As this case demonstrates, the prominence of liberal ideas in recent decades has transformed the immigration policy debate in the United States and has contributed to liberal immigration policies. In this way, the ascendance of liberal ideas helps to explain the high levels of illegal and legal immigration to this country since the 1960s.

NOTES

1. Frank D. Bean, Barry Edmonston, and Jeffrey S. Passel, eds., *Undocumented Migration to the United States: IRCA and the Experience of the 1980s* (Washington, D.C.: The Urban Institute; Santa Monica: The RAND Corporation, 1990): 1–2; Vernon M. Briggs, Jr., *Mass Immigration and the National Interest* (Armonk, NY: M.E. Sharpe, Inc., 1992): 150–154; John Crewdson, *The Tarnished Door* (New York: Times Books, 1983): 98–111; Elizabeth S. Rolph, *Immigration Policies: Legacy from the 1980s and Issues for the 1990s* (Santa Monica, CA: The RAND Corporation, 1992): 10.

2. The focus on employer sanctions was initiated at the state and not the federal level. On November 8, 1971, California became the first governmental body in the United States to adopt employer sanctions legislation, though the law was never strongly enforced. Kitty Calavita, "California's 'Employer Sanctions' Legislation: Now You See It, Now You Don't," *Politics and Society* 12:2 (1983): 205–230. Several states followed California's lead by adopting employer sanctions legislation in the 1970s, and, in each case, the legislation was not enforced effectively as a result of court challenges based on due process and civil rights claims and opposition to sanctions among Hispanic organizations, civil rights groups, and employer associations. Carl E. Schwarz, "Employer Sanctions Laws: The State Experience as Compared with Federal Proposals," in Wayne A Cornelius and Ricardo Anzaldúa Montoya, eds., *America's New Immigration Law: Origins, Rationales, and Potential Consequences* (San Diego: University of California, Center for U.S.-Mexican Studies, 1983): 83–101. The failure of state employer sanctions laws previewed the ineffectiveness of employer sanctions at the federal level.

3. E.P. Hutchinson, *Legislative History of American Immigration Policy: 1798–1965* (Philadelphia: University of Pennsylvania Press, 1981): 218, 228, 240.

4. Ellis W. Hawley, "The Politics of the Mexican Labor Issue, 1950–1965," in George C. Kiser and Martha Woody Kiser, eds., *Mexican Workers in the United States* (Albuquerque: University of New Mexico Press, 1979): 99.

5. Hutchinson: 301–303, 600–603.

6. Ibid.: 322–323.

7. U.S. Congress, House Subcommittee on Immigration and Nationality, *Hearings on Illegal Aliens*, 92d Cong., 1st and 2d sess., Parts 1–5 (Washington, D.C.: U.S. Government Printing Office, 1971, 1972).

8. Ibid., Part 1: 109.

9. Ibid., Part 2: 1183–1186.

10. For example, Dean Kittel, an administrative officer with the Colorado Farm Bureau, testified: "We heard people who are professional interrogators this morning say that it is difficult to know. I have heard, and this is strictly rumor, but I have heard in California you can buy a green card for $1.50. Now, if a man has a social security card and green card, which is basically the proof that he is a legal alien, how much trouble am I in as an employer if I hire him? If he's chicano, should I just not take the chance at all? And would this not be discriminatory?" Ibid., Part 2: 342.

11. See U.S. Congress, Congressional Research Service, *U.S. Immigration Law and Policy: 1952–1979*, 96th Cong., 1st sess. (Washington: U.S. Government Printing Office, 1979): 74.

12. U.S. Congress, Congressional Research Service, *U.S. Immigration Law*: 74–76.

13. See U.S. Congress, House Subcommittee on Immigration, Citizenship, and International Law, *Hearings on H.R. 982 and Related Bills*, 94th Cong., 1st sess. (Washington, D.C.: U.S. Government Printing Office, 1975) for summaries of the positions of various interest groups on employer sanctions legislation.

14. For an overview of congressional discussion on the issue of legalization, see *Congressional Digest*, 56:10 (October 1977): 235–255 cited in U.S. Congress, Congressional Research Service, *Selected Readings on U.S. Immigration Policy and Law*, 96th Cong., 2d sess. (Washington, D.C.: U.S. Government Printing Office, 1980): 177–187.

15. For example, the National Federation of Independent Business testified that a majority of its members were concerned about illegal immigration and favored employer sanctions legislation under which they would not be penalized if they could certify that they had seen the proper documentation. U.S. Congress, Senate Select Committee on Small Business, *Hearings on the Effects of Proposed Legislation Prohibiting the Employment of Illegal Aliens on Small Business*, 94th Cong., 2d sess. (Washington, D.C.: U.S. Government Printing Office, 1977): 11–14, 115–125.

16. Edwin Harwood, "American Public Opinion and U.S. Immigration Policy," *The Annals of the American Academy of Political and Social Science* 487 (September 1986): 204–207.

17. Select Commission on Immigration and Refugee Policy, *U.S. Immigration Policy and the National Interest*, The Final Report and Recommendations of the Select Commission on Immigration and Refugee Policy to the Congress and President of the United States, March 1, 1981.

18. Ibid.: 72–85.

19. Ibid.: 42–43.

20. Ibid.: 226–229.

21. The Simpson-Mazzoli legislation also would have given temporary legal status to illegal immigrants who could show continuous residence since January 1, 1980.

22. Nancy Humel Montweiler, *The Immigration Reform Law of 1986* (Washington, D.C.: The Bureau of National Affairs, Inc., 1987): 8.

23. This discussion of the interest group alignments in the debate over the Simpson-Mazzoli legislation draws on congressional hearings on this legislation in the early 1980s. The following hearings were the primary sources: U.S. Congress, Senate Subcommittee on Immigration and Refugee Policy, *Hearings on the Knowing Employment of Illegal Immigrants*, 97th Cong., 1st sess. (Washington, D.C.: U.S. Government Printing Office, 1982); U.S. Congress, House Subcommittee on Immigration, Refugees, and International Law and Senate Subcommittee on Immigration and Refugee Policy, *Joint Hearings on H.R. 5872 and S. 2222 (Immigration Reform and Control Act of 1982)*, 97th Cong., 2d sess. (Washington, D.C.: U.S. Government Printing Office, 1982); and, U.S. Congress, House Subcommittee on Immigration, Refugees, and International Law, *Hearings on H.R. 1510 (Immigration Reform and Control Act of 1983)*, 98th Cong., 1st sess. (Washington, D.C.: U.S. Government Printing Office, 1983).

24. In spite of the NAACP's support for employer sanctions and public opinion polls which indicated that a majority of African Americans favored employer sanctions, the Congressional Black Caucus opposed early employer sanctions legislation because of alliances with Hispanic representatives, the fact that many African American representatives had large numbers of Hispanics in their districts, and support of the argument that sanctions might lead to discrimination. Gary P. Freeman and Katharine

Betts, "The Politics of Interests and Immigration Policymaking in Australia and the United States," in Gary P. Freeman and James Jupp, eds., *Nations of Immigrants: Australia, the United States, and International Migration* (Oxford: Oxford University Press, 1992): 85–86.

25. The United Farm Workers did not demonstrate consistent support for employer sanctions. In California, for example, though the organization initially had supported the state's employer sanctions law, the United Farm Workers came to criticize employer sanctions after it became evident that the law was not being enforced. The organization argued that employer sanctions divided the working class and might lead to discrimination against ethnic minorities. Calavita, "California's 'Employer Sanctions Legislation'": 221.

26. John Tanton, a former president of Zero Population Growth, founded FAIR in 1978. Dr. Tanton, an ophthalmologist, has been involved with several organizations concerned with environmental protection, population growth, immigration, and cultural preservation. FAIR bases its anti-immigrant message largely on the argument that illegal immigration aggravates overpopulation in the United States, thereby contributing to environmental degradation in this country. The concerns of environmental groups and FAIR clearly overlap, and Garrett Hardin, the prominent ecologist who pushed the notion of "lifeboat ethics" in the 1980s, has served on the board of directors for FAIR. In addition to the environmental argument, FAIR pushes the view that illegal immigrants pose a threat to cultural and political stability in this country. In this way, FAIR's arguments represent a new form of nativism in the debate over immigration policy. An indication of its ideological ties with the nativist groups of the past is the fact that FAIR has received funding from the Pioneer Fund, which funded eugenics research in the 1930s and continues to fund such research today. Though their concerns are not stated in explicitly racial terms like nativist arguments early in this century, FAIR clearly discusses the problem of illegal immigration in terms of "natives" versus "aliens." See Ruth Conniff, "The War on Aliens: the Right Calls the Shots," *The Progressive* (October 1993): 22–29 reprinted in Robert M. Jackson, ed., *Global Issues 94/95* (Guilford, CT: The Dushkin Publishing Group, Inc. 1994): 51–57.

27. Employers were not unanimous in their opposition to sanctions. Many other employer associations (including the American Council on International Personnel; the Alliance for Immigration Reform, which represents several large multinational corporations including Ford, Xerox, and Union Carbide; and the National Association of Manufacturers) testified that they would accept sanctions if due process rights of employers were protected. U.S. Congress, House Subcommittee on Immigration, Refugees, and International Law and Senate Subcommittee on Immigration and Refugee Policy, *Joint Hearings on H.R. 5872 and S.2222.*

28. U.S. Congress, House Subcommittee on Immigration, Refugees, and International Law, *Hearings on H.R. 1510*; Philip L. Martin, "Good Intentions Gone Awry: IRCA and U.S. Agriculture," *The Annals of the American Academy of Political and Social Science* 534 (July 1994): 47–49.

29. Delegates from the Hispanic community threatened to withhold their votes at the Democratic National Convention in protest of the Simpson-Mazzoli legislation. Given the intensity of critics of the legislation, Walter Mondale and Geraldine Ferraro, the Democratic ticket for president and vice-president, emphasized their opposition to the legislation. Montweiler: 9–10.

30. Ibid.

31. Ibid.: 10–12.

32. This compromise had many opponents, including Representative Mazzoli. Ibid.: 16–18.

33. Ibid.

34. These compromises were especially crucial in gaining the votes of some Hispanic and African American representatives who previously opposed the Simpson-Mazzoli legislation. Jacquelyne Johnson Jackson, "Seeking Common Ground for Blacks and Immigrants," in David E. Simcox, ed., *U.S. Immigration in the 1980s: Reappraisal and Reform* (Boulder: Westview Press; Washington, D.C., Center for Immigration Studies, 1988): 98–100.

35. Robert Pear, "Congress, Winding Up Work, Votes Sweeping Aliens Bill: Reagan Expected to Sign It," *The New York Times*, 18 October 1986: 1 (Section 1).

36. Montweiler: 18.

37. Ibid.: 23–30.

38. "Freedom Day," *The New York Times*, 19 October 1986: 22 (Section 4).

39. Patrick G. Marshall, "The Immigration Reform Act Appears to Be Doomed to Failure," *Chicago Tribune*, 18 November 1986: C19.

40. Jorge G. Castaneda, "A Flawed Immigration Law," *The New York Times*, 13 November 1986: A31.

41. Both quotations were cited in Robert Pear, "President Signs Landmark Bill on Immigration," *The New York Times*, 7 November 1986: A12.

42. Frank D. Bean, Thomas J. Espenshade, Michael J. White, and Robert F. Dymowski, "Post-IRCA Changes in the Volume and Composition of Undocumented Migration to the United States: An Assessment Based on Apprehensions Data," in Bean, Edmonston, and Passel, eds.: 114; David S. North, *Immigration Reform in Its First Year*, (Washington, D.C.: Center for Immigration Studies, November 1987): 9–15.

43. U.S. Immigration and Naturalization Service, *Statistical Yearbook of the Immigration and Naturalization Service, 1992* (Washington, D.C.: U.S. Government Printing Office, 1993): 156.

44. Unlike aggregate apprehensions data, the average number of Border Patrol apprehensions per hour controls for changes in I.N.S. funding and staff. Michael D. Hoefer, "Background of U.S. Immigration Policy Reform," in Francisco L. Rivera-Batiz, Selig L. Sechzer, and Ira N. Gang, eds., *U.S. Immigration Policy Reform in the 1980s: A Preliminary Assessment* (New York: Praeger, 1991): 39–43.

45. Keith Crane, Beth J. Asch, Joanna Zorn Heilbrunn, and Danielle C. Cullinane, *The Effect of Employer Sanctions on the Flow of Undocumented Immigrants to the United States* (Washington, D.C.: The Urban Institute; Santa Monica, CA: The RAND Corporation, April 1990): 42–46.

46. Thomas J. Espenshade, "Undocumented Migration to the United States: Evidence from a Repeated Trials Model," in Bean, Edmonston, and Passel, eds.: 168–178.

47. Karen A. Woodrow and Jeffrey S. Passel, "Post-IRCA Undocumented Immigration to the United States: An Assessment Based on the June 1988 CPS," in Bean, Edmonston, and Passel, eds.: 56–57.

48. Katharine M. Donato, Jorge Durand, and Douglas S. Massey, "Stemming the Tide? Assessing the Deterrent Effects of the Immigration Reform and Control Act," *Demography* 29:2 (May 1992): 139–157; Wayne A. Cornelius, "Impacts of the 1986 U.S. Immigration Law on Emigration from Rural Mexican Sending Communities," in Bean, Edmonston, and Passel, eds.: 230–235.

49. Douglas S. Massey, Katharine M. Donato, and Zai Liang, "Effects of the Immigration Reform and Control Act of 1986: Preliminary Data from Mexico," in Bean, Edmonston, and Passel, eds.: 197–198.

50. David S. North, *Immigration Reform in Its First Year* (Washington, D.C.: Center for Immigration Studies, November 1987): 10–15. See also Sherrie A. Kossoudji, "Playing Cat and Mouse at the U.S.-Mexican Border," *Demography* 29:2 (May 1992): 159–180.

51. The photographic monitoring of Zapata Canyon, one of the most widely used border crossings for undocumented immigrants who enter the United States from Mexico, provides inconclusive evidence on the question of whether the flows of illegal immigrants declined in the years following IRCA's passage. On the one hand, this project's data suggests that undocumented immigration by males across this border generally declined from 1986 to 1988. On the other hand, the data on undocumented immigration by women across this border shows that the figures for 1987 are higher than those for 1986 while the figures for 1988 are lower than both previous years. Jorge A. Bustamente, "Undocumented Migration from Mexico to the United States: Preliminary Findings of the Zapata Canyon Project," in Bean, Edmonston, and Passel, eds.: 218.

52. *Statistical Yearbook of the Immigration and Naturalization Service, 1992*: 156.

53. It is important to distinguish between the flow and the stock of immigrants. The flow of undocumented immigrants refers to the number of individuals entering a country illegally during a particular period of time. The stock of undocumented immigrants refers to the number of individuals residing illegally in a country at a specific time. Bean, Edmonston, and Passel, eds.: 6.

54. Robert L. Bach and Doris Meissner, *Employment and Immigration Reform: Employer Sanctions Four Years Later* (Washington, D.C.: Immigration Policy Project of the Carnegie Endowment for International Peace, September 1990): 9; Woodrow and Passel: 47–51.

55. *Statistical Yearbook of the Immigration and Naturalization Service, 1992*: 32.

56. Rolph: 39–40.

57. Susan González Baker, "The 'Amnesty' Aftermath: Current Policy Issues Stemming from the Legalization Programs of the 1986 Immigration Reform and Control Act," *International Migration Review* 31:1 (Spring 1997): 6.

58. Instead, many unemployed illegal immigrants remain in this country and are supported by relatives. Bach and Meissner: 10; Rolph: 50.

59. Rolph: 53–54.

60. Kitty Calavita, "Employer Sanctions Violations: Toward a Dialectical Model of White-Collar Crime," *Law and Society Review* 24:4 (1990): 1050–1055.

61. For example, a study of the labor market effects of IRCA found no significant changes in the predominant wage rates for legal workers in cities with industries highly reliant on undocumented workers. Crane et al.: 47–68. Similarly, no increase in agricultural wages was evident in the first year after IRCA's implementation. See North, *Immigration Reform*: 30–36. See also Bach and Meissner: 9.

62. Elaine Sorensen and Frank D. Bean, "The Immigration Reform and Control Act and the Wages of Mexican Origin Workers: Evidence from Current Population Surveys," *Social Science Quarterly* 75:1 (March 1994): 1–17.

63. Katharine M. Donato and Douglas S. Massey, "Effect of the Immigration Reform and Control Act on the Wages of Mexican Migrants," *Social Science Quarterly* 74:3 (September 1993): 539.

64. Frank D. Bean, Georges Vernez, and Charles B. Keely, *Opening and Closing the Doors: Evaluating Immigration Reform and Control* (Washington, D.C.: The Urban Institute; Santa Monica, CA: The RAND Corporation, 1989): 53. The average size of fines varied by I.N.S. districts from a low of $850 per violation to $45,000 per notice. Bach and Meissner: 21.

65. Bach and Meissner: 9–10, 19; Cornelius, "Impacts of the 1986 U.S. Immigration Law": 234; Rolph: 41–42. In general, a steady increase in the total number of immigrant and non-immigrant visa applications since the 1970s has made it more difficult for consular officials to identify fraudulent documents. Milton D. Morris, *Immigration—The Beleaguered Bureaucracy* (Washington, D.C.: The Brookings Institution, 1985): 94–102.

66. Michael Fix and Paul Hill, *Enforcing Employer Sanctions: Challenges and Strategies* (Washington, D.C.: The Urban Institute; Santa Monica, CA: The RAND Corporation, 1990); Bach and Meissner: 17–18.

67. Rolph: 43.

68. Bach and Meissner note that the I.N.S. had no previous institutional experience in enforcing legislation involving the domestic labor market and argue that a lack of "institutional authority" may have hindered the effective implementation of employer sanctions. Bach and Meissner: 21–23.

69. Jason Juffras, *Impact of the Immigration Reform and Control Act on the Immigration and Naturalization Service* (Washington, D.C.: The Urban Institute; Santa Monica, CA: The RAND Corporation, January 1991): 23–26.

70. Bean, Vernez, and Keely: 51–52.

71. Bach and Meissner: 9–10, 19.

72. Rosanna Perotti, "Employer Sanctions and the Limits of Negotiation," *The Annals of the American Academy of Political and Social Science* 534 (July 1994): 40–41; Rolph: 47.

73. Juffras: 31–32.

74. Ibid.: 31–34.

75. By the end of the 1980s, concern over international drug trafficking had displaced the employment of undocumented workers as a priority in the I.N.S. The I.N.S. received supplemental appropriations in the late 1980s for their role in trying to crack down on drug smuggling and in deporting immigrants who had violated narcotics laws. Ibid.: 34–44.

76. Ibid.: 39, 46–47.

77. Woodrow and Passel: 66.

78. Susan González Baker, *The Cautious Welcome: The Legalization Programs of the Immigration Reform and Control Act* (Washington, D.C.: The Urban Institute; Santa Monica, CA: The RAND Corporation, 1990). By 1992, approximately 1.6 million individuals legalized under IRCA's general amnesty provision had adjusted their status to become permanent residents. Almost 1.1 million legalized under IRCA's Seasonal Agricultural Worker provision had become legal permanent residents. *Statistical Yearbook of the Immigration and Naturalization Service, 1992*: 32.

79. Bach and Meissner: 5. Bach and Meissner note that many of the illegal immigrants who did not qualify for amnesty under IRCA were Central Americans fleeing political violence and economic degradation in that region in the mid-1980s.

80. Wilbur A Finch, Jr., "The Immigration Reform and Control Act of 1986: a Preliminary Assessment," *Social Science Review* (June 1990): 249–250.

81. The fact that IRCA did not provide derivative legal status posed many potential problems for families. For example, because IRCA provides that legalized immigrants are not eligible for public assistance for five years, a mother who obtained amnesty could not apply for public assistance to help her support her children, even if they are native-born citizens. Under this scenario, the mother might have chosen not to apply for amnesty. Judith L. Fischer, "Effects of the Immigration Reform and Control Act on Families," *Marriage and Family Review* 19:3/4 (1993): 234–237.

82. Pre-implementation estimates suggested that fifty percent of the undocumented population was Mexican, but seventy percent of legalization applications came from Mexicans. This discrepancy might suggest that I.N.S. outreach programs were not targeted as effectively at other groups. Critics have also charged that legalization was biased against women in that applications required documentation, such as paycheck stubs, rent receipts, and utility bills, which many women did not have either because they worked in the underground economy or because their bills and rent receipts were in the name of male partners. Susan González Baker, "The 'Amnesty' Aftermath": 13–15.

83. Finch: 249–250. Immigrant advocacy groups brought suits in the courts in an effort to liberalize the implementation of legalization. One of the most famous court cases regarding legalization is *Haitian Refugee Center v. Nelson*, in which the I.N.S. was charged to review a number of SAW cases which they had previously denied because the court decided that the agency had violated the applicants' due process rights. In its decision, the court asserted applicants' rights to hear and rebut evidence regarding their case. Bean, Vernez, and Keely: 48–50, 54; and Juffras: 59 (see footnote 3), 68; Jacqueline Maria Hagan and Susan González Baker, "Implementing the U.S. Legalization Program: The Influence of Immigrant Communities and Local Agencies on Immigration Policy Reform," *International Migration Review* 27:3 (Fall 1993): 526–528.

84. Hagan and Baker: 529.

85. Lawrence H. Fuchs, *The American Kaleidoscope: Race, Ethnicity, and the Civic Culture* (Hanover, NH: University Press of New England, 1990): 474; Juffras: 61–64.

86. Bean, Vernez, and Keely: 39.

87. Woodrow and Passel: 60–61. Most fraudulent applications were submitted under the SAW provision because it did not contain the language and civics requirements of the general legalization provision.

88. Mercedes González de la Rocha and Agustín Escobar Latapí, "The Impact of IRCA on the Migration Patterns of a Community in Los Altos, Jalisco, Mexico," in Sergio Díaz-Briquets and Sidney Weintraub, eds., *The Effects of Receiving Country Policies on Migration Flows* (Boulder: Westview Press, 1991): 221–223, 228–229; Cornelius, "Impacts of the 1986 U.S. Immigration Law": 236–237; Georges Vernez, ed., *Immigration and International Relations: Proceedings of a Conference on the International Effects of the 1986 Immigration Reform and Control Act (IRCA)* (Washington, D.C.: The Urban Institute; Santa Monica, CA: The RAND Corporation, May 1990): 49.

89. Perotti: 38–39.

90. Martin, "Good Intentions Gone Awry": 51–53; Perotti: 39–40.

91. For example, Cornelius argues that a trend towards permanent settlement by Mexican immigrants may have been reinforced by IRCA. Cornelius, "Impacts of the 1986 U.S. Immigration Law": 238–241. See also Vernez: 49–50.

92. Bach and Meissner: 1–3; Juffras: 59.

93. Bach and Meissner: 1, 10–17; Frank D. Bean and Michael Fix, "The Significance of Recent Immigration Policy Reforms in the United States," in Gary P. Freeman and James Jupp, eds., *Nations of Immigrants: Australia, the United States, and International Migration* (Oxford: Oxford University Press, 1992): 47–48.

94. Vernon M. Briggs, Jr., "Employer Sanctions and the Question of Discrimination," *International Migration Review* 24:4 (Winter 1990): 808.

95. Ibid.: 810–811.

96. Bach and Meissner: 23; Bean, Vernez, and Keely: 42; Juffras: 42.

97. Rolph: 43.

98. Perotti: 41.

99. Juffras: 45–46.

100. Bach and Meissner: 14.

101. Ibid.: 1–2.

102. Realists might respond that foreign policy considerations did not fundamentally shape IRCA because illegal immigration is not truly relevant to national security. However, because the ability to regulate its borders is a major component of a state's sovereignty and given widespread public opinion suggesting that illegal immigration has been a major public concern in the United States since the 1960s, this response is not persuasive.

Chapter 4

Domestic Politics, Liberal Ideas, and the Immigration Act of 1990

PUBLIC OPINION AND LEGAL IMMIGRATION

In the 1960s, approximately 3.3 million legal immigrants arrived in the United States. This number increased to nearly 4.5 million in the 1970s. The admission of legal immigrants to the United States rose to over 7.3 million in the 1980s, a number exceeded only by the nearly 8.8 million legal immigrants admitted to the United States between 1901 and 1910.[1] (See Figure 4.1.)[2] The steady rise in the number of legal immigrants to the United States since the 1960s has been paralleled by a significant increase in public support for new restrictions on legal immigration. According to a 1965 Gallup poll, only one-third of the American public supported reductions in legal immigration. In contrast, a 1977 Gallup poll found that forty-two percent of those Americans surveyed believed legal immigration should be reduced.[3] Opposition to increasing numbers of legal immigrants continued to grow in ensuing years. In a 1990 Roper poll, seventy-five percent of those polled said legal immigration should not be increased, and almost one-half stated that legal immigration should be reduced.[4] As was the case with illegal immigration, public concern over rising numbers of legal immigrants has been exacerbated by the perception that these immigrants generate net costs for American society. Recent public opinion polls indicate that a majority of Americans believe that immigrants displace U.S. workers, burden social welfare systems, and threaten American culture.[5] Since the 1980s, then, public opinion polls generally have indicated that, at the very least, a majority of the U.S. public favors stabilizing current legal immigration levels, and significant numbers of Americans prefer a reduction in legal immigration to this country.[6]

Figure 4.1
Legal Immigration to the United States: 1821–1990

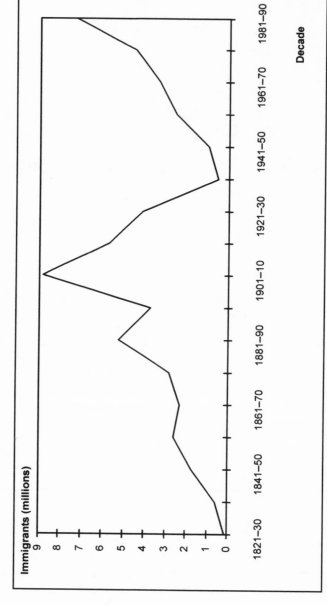

Source: U.S. Immigration and Naturalization Service, *Statistical Yearbook of the Immigration and Naturalization Service, 1992):* 26–29.

In response to public demands for the reform of legal immigration policy, Congress passed the Immigration Act of 1990. However, even though public opinion polls in the 1980s indicated majority support for new restrictions on legal immigration, the liberal provisions of the Immigration Act of 1990 actually increased the number of visas available for legal immigration to the United States. As in the case of the Immigration Reform and Control Act of 1986, Congress's passage of this liberal policy in spite of popular support for immigration restrictions can be attributed to interest group politics and liberal norms. While public support for a reduction in legal immigration was broad, it was not well-organized. Only a few interest groups, including FAIR and some environmental groups, actively advocated new restrictions on legal immigration. In contrast, a liberal coalition of well-organized groups, including ethnic organizations, churches, and employer associations, articulated strong opposition to proposals for restricting legal immigration. In fact, this liberal coalition urged Congress to expand annual limits on legal immigration in order to facilitate family reunification, to meet the nation's economic needs, and to increase the diversity of immigration flows to the United States.

Rather than addressing widespread public support for new restrictions on legal immigration, Congress acknowledged the demands of ethnic organizations, churches, and employer associations in formulating the main provisions of the Immigration Act of 1990. This legislation maintained the emphasis on family reunification in U.S. immigration policy. At the same time, the 1990 legislation increased the number of visas available for employment-based immigration and created a new "diversity program" which provides additional visas to individuals from countries that have been underrepresented in immigration flows to the United States in recent years. As the liberal provisions of the Immigration Act of 1990 illustrate, liberal norms at the domestic level have prevented the United States government from adopting new restrictions on legal immigration.

THE POLICY DEBATE OVER LEGAL IMMIGRATION IN THE 1970s

The origins of the Immigration Act of 1990 can be traced to the 1965 amendments to the Immigration and Nationality Act. While the 1952 Immigration and Nationality Act had reserved up to fifty percent of visa preferences for immigrants with special occupational skills, the 1965 amendments gave a higher priority to family reunification. The immigrant admissions system created in 1965 exempted spouses and minor children of U.S. citizens from numerical limitation and reserved approximately seventy-five percent of all preference visas for other types of family migration. Under this preference system, only twenty percent of the visas for legal immigration were set aside for employment-based immigration. Thus, the 1965 amendments to the Immigration and Nationality Act established family ties as the primary criteria for obtaining permanent residence in the United States.

A number of interest groups supported the emphasis on family reunification in the 1965 legislation for a variety of reasons. Opponents of the national origins system, including churches, ethnic organizations, and civil rights groups, advocated a quota system that gave preference to family reunification as a fair method for regulating legal immigration without blatantly discriminating against individuals from specific countries. Interestingly, several groups that initially opposed the elimination of the national origins system, including the Daughters of the American Revolution and the American Legion, also came to support the emphasis on family reunification in the 1965 legislation because they anticipated that this emphasis would ensure that the ethnic composition of immigration flows to the United States would not change dramatically. Since only a small proportion of immigrants from Asia and Africa resided in the United States in the 1960s, few immigrants from these regions were expected to have the family ties to attain visas for legal immigration. Therefore, while churches, ethnic organizations, and civil rights groups advocated family criteria as a fair, humane way to regulate legal immigration to the United States, other interest groups that traditionally opposed liberal immigration policies accepted the 1965 legislation's emphasis on family reunification because they viewed this change primarily as a symbolic measure that would not significantly alter the status quo.[7]

Contradicting the expectations of restrictionist groups, the ethnic composition of immigration flows to the United States clearly has changed since the national origins system was eliminated in 1965. The most significant change resulting from the elimination of the restrictive national origins system was the rise in immigration from previously underrepresented regions. The increase in immigration from Asia is the most striking example of the extent to which the ethnic composition of immigration flows to the United States has changed since 1965. While only roughly 150,000 Asian immigrants entered the United States in the 1950s, this number had risen to over 2.7 million by the 1980s. Legal immigration from the Americas also has increased since the 1960s. Even though the 1965 legislation placed a ceiling on Western Hemisphere immigration for the first time, the number of immigrants from this region has increased steadily since the 1960s. During the 1950s, just under 1 million immigrants from the Americas entered the United States. This number was roughly 1.7 million in the 1960s and over 1.9 million in the 1970s. Immigration from the Americas reached an all-time high during the 1980s when over 3.6 million individuals from this region attained permanent residence in the United States. Though not as dramatic in terms of aggregate numbers, immigration from Africa also has increased significantly since the 1960s. Almost 200,000 African immigrants entered the United States in the 1980s, compared to under 15,000 in the 1950s.[8] Although a lack of family ties was expected to hinder immigration from previously underrepresented areas, individuals from these regions, especially Asia, commonly immigrated to the United States either under the occupational preference categories or as refugees. These immigrants later petitioned for the entry of other family members.[9]

While immigration from Asia, the Americas, and Africa has increased since the 1960s, immigration from Europe declined significantly after 1965. Fewer than 400,000 immigrants from countries in northern and western Europe entered the United States in the 1980s, compared to over 900,000 in the 1950s. Many individuals who would have been likely to emigrate from this region, unskilled workers in Ireland, for example, did not have close family ties or the necessary occupational skills to obtain a visa under the new preference system.[10] Immigration from southern and eastern Europe increased modestly after the creation of the new preference system in 1965. While under 400,000 individuals had immigrated from this region in the 1950s, over 500,000 immigrants from southern and eastern Europe entered the United States during both the 1960s and the 1970s.[11] Nevertheless, a marked decline in total European immigration to the United States has been evident since the 1960s. Since the passage of the 1965 legislation, then, the ethnic composition of immigration flows to the United States has changed dramatically. In contrast to the historical dominance of immigration from Europe, especially northern and western Europe, a large majority of legal immigrants in recent decades have come from Asia and the Americas. (See Figure 4.2.)

The emphasis on family reunification in the 1965 legislation and the increasing ethnic diversity of immigration flows to the United States have reinforced each other. Immigrants from Asia and the Americas, who have dominated immigration flows in the years following the passage of the 1965 legislation, continue to benefit from the emphasis on family reunification in U.S. immigration policy. Since 1965, a vast majority of legal immigrants have received visas because of family ties. For example, throughout most of the 1980s, annual legal immigration to the United States averaged between 500,000 and 600,000, but only approximately 50,000 immigrants annually entered the United States under occupational preference categories.[12] Since at least the end of the 1970s, most of the immigrants entering the United States as immediate relatives of U.S. citizens or under the family preference categories have come from Asia and North America.[13] In recent years, then, individuals from countries in these areas have established family ties in the United States that have facilitated further immigration from these regions.

The issues of family reunification and ethnic diversity have been at the foundation of the debate over legal immigration policy reform since 1965. Almost immediately after the 1965 amendments to the Immigration and Nationality Act were implemented, a variety of interest groups began to complain about the legislation's effects. In 1968, the Irish American National Immigration Committee complained to Congress that the new policy unfairly limited immigration from Ireland.[14] In the 1970s, a number of churches, Hispanic groups, and the American Civil Liberties Union criticized the 1965 legislation for failing to apply preference categories within the new ceiling on Western Hemisphere immigration. Because visas for this hemisphere were not allocated according to a preference system, relatives of Western Hemisphere immigrants competed with workers and other individuals for the limited number of visas each year, and large backlogs in visa applications developed, which often kept family members apart for years. In response to the emergence of lengthy waiting periods for family reunification, churches, Hispanic groups, and

Figure 4.2
Immigration to the United States by Region of Origin: 1901–1990

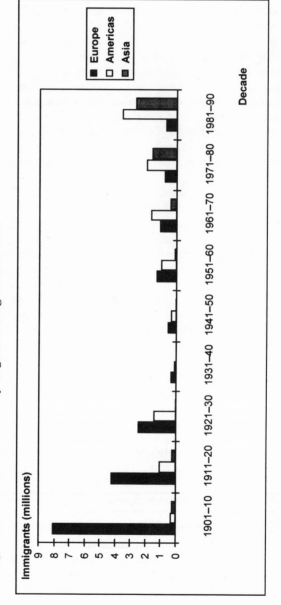

Source: U.S. Immigration and Naturalization Service, *Statistical Yearbook of the Immigration and Naturalization Service,1992*: 26–29.

the ACLU urged Congress to extend the preference categories to the Western Hemisphere. In addition, Mexican-American groups contended that Mexico should be given a larger per-country limit not only because of the large backlogs in visa applications for this country but also in recognition of Mexico's historical relationship with the United States. The AFL-CIO, Zero Population Growth, and other restrictionist groups countered that the imposition of equal per-country limits was necessary in order to limit immigration and to ensure that U.S. immigration policy was fair and equitable. Ultimately, Congress attempted to balance the concerns of all of these interest groups by passing the 1976 amendments to the Immigration and Nationality Act which extended both the preference categories *and* per-country limits to the Western Hemisphere in order to facilitate family reunification and to eliminate the differential treatment of the Western and Eastern Hemispheres in U.S. immigration policy. [15]   In the 1978 amendments to the Immigration and Nationality Act, Congress further eliminated blatant discrimination from the immigrant admissions system by replacing the inequitable hemispheric ceilings with an overall global ceiling of 290,000.[16]

By the end of the 1970s, then, U.S. policy towards legal immigration was based on equitable national quotas within an overall global ceiling on immigration. Though each country received an equal number of quota allowances under this ceiling, a variety of interest groups continued to charge that this system was discriminatory. Civil rights advocates argued that equal per-country limits hindered family reunification for individuals from countries where the demand for visas was especially high. These critics argued that per-country limits should be eliminated and that, instead, the granting of visas within the preference system should take place on a first-come, first-served basis.[17] Conversely, some ethnic organizations, especially Irish groups, argued that the emphasis on family reunification in the immigrant admissions system minimized ethnic diversity in immigration flows to the United States and discriminated against individuals who did not have family ties in this country. At the same time, the growing political power of new immigrant groups, including Asians and Latin Americans, bolstered support for continuing emphasis on family reunification in U.S. immigration policy. The generally negative economic climate of the 1970s and public preoccupation with the issue of illegal immigration prevented Congress from seriously considering any proposals for major reforms of U.S. policy towards legal immigration. Nevertheless, the growing prominence of the issues of family reunification and ethnic diversity in the debate over legal immigration in the 1970s set the stage for the immigration reform movement of the 1980s.

THE SELECT COMMISSION ON IMMIGRATION AND REFUGEE POLICY

In spite of widespread public agreement that existing U.S. immigration policy needed to be reformed, Congress was unable to pass comprehensive immigration policy reforms in the 1970s. Therefore, in 1978, Congress created the Select Commission on Immigration and Refugee Policy to study, evaluate, and recommend changes in U.S. immigration policy. In the introduction to the commission's final report, submitted in 1981, the Reverend Theodore Hesburgh, chairperson of the commission, wrote:

To the question: Is immigration in the U.S. national interest?, the Select Commission gives a strong but qualified yes. A strong yes because we believe there are many benefits which immigrants bring to U.S. society; a qualified yes because we believe there are limits on the ability of this country to absorb large numbers of immigrants effectively.[18]

One of the fundamental goals of the Select Commission, then, was to recommend a reformulation of U.S. immigration policy designed to advance the national interest.

With this goal framing their recommendations, the Select Commission concluded that a modest increase in legal immigration would contribute to the national interest by stimulating economic growth, providing needed skilled workers, fostering positive relations with other countries and the vision of the United States as a world leader, reunifying families of citizens and permanent residents, and enriching U.S. culture.[19] To this end, the commission recommended legislation increasing the annual ceiling on legal immigration from 270,000 to 350,000, with an extra 100,000 visas annually for five years to facilitate family reunification for countries that had large backlogs in visa applications. Although it recommended an increase in the ceiling on legal immigration, the Select Commission resisted proposals to expand legal immigration even further because most commissioners believed that too much immigration displaces native workers, especially in specific regions and employment sectors, and that higher levels of immigration might aggravate social tensions and population problems in this country.[20]

In addition to recommending an increase in the overall immigration ceiling, the Select Commission concluded that family reunification should continue to be a principal factor guiding the admission of legal immigrants to this country. In supporting this principle, the commission cited U.S. commitment to promoting family reunification under the Helsinki Accords[21] and argued that family reunification advanced the national interest by contributing to public order, health, and social welfare.[22] In order to promote family reunification, the Select Commission recommended that the immigration of immediate relatives of U.S. citizens should continue to be exempt from the overall immigration ceiling. In fact, a majority of commissioners argued that exemptions from numerical limitations should be extended to unmarried adult children and grandparents of adult U.S. citizens. Most commissioners agreed that the preference categories for other relatives of citizens and permanent residents should be maintained. Thus, the Select Commission rejected calls by restrictionist groups to eliminate the preference category for brothers and sisters of adult U.S. citizens.[23] Instead of recommending a reduction in the number of preference categories, a majority of the commissioners argued that a new preference category for parents of permanent residents should be created. In sum, not only did the Select Commission recommend that the emphasis on family reunification in U.S. immigration policy be maintained, but it also suggested that Congress should adopt measures exempting additional relative categories from numerical limitation and creating a new category of family members eligible for preference visas.[24]

While advocating continuing emphasis on family reunification in U.S. immigration policy, the Select Commission also recommended that the entry of "independent" immigrants, individuals without family ties in this country, should be promoted. To this end, the Select Commission unanimously voted that two separate admissions categories should be created for "family" and "independent" immigrants so that individuals applying in each category would not be competing against each other for a limited number of visas.[25] According to the commission's report, immigration in the independent category would be designed to meet the country's labor market needs and to foster cultural diversity. In place of the third preference category for immigrants with exceptional abilities and the sixth preference category for skilled and unskilled workers, the new independent immigration category would include preferences for immigrants with exceptional qualifications, investors, and other immigrants selected based on either labor market needs or the objective of increasing the diversity of immigration flows to this country. Although the Select Commission did not recommend an exact number of visas that should be made available under this category, the majority of commissioners clearly believed that existing restrictions on the entry of independent immigrants should be eased.[26]

The Select Commission on Immigration and Refugee Policy viewed its recommended changes to the immigrant admissions system as part of comprehensive immigration policy reforms. A modest increase in the annual ceiling on legal immigration coupled with minor expansions in the criteria for admission were designed to reduce backlogs in visa applications and to prevent the development of major backlogs in the future. The Select Commission also believed that a modest liberalization of the immigrant admissions system would reduce some of the pressure for illegal entry to this country.[27] Thus, the Select Commission presented its recommendations on reducing undocumented immigration and modifying the system for the admission of legal immigrants as part of a coherent approach to immigration policy reform. However, the political obstacles to comprehensive immigration policy reform would prove to be too great, and Congress would not reform legal immigration policy until almost a decade after the Select Commission submitted its final report.

THE POLICY DEBATE OVER LEGAL IMMIGRATION IN THE 1980s

Early versions of the Simpson-Mazzoli legislation, which provided for sanctions against employers who knowingly hire undocumented workers, as discussed in Chapter 3, also included provisions designed to modify the system for admitting legal immigrants. The 1982 Simpson bill in the Senate would have imposed an overall ceiling of 425,000 on total immigration. Though this ceiling was higher than the overall limit of 350,000 recommended by the Select Commission on Immigration and Refugee Policy, this bill was more restrictive than the Select Commission's proposal because it included the immediate relatives of U.S. citizens under this immigration ceiling, while the Select Commission had recommended that immediate relatives continue to be exempted from the overall immigration ceiling. It also diverged from the Select Commission's proposals by eliminating the fifth preference category for the brothers and sisters of adult U.S. citizens. While differing in these respects, the Simpson bill adopted the Select Commission's recommendations by creating two separate admissions categories for family reunification and independent immigration. The bill reserved 350,000 visas for family reunification and 75,000 visas for independent immigrants. Senator Simpson submitted an identical bill in 1983, with the exception that this bill reserved the fifth preference for siblings of adult U.S. citizens.[28] Each of these bills passed in the Senate but failed in the House.

The 1982 and 1983 Simpson bills were blocked in the House because legislators were unable to negotiate a compromise acceptable to the competing interest groups involved in shaping the immigration policy debate. Ethnic organizations and church groups generally were opposed to the creation of a ceiling on legal immigration that included immediate relatives of U.S. citizens because such a ceiling would hinder family reunification. FAIR, the Environmental Fund, and Zero Population Growth remained opposed to legislation that did not include a rigid ceiling on all types of immigration and criticized the continued emphasis on family reunification in the Simpson bills. Employer associations favored the creation of a new category for independent immigration, though ethnic groups and churches criticized early proposals for the establishment of an independent immigration category because English language skills would have been one of the criteria for allocating visas under this category.[29] Ultimately, Congress dropped the provisions relating to the modification of the system for admitting legal immigrants in order to facilitate the passage of employer sanctions legislation.[30]

After passing the Immigration Reform and Control Act in 1986, Congress was able to return to a consideration of comprehensive legal immigration policy reform and clearly faced conflicting interests in this legislative task. The debate over legal immigration policy reform in ensuing years centered on three basic issues: family reunification, labor migration, and the diversity of immigration flows to the United States. In each case, domestic interest group politics favored the liberalization of immigration policy rather than new restrictions on the admission of legal immigrants.[31] Because a return to the discriminatory national origins system created in the 1920s would not have been politically feasible, Congress would have had to restrict the number of visas for family reunification and/or labor migration in order to reduce legal immigration. While FAIR and some environmental groups favored such limitations, most interest groups opposed new restrictions on legal immigration. Indeed, a variety of interest groups contended that an increase in legal immigration was necessary to facilitate family reunification, to meet the nation's economic needs, and to rectify unintended discriminatory consequences of the 1965 legislation.

In regard to family migration, broad, organized support for the principle of family reunification impeded congressional efforts to restrict legal immigration. Legislative proposals to reduce legal immigration typically included measures to restrict family reunification, and these proposals met strong resistance from ethnic organizations and religious groups, including the National Council of La Raza, the Organization of Chinese Americans, the American Committee on Italian Migration, the American Jewish Committee, and Migration and Refugee Services of the U.S. Catholic Conference. These groups insisted that U.S. immigration policy should continue to emphasize the humanitarian principle of family reunification. Indeed, many ethnic organizations and churches argued that an expanded number of visas should be set aside for family reunification in an effort to alleviate visa application backlogs in many countries that often kept families apart for years.[32] Thus, legislative proposals to restrict family migration faced strong, well-organized opposition.

Well-organized opposition among employer associations also provided an obstacle to new restrictions on the admission of legal immigrants. Labor migration had not been a central issue in the debate over legal immigration policy reform in the 1970s primarily because negative economic conditions in that decade would have precluded any serious discussion of an increase in the number of visas available for independent immigrants. In the 1980s, however, labor migration again emerged as a prominent issue in the debate over legal immigration reform. Critics of the existing preference system argued that limitations on the number of immigrant visas for individuals with special occupational skills hindered the ability of the United States to compete in a globalized economy by restricting the entry of highly-skilled labor.[33] For example, *Workforce 2000*, a 1987 Hudson Institute Report funded by the Department of Labor, estimated that a shortage of skilled labor would develop by the year 2000.[34] Therefore, many employer associations, including the Chamber of Commerce, the National Association of Manufacturers, and the American Council on International Personnel, urged Congress to increase the number of visas available for employment-based immigration, especially for the entry of immigrants with special managerial or technological skills or knowledge of specific markets. Importantly, employer associations did not argue that employment-based immigration should be increased at the expense of family migration. Because proposals for an expansion of employment-based immigration typically did not call for a parallel reduction in family immigration, many ethnic organizations and church groups vocalized their support for these proposals.[35]

In addition to well-organized support for family reunification and renewed emphasis on the admission of skilled workers, political support for diversity in immigration flows to the United States impeded the passage of restrictive immigration policy reforms in the 1980s. In response to the declining proportion of "traditional" immigrant groups in immigration flows to the United

States, several ethnic organizations representing these immigrant groups called for policy reforms that would diversify the ethnic composition of immigration flows. Irish organizations, like the Irish Immigration Reform Movement, were the most vocal advocates of policies for the diversification of the ethnic origins of immigrants to the United States. Though these groups called for increased diversity in legal admissions to this country, they did not argue that the existing preference system should be replaced. Rather, these organizations urged Congress to supplement the existing preference system with additional visas for immigrants from countries that had been underrepresented in immigration flows to the United States since the 1960s. Ethnic organizations representing groups that generally had benefited from the elimination of the discriminatory national origins system, including the Organization for Chinese Americans and the American Jewish Committee, typically supported efforts to increase the diversity of immigration flows as long as U.S. immigration policy maintained its priority for family reunification.[36]

With a complex set of interests framing the debate, Congress began to consider the reform of legal immigration policy soon after the Immigration Reform and Control Act was passed in 1986. In 1988, Senators Alan Simpson and Edward Kennedy submitted a bill which attempted to address widespread restrictionist sentiment while acceding to the demands of interest groups that favored an expansion in the immigrant admissions system. In an effort to acknowledge the public desire for a reduction in legal immigration, this bill provided for an overall cap on annual immigration that would have included immediate relatives of U.S. citizens. However, because the overall cap on legal immigration was set at nearly 600,000, which was the average number of legal immigrants including immediate relatives in the 1980s, this change would not have represented a truly important restriction on legal immigration. Moreover, while it reduced the number of visas available for siblings of citizens, the bill increased the number of visas available for the children and spouses of permanent residents. Finally, this bill created a separate category for independent immigration, under which 55,000 visas would be allocated annually on the basis of a point system that took into account the age, skills, education, and English-speaking ability of potential immigrants. Though generally expansive, this provision was opposed by many interest groups because its emphasis on English-speaking ability was viewed as discriminatory. Ultimately, then, the bill did not satisfy either restrictionist or pro-immigration forces. Although it passed in the Senate, it was not acted on in the House.[37]

Another Kennedy-Simpson bill that clearly attempted to address the demands of pro-immigration forces passed the Senate in 1989. This legislation provided for a 630,000 cap on overall immigration, including immediate relatives of citizens. Not only did this legislation provide for a higher ceiling on legal immigration than the previous Kennedy-Simpson bill, but it also defined this ceiling as "flexible." Under this flexible ceiling, the migration of immediate family members of citizens would be unlimited, and the number of immigration visas allotted to other family members of citizens and permanent residents could not fall below 216,000. Again, the Kennedy-Simpson legislation would have increased the number of visas available to immediate family members of permanent residents, but, unlike the previous bill, this legislation maintained the same number of preference visas for siblings of U.S. citizens.   The 1989 Kennedy-Simpson legislation provided for an independent immigration category that would have been allotted 150,000 visas per year. Preference visas within this category were reserved for immigrants with exceptional abilities, skilled workers, investors, special immigrants, including ministers and former embassy employees, rural medical personnel, and immigrants selected by a point system. Unlike the 1988 bill, this legislation did not include English literacy as one of the criteria to be considered under the point system. This modified version of the Kennedy-Simpson bill was opposed by restrictionist forces, which viewed it as too expansive, and pro-immigration groups, which generally preferred an even more expansive House bill that would have raised the number of immigrant visas to almost 800,000 annually. In light of continued opposition, the House did not act on the Kennedy-Simpson bill in 1989.[38]

The following year, congressional leaders involved in the debate over legal immigration policy were able to forge an agreement on the reform of the immigrant admissions system. A solid majority of the House and the Senate passed a modified version of the Kennedy-Simpson bill at the end of October, and President Bush signed this legislation into law on November 29, 1990.[39] Like the Immigration Reform and Control Act of 1986, the Immigration Act of 1990 can be depicted as compromise legislation that attempted to acknowledge the concerns of restrictionist as well as pro-immigration forces. However, this compromise agreement was skewed in favor of advocates of liberal immigration policies. Though it did not completely satisfy the demands of ethnic groups, churches, or employer associations, the legislation finally passed by Congress in 1990 provided for only a few restrictive measures. For example, this legislation authorized increased funding for border control personnel in the Immigration and Naturalization Service. Moreover, it placed a cap of 10,000 visas per year on the immigration of unskilled workers. Furthermore, it required the Secretary of Labor to use aggregate data in deciding whether to certify that immigrant workers are needed in various occupations.[40]   Although this legislation contained some restrictive measures, the major provisions of the Immigration Act of 1990 provided for an expansion in legal immigration to the United States.

The Immigration Act of 1990 created an overall annual cap on legal immigration of 675,000, with a transitional cap of 700,000 between 1992 and 1994.   Though this cap represents an increase from the previous overall immigration ceiling of 270,000, it applies to the immigration of immediate family members of U.S. citizens. Thus, under the overall ceiling on legal immigration, Congress created a cap of 480,000 on family immigration.[41] By creating an overall immigration ceiling which applied to immediate family members and an annual cap on family immigration, Congress was attempting to address the public desire for restrictions on legal immigration and to assert the appearance of control.

However, the Immigration Act of 1990 actually authorized a slight increase in family immigration. Congress defined the annual ceiling on overall immigration and the cap on family immigration as "flexible." Immediate family members of U.S. citizens continue to be admitted without numerical limitation, and the number of visas available for other family members of U.S. citizens and permanent residents each year cannot fall below a floor of 226,000. Therefore, the "flexible ceiling" of 480,000 can be pierced if a large number of immediate relatives of U.S. citizens enter in a particular year. Under the previous law, only 216,000 family-preference visas were available each year. Thus, the floor of 226,000 on family-preference immigration represents a modest increase in the visa allowances for family-preference categories. In addition to increasing the number of family-preference visas, the 1990 Immigration Act increased the number of visas available for the immediate relatives of permanent residents, a category that had been oversubscribed in many countries for several years, from just over 70,000 to more than 114,000.[42] Moreover, the legislation provided that seventy-five percent of the spouses and children of permanent residents admitted would be exempt from the per-country limits. Finally, the 1990 legislation facilitated family migration by allowing spouses and minor children of immigrants who had received amnesty under IRCA's legalization programs to apply for permanent residence.[43] Although it did not include stronger measures designed to facilitate family reunification, such as the elimination of per-country limits, one of the primary features of the Immigration Act of 1990 was a fundamental emphasis on family reunification.

While continuing to emphasize family reunification, the 1990 Immigration Act also increased the number of visas available for employment-based immigration. The 1990 Immigration Act allotted 140,000 visas annually for employment-based immigration, slightly less than the 150,000 independent immigrant visas called for in the 1989 Kennedy-Simpson legislation. As in earlier versions of the legislation, the 1990 Immigration Act gave preference within the employment-based immigration category to individuals with special abilities, professionals, and skilled workers.[44] Although the employment-based category stresses occupational skills or other economic criteria, family reunification is taken into consideration even in this category in that the 140,000 annual limit covers not only workers but also their families.[45] In fact, family members traditionally have comprised the majority of immigrants who enter under employment-based preference categories.[46]

Finally, the Immigration Act of 1990 created a permanent diversity program through which additional visas are made available annually in an effort to diversify the ethnic composition of immigrants to the United States. Between 1992 and 1994, 40,000 visas were made available each year to immigrants from countries, especially Ireland, which have had a proportionally low number of immigrants to the United States since 1965. Beginning in 1995, the Immigration Act of 1990 made 55,000 visas available annually to individuals from countries that have been underrepresented in immigration flows to the United States in recent years. These diversity visas are allocated by a lottery system and are not included under the "flexible ceiling" on legal immigration to the United States.[47]

The Immigration Act of 1990 included a variety of other provisions that liberalized U.S. immigration policy. It created a separate per-country ceiling of 10,000 for Hong Kong and provided an additional 12,000 visas per year between 1991 and 1993 for Hong Kong nationals employed in multinational corporations in the United States. This legislation increased the cap on asylee adjustments from 5,000 to 10,000 per year and also authorizes the Attorney General to grant temporary protected status and work authorization to immigrants in the U.S. who are from countries that the Attorney General and other relevant cabinet members determine to be subject to war, natural disaster, or other emergency situations. The 1990 act specifically provided that Salvadorans who had resided in the United States since September 19, 1990, qualified for temporary protected status, which was authorized until June 30, 1992. Finally, the Immigration Act of 1990 removed the exclusion against the admission of homosexuals for permanent residence.[48]

Congress passed this generally liberal legislation in spite of widespread public support for restrictions on legal immigration because of the strength of opposition to immigration restrictions among a liberal coalition of interest groups. Broad public support for a reduction in legal immigration existed in the abstract. Specific proposals to limit family reunification or place an inflexible cap on overall migration received minimal organized support. In contrast, ethnic organizations, churches, and employer associations not only opposed specific proposals to reduce legal immigration but, in fact, advocated an expansion in the number of visas available for legal immigration. Though the legislation was not as liberal as many pro-immigration groups would have liked, it demonstrates the way in which a liberal coalition of interest groups has prevented the U.S. government from adopting a policy designed to reduce legal immigration to this country.

THE EFFECTS OF THE IMMIGRATION ACT OF 1990

Upon signing the Immigration Act of 1990 into law, President Bush hailed the benefits of this legislation for the nation, saying, "This act recognizes the fundamental importance and historic contributions of immigrants to our country" and "is good for families, good for business, good for crime fighting, and good for America."[49] President Bush's praise for the legislation was not echoed by everyone who had been involved in the debate over legal immigration policy reform. Employers, contending that the law would contribute to economic growth, generally expressed the most satisfaction with the legislation.[50] Most interest groups, however, maintained some reservations about the Immigration Act of 1990. The few restrictive provisions in this legislation clearly did not satisfy interest groups like FAIR and Zero Population Growth, which favored stronger restrictions on legal immigration. At the same time, ethnic organizations and churches expressed concern that the immigration reforms did not go far enough to reduce the visa backlogs that were hindering family reunification and complained that temporary protected status for Salvadorans should have been granted for a longer period.[51]   Irish-American organizations obviously were supportive of the creation of the diversity program but had preferred an even more liberal House version of the legislation.[52]   As indicated by persistent concerns among a variety of interest groups, the Immigration Act of 1990 has not resolved the debate over legal immigration policy reform.

Information on immigration flows to the United States since the passage of the Immigration Act of 1990 indicates that it has had mixed results in terms of meeting the objectives of advocates of immigration reform. Immigration to the United States has increased significantly since 1990. During the 1980s, an average of only approximately 600,000 immigrants entered the United States annually. In contrast, over 1.8 million legal immigrants attained permanent residence in the United States in 1991. In 1992, this number remained at nearly 1 million. Aside from the high numbers of legal immigrants in 1989 and 1990, the immigration figures for 1991 and 1992 represent the highest annual levels of immigration since the first decades of the twentieth century.[53]

While legal immigration has been near record-highs in recent years, this increase cannot generally be attributed to the effects of the Immigration Act of 1990. Rather, most of the increase in legal immigration since the end of the 1980s has resulted from the legalization programs created by the Immigration Reform and Control Act of 1986. For example, in 1991, over 1.1 million immigrants, representing over sixty percent of total immigration, were legalized under the provisions of IRCA. In addition to increases attributable to legalization, slight increases in refugee and asylee admissions since 1990 have contributed to the overall increase in legal immigration.[54]

When legalized immigrants, refugees, and asylees are excluded from the analysis, the increase in legal immigration since 1990 becomes less dramatic. In 1992, the first year the major provisions of the legislation went into effect, 693,598 legal immigrants, excluding the categories of legalized immigrants, refugees, and asylees, were admitted to the United States compared to 564,926 legal immigrants in 1991. This number represents almost a nineteen percent increase in legal immigration after the implementation of the Immigration Act of 1990.   However, legal immigration for this year did not even reach the transitional "flexible ceiling" of 700,000 authorized by Congress for 1992 through 1994.[55]   Thus, the Immigration Act of 1990 was designed to increase modestly the levels of legal immigration to the United States, and it has been relatively effective in this regard so far.

In addition to providing for an increase in overall immigration levels, the Immigration Act of 1990 maintained the emphasis on family reunification in U.S. immigration policy. Family reunification has led to a modest increase in overall immigration since 1990. Family immigration to the United States averaged under 430,000 per year during the 1980s. In 1992, nearly 448,607 family immigrants were admitted to the United States. In spite of this slight increase, the proportion of family immigrants in the overall number of immigrants to this country has decreased. In 1987, family immigrants still constituted over seventy percent of the total number of immigrants to this country. In 1990 and 1991, this number declined to under thirty percent as legalized immigrants came to dominate immigration flows to this country. In 1992, though the overall number of family immigrants was higher than the annual average for the 1980s, family immigration constituted only forty-six percent of total immigration that year.[56] Although significant numbers of legalized immigrants were still entering the country in 1992, the expansion in employment-based immigration and the issuance of the first diversity visas provided for under the Immigration Act of 1990 ensured that rising numbers of family immigrants represented a smaller percentage of overall immigration.

Even though the Immigration Act of 1990 provided for a modest increase in family immigration, it has not alleviated the backlogs in visa applications so strongly criticized by ethnic organizations and churches in the debate over legal immigration policy reform. In January 1993, the number of backlogged visas was almost 3.4 million, which represents a sixteen percent increase over the previous year. Visa applications in a relatively small number of countries, especially Mexico, the Philippines, India, China, Korea, Taiwan, and Vietnam, account for the largest proportion of the total backlog.[57] For example, as of April 1994, Mexico and the Philippines had visa backlogs in all family-preference categories. Visa applications in China, the Dominican Republic, and India were backlogged for every category except the first preference for unmarried adult children of U.S. citizens. The backlogs for preference visas for siblings of adult U.S. citizens were especially large, extending all the way back to June 1977 for the Philippines. Concerning visa preferences for spouses and children of permanent residents from a number of countries, applicants for visas who applied in 1991 are still waiting to be reunited with their families.[58] Unused visas remain available under the ceiling on family immigration in spite of the persistent backlogs in family-preference categories because some countries commonly do not reach the per-country limits in the family-preference categories.

Employment-based immigration has increased significantly since the implementation of the 1990 Immigration Act began in 1992. Prior to 1992, employment-based immigration consistently was below 60,000 per year.   In 1992, this number jumped to 116,198, though employment-based immigration still represented only twelve percent of total immigration for that year because of the continuing emphasis on family immigration as well as legalizations under IRCA.[59]   The growth in employment-based immigration resulting from the Immigration Act of 1990 has reflected primarily an increase in the immigration of professionals with advanced degrees and skilled workers. In general, then, employers' demands for increased access to skilled workers and professionals deemed necessary for economic competition in a globalized economy generally have been met by the admission system created in 1990.

In terms of diversifying the ethnic origins of current immigrants to the United States, the Immigration Act of 1990 has resulted in only minor changes in the ethnic composition of immigration flows to the United States. Specifically, immigration from Europe has increased since this legislation was passed. While fewer than 70,000 European immigrants arrived in the United States in

1987, over 150,000 European immigrants were granted visas for permanent residence in 1992.[60]   Even before the Immigration Act of 1990, European immigration to this country had begun to increase.   This gradual rise in immigration from Europe can be attributed, in part, to legalizations under the Immigration Reform and Control Act of 1986. However, the diversity program created by the Immigration Act of 1990 explains most of the sustained increase in European immigration since 1990. Most of the diversity visas under the transitional diversity program went to European countries, partly because forty percent of the transitional diversity visas were set aside for Ireland.   In 1992, for example, over 25,000 of a total of approximately 34,000 diversity visas were granted to individuals from Europe.[61]

In spite of the increase in immigration from Europe since 1990, the Immigration Act of 1990 has not dramatically altered the ethnic origins of current immigrants to the United States. In fact, the continued emphasis on family reunification in this legislation has ensured that the post-1965 dominance of Asians and Latin Americans in immigration flows to this country generally has been maintained. In 1987, while only roughly eleven percent of all visas went to European immigrants, immigrants from Asia and the Americas received over forty percent of legal immigration visas. By 1992, these proportions had been altered only slightly. The proportion of legal immigration visas going to Europe increased to sixteen percent while the proportion received by Asian countries declined to thirty-five percent. Throughout this period, the number of visas for all African countries has averaged roughly two percent of the overall number of visas.[62] Thus far, then, the ethnic origins of immigrants to the United States have not changed significantly in response to the modification of U.S. immigration policy in 1990. However, the transitional diversity program has increased slightly the proportion of legal immigration visas received by European countries. The impact, though modest, of the transitional diversity program suggests that the permanent diversity program, which went into effect in 1995, may lead gradually to the further diversification of the ethnic origins of immigrants to the United States.

In conclusion, the data on immigration flows to the United States since the implementation of the Immigration Act of 1990 suggests that, thus far, neither the goals of anti-immigration nor pro-immigration forces have been completely met. To the chagrin of advocates of restriction, total immigration has increased since 1990 not only because of legalizations under the Immigration Reform and Control Act of 1986 and a growing number of refugee and asylee admissions but also because of the expansion in family immigration and employment-based immigration authorized by the 1990 legislation. However, confirming the fears of churches and ethnic organizations, significant obstacles to family reunification remain, especially the per-country limits, even after the legal immigration policy reforms of 1990. Moreover, the diversity program has not yet resulted in a significant diversification of the ethnic origins of immigrants to this country, though it is still far too early to evaluate the long-term effects of this provision. Because the Immigration Act of 1990 has not fulfilled the objectives of either restrictionist or pro-immigration forces, legal immigration policy reform remains a fundamental issue in public policy debates today.

DOMESTIC POLITICS, LIBERAL IDEAS, AND THE REGULATION OF LEGAL IMMIGRATION

Rising numbers of legal immigrants after 1965 precipitated an increase in public support for new restrictions on legal immigration. However, this broad public support for restrictions on legal immigration existed in the abstract. Some of the same public opinion polls conducted in the 1980s which indicated that a majority of Americans believe immigrants have a negative impact on U.S. society also suggested that a majority of the U.S. public believes that immigrants frequently work in jobs that U.S. workers do not want and that the cultures and talents of immigrants have improved our country.[63]   Moreover, two recent Roper polls suggest that many Americans oppose illiberal measures which would hinder the reunification of families. In a 1990 Roper poll that asked which immigrants beyond immediate family should be given preference under U.S. immigration policy, a strong majority of the respondents indicated that extended family, individuals with skills needed by the United States, or both groups should be given preference. Only twenty percent of the respondents answered that neither group should be given preference.[64] A 1995 Roper poll also suggests that most Americans favor family reunification. Sixty-one percent of the respondents to this survey disapproved of eliminating the emphasis on family reunification in U.S. immigration policy. Moreover, the responses to one question in this survey suggest that many Americans might oppose immigration restrictions based on ethnic discrimination. Asked about whether the federal government should act on Census Bureau estimates that Anglo-Americans will comprise only half of the population in fifty years, sixty-one percent of the respondents said that the U.S. government should not try to prevent this predicted decline of non-Hispanic white people as a proportion of the overall population in the United States.[65] Thus, though broad generalizations should not be drawn from only a couple of public opinion surveys, these polls suggest that a majority of the American public may support some of the liberal norms advanced by churches, civil rights groups, and ethnic organizations in the immigration policy debate in the 1980s.

In the congressional debate over immigration policy reform in the 1980s, support for new immigration restrictions diminished when specific proposals for reducing legal immigration were discussed. Legislators could have turned to several mechanisms to restrict legal entry into this country. Congress could have explicitly limited the entry of individuals from specific countries. Alternatively, it could have adopted a system that limited family reunification. Finally, Congress could have reduced labor migration even further than it had been cut back in 1965. None of these mechanisms was politically feasible. A return to the discriminatory national origins system of the 1920s clearly could not have attained the necessary political support in Congress by the 1980s. Similarly, efforts to place new restrictions on family reunification or labor migration also faced insurmountable opposition in the debate over legal immigration policy reform in the 1980s. In fact, churches, ethnic organizations, and employers associations urged Congress to expand legal immigration allowances in order to facilitate family reunification, to meet the nation's economic needs, and to diversify the ethnic origins of recent immigrants to the United States.

The Immigration Act of 1990 is compromise legislation which acceded to many of the demands of the interest groups that favored the liberalization of U.S. immigration policy. This legislation increased the overall allowances for annual immigration to this country. In doing so, it maintained the emphasis on family reunification in U.S. immigration policy while increasing the number of visas for employment-based immigration and authorizing additional visas for individuals from countries that have been underrepresented in immigration flows to the United States in recent years.

The data on immigration flows to the United States since the Immigration Act of 1990 suggest that the government has been able to regulate legal immigration effectively. This legislation was designed to encourage a modest increase in legal immigration, to emphasize the importance of family reunification, to increase employment-based immigration, and to provide a new means of entry for "diversity immigrants." All of these goals have been accomplished. Backlogs in visa applications remain a problem, and the ethnic composition of immigrants to this country has not changed dramatically. However, the policy was not designed to accomplish these far-reaching goals. Rather, this legislation was a political compromise designed to achieve only modest reforms of immigration policy.

Although the modest objectives of the Immigration Act of 1990 appear to have been met, this analysis of the interest group politics leading to the passage of this legislation contradicts realist explanations of immigration policy. Contrary to realist assumptions, this legislation does not represent a clear, rational approach to the regulation of legal immigration based on precise considerations of the national interest. The debate over legal immigration policy reform in the 1980s indicates that no consensus exists on what the national interest is in regard to immigration. According to several public opinion polls and a number of interest groups, a reduction in legal immigration would have been in the national interest, but political obstacles to new immigration restrictions were too strong. Congress emphasized family reunification in the 1990 Immigration Act because of lobbying by churches, ethnic organizations, and civil rights groups—not because family immigration necessarily represents a clear, well-defined national interest.

The key role of liberal ideas and interest group politics in shaping the Immigration Act of 1990 also challenges Marxist explanations of U.S. immigration policy, which strictly emphasize the economic interests of capitalists as the major determinant of policy. Though it is true that Congress authorized higher levels of employment-based immigration in the 1990 act largely because of lobbying by influential employer associations, these groups were not the only or even the most important actors shaping the provisions of this legislation. In spite of the fact that some employer groups have argued that the fundamental criteria for the admission of legal immigrants should be whether immigrants offer skills needed by American businesses, the Immigration Act of 1990 retained a solid majority of annual immigration visas for immediate family members of citizens and permanent residents, without reference to the skills these immigrants can provide in the labor market. Similarly, the diversity program provision in the Immigration Act of 1990 also challenges the notion that civil rights rhetoric has been used merely to justify immigration increases favored by the business community. Visas under the diversity program are allocated by a lottery that does not take into consideration the occupational characteristics of applicants, which suggests that the program was not shaped strictly by economic considerations. The continued emphasis on family reunification in U.S. immigration policy reflects the influence of churches, ethnic groups, and civil rights organizations—not the dominance of the capitalist class in the immigration policy debate.

Although this analysis points to the importance of domestic politics, it is important to note that global political and economic forces have had a significant impact on the interest group debate over U.S. immigration policy. The emergence of growing international support for family reunification as a humanitarian norm, as embodied in the Helsinki Accords, provided moral weight to the claims of churches and ethnic organizations that family immigration should be emphasized in U.S. immigration policy. While this provision of the Helsinki Accords does not reflect the existence of a formal international migration regime that directly led the United States to continue to support family reunification in the Immigration Act of 1990, it does represent an important transnational norm that was incorporated by important interest groups into the immigration policy debate in this country and that contributed to the liberalization of U.S. policy towards legal immigration in 1990. While growing international support for the norm of family reunification shaped the strategies of humanitarian groups involved in the debate over immigration policy reform, increasing competition in the global economy underlay employers' demands for increased access to skilled workers. Employers' groups relied on the rhetoric of interdependence and competition to support their claims that the United States needed to foster the immigration of skilled workers. Finally, previous immigration flows to this country have increased the cultural, religious, and ethnic diversity in this country. As a result, a variety of ethnic organizations have attained increased political influence in American politics and continue to argue for the desirability of diversity in immigration flows to this country. In sum, global economic and political developments contributed to the strength of the liberal coalition of ethnic organizations, churches, and employer associations in the debate over legal immigration policy reform in recent decades.

While legal immigration in recent years generally reflects the objectives defined in the Immigration Act of 1990 and indicates that the government has been relatively effective in regulating legal immigration, the content of this policy can be explained primarily by interest group politics and the prominence of liberal ideas in the immigration policy debate in the 1980s. Civil rights considerations and non-discrimination have become important values among significant segments of the U.S. population. The ascendance of liberal ideas helps to explain not only the liberalization of U.S. immigration policy towards legal immigrants in 1990 but also the concomitant rise in legal immigration to this country in recent years.

NOTES

1. U.S. Immigration and Naturalization Service, *Statistical Yearbook of the Immigration and Naturalization Service, 1992* (Washington, D.C.: U.S. Government Printing Office, 1993): 27–28.

2. Figures cover admission for permanent legal residence and represent immigration admissions by decade from 1820–1990.

3. Edwin Harwood, "The Crisis in Immigration Policy," *Journal of Contemporary Studies* 6:4 (Fall 1983): 45.

4. Thomas J. Espenshade and Katherine Hempstead, "Contemporary American Attitudes Toward U.S. Immigration," *International Migration Review* 30:2 (Summer 1996): 538.

5. Edwin Harwood, "American Public Opinion and U.S. Immigration Policy," *The Annals of the American Academy of Political and Social Science* 487 (September 1986): 207–208; Roper Center for Public Opinion Research, "Immigration," *Public Perspective* 5:2 (January/ February 1994): 98.

6. Harwood, "American Public Opinion": 202–203; Roper Center for Public Opinion Research, "Immigration": 97.

7. Vernon M. Briggs, Jr., *Mass Immigration and the National Interest* (Armonk, NY: M.E. Sharpe, Inc., 1992): 106–113; David M. Reimers, *Still the Golden Door: The Third World Comes to America*, 2d ed. (New York: Columbia University Press, 1992): 67–76.

8. U.S. Immigration and Naturalization Service, *Statistical Yearbook of the Immigration and Naturalization Service, 1990* (Washington, D.C.: U.S. Government Printing Office, 1991): 49–50.

9. Vernon M. Briggs, Jr., *Immigration Policy and the American Labor Force* (Baltimore: The Johns Hopkins University Press, 1984): 78–82; Lawrence H. Fuchs, *The American Kaleidoscope: Race, Ethnicity, and the Civic Culture* (Hanover, NH: University Press of New England, 1990): 278–283; David M. Reimers, "An Unintended Reform: The 1965 Immigration Act and Third World Immigration to the United States," *Journal of American Ethnic History* 3:1 (Fall 1983): 15–16.

10. Reimers, *Still the Golden Door*: 89–91.

11. Restrictions on emigration from many eastern European countries may have prevented an even greater increase in immigration from this region to the United States. Alan Dowty, *Closed Borders: The Contemporary Assault on Freedom of Movement* (New Haven: Yale University Press, 1987): 113–118. By the 1980s, immigration from southern and eastern Europe had declined again to under 400,000. This decline may be attributable, in part, to the demise of authoritarian governments in eastern Europe in the 1980s.

12. *Statistical Yearbook of the Immigration and Naturalization Service, 1990*: 54–55.

13. Ibid.: 54–63.

14. Reimers, *Still the Golden Door*: 89–91.

15. U.S. Congress, Senate Subcommittee on Immigration and Naturalization, *Hearings on S. 3074 to Amend the Immigration and Nationality Act and for Other Purposes*, 94th Cong., 2d sess. (Washington, D.C.: U.S. Government Printing Office,

1976.); U.S. Congress, Congressional Research Service, *U.S. Immigration Law and Policy: 1952–1979*, 96th Cong., 1st sess. (Washington: U.S. Government Printing Office, 1979): 62–70; Reimers, *Still the Golden Door*: 85–87.

16. Many congressional leaders supported this change as a way of removing the last vestiges of blatant discrimination in U.S. immigration policy. However, another reason this policy was adopted was to give refugees from the Eastern Hemisphere access to unused refugee visas from the Western Hemisphere. U.S. Congress, Congressional Research Service, *U.S. Immigration Law*: 62–70.

17. U.S. Commission on Civil Rights, *The Tarnished Door: Civil Rights Issues in Immigration* (Washington, D.C.: U.S. Government Printing Office, 1980): 17–19.

18. Select Commission on Immigration and Refugee Policy, *U.S. Immigration Policy and the National Interest*, The Final Report and Recommendations of the Select Commission on Immigration and Refugee Policy to the Congress and President of the United States, March 1, 1981: 5.

19. Ibid.: 103.

20. Ibid.: 103–107.

21. William Korey, *The Promises We Keep: Human Rights, the Helsinki Process, and American Foreign Policy* (New York: St. Martin's Press in association with the Institute for East West Studies, 1993): xxiv–xxv, 8.

22. Select Commission on Immigration and Refugee Policy: 112.

23. The Reverend Theodore Hesburgh disputed the majority view and argued that visa allowances for brothers and sisters of citizens limited the number of visas that would be available for other categories of family members, including spouses and minor children. Ibid.: 334–335.

24. Ibid.: 112–122.

25. Ibid.: 111.

26. Ibid.: 127–139.

27. Ibid.: 14–15, 145.

28. Briggs, *Immigration Policy*: 91–92.

29. Two key interest groups generally were silent in the debate over legal immigration in the 1980s. The testimony of the AFL-CIO and the ACLU before the House immigration subcommittee focused primarily on legislative proposals for addressing illegal immigration. U.S. Congress, House Subcommittee on Immigration, Refugees, and International Law, *Hearings on Immigration Reform*, 97th Cong., 1st sess. (Washington, D.C.: U.S. Government Printing Office, 1982); U.S. Congress, House Subcommittee on Immigration, Refugees, and International Law, *Hearings on H.R. 1510 (Immigration Reform and Control Act of 1983)*, 98th Cong., 1st sess. (Washington, D.C.: U.S. Government Printing Office, 1983).

30. Reimers, *Still the Golden Door*: 253.

31. Michael Fix and Jeffrey S. Passel, *The Door Remains Open: Recent Immigration to the United States and a Preliminary Analysis of the Immigration Act of 1990* (Washington, D.C.: Program for Research on Immigration Policy, The Urban Institute, January 1991): 8–12.

32. U.S. Congress, House Subcommittee on Immigration, Refugees, and International Law, *Hearings on the Immigration Act of 1989*, 101st Cong., 1st sess. (Washington, D.C.: U.S. Government Printing Office, 1989); U.S. Congress, Senate Subcommittee on Immigration and Refugee Affairs, *Hearings on Immigration Reform (S. 358 and S. 448)*, 101st Cong., 1st sess. (Washington, D.C.: U.S. Government Printing Office, 1990).

33. Briggs, *Immigration Policy*: 256–257.

34. Reimers, *Still the Golden Door*: 254–255.

35. U.S. Congress, House Subcommittee on Immigration, Refugees, and International Law, *Hearings on the Immigration Act of 1989*; U.S. Congress, Senate Subcommittee on Immigration and Refugee Affairs, *Hearings on Immigration Reform (S. 358 and S. 448)*.

36. Ibid.

37. Reimers, *Still the Golden Door*: 255–256.

38. Frank D. Bean, Georges Vernez, and Charles B. Keely, *Opening and Closing the Doors: Evaluating Immigration Reform and Control* (Washington, D.C.: The Urban Institute; Santa Monica, CA: The RAND Corporation, 1989): 101–108.

39. Briggs, *Mass Immigration*: 167–172.

40. Joyce C. Vialet and Larry M. Eig, "Immigration Act of 1990 (P.L. 101–649)," (Washington, D.C.: Congressional Research Service, Library of Congress): 4, 13.

41. The legislation provided for a transitional ceiling on family immigration of 465,000 between 1992 and 1994.

42. Stephen H. Legomsky, *Immigration Law and Policy* (Westbury, NY: The Foundation Press, Inc., 1992): 134.

43. Vialet and Eig: 2–4.

44. This act set aside 40,000 first-preference visas for immigrants of outstanding ability, 40,000 second-preference visas for professionals with advanced degrees or immigrants with exceptional abilities, 40,000 third-preference visas for skilled workers or unskilled shortage workers, 10,000 fourth-preference visas for special immigrants, including ministers, and 10,000 fifth-preference visas for investors. The first three preference categories receive the unused visas from the other preference categories. Under this legislation, the allocation of visas to unskilled workers cannot rise above ten percent, and visas issued to individuals in the second and third employment-based preference categories require certification by the Department of Labor that native workers are not available. Ibid.: 4–5.

45. Frank D. Bean and Michael Fix, "The Significance of Recent Immigration Policy Reforms in the United States," in Gary P. Freeman and James Jupp, eds., *Nations of Immigrants: Australia, the United States, and International Migration* (Oxford: Oxford University Press, 1992): 49–52.

46. Fix and Passel: 14.

47. Vialet and Eig: 5.

48. Briggs, *Mass Immigration*: 233–239.

49. Cited in Ronald J. Ostrow, "Bush Signs Law Boosting Immigration Quotas by 40%," *Los Angeles Times*, 30 November 1990: A39.

50. George White, "State Hopes to Attract Foreign Entrepreneurs," *Los Angeles Times*, 20 December 1990: D2;   William Flannery, "Visa Law Called Good for Business," *St. Louis Post-Dispatch*, 2 December 1990: 1E.

51. George Ramos, "Broad New Law Changes Policies on Immigration," *Los Angeles Times* Nuestro Tempo ed., 6 December 1990: 1; George Papajohn, "Lawyers, Advocates Sort Out Changes in Immigration Code," *Chicago Tribune*, 5 December 1990: 4; Ostrow: A39.

52. Marvin Howe, "Irish-Americans Praise New Immigration Bill," *The New York Times*, 7 October 1990: 1 (Section 1).

53. Prior to 1989, annual immigration to the United States had topped 1 million only six times, in 1905,1906, 1907, 1910, 1913, and 1914.   *Statistical Yearbook of the Immigration and Naturalization Service, 1992*: 25.

54. Consistently under 100,000 in the 1980s, refugee and asylee admissions were nearly 140,000 in 1991 and just under 120,000 in 1992.

55. *Statistical Yearbook of the Immigration and Naturalization Service, 1992*: 13, 25, 32.

56. Ibid.: 32.

57. U.S. Department of Labor, Bureau of International Labor Affairs, *Developments in International Migration to the United States: 1993*, by Roger G. Kramer, (Washington, D.C.: U.S. Department of Labor, 1993): 13–16.

58. U.S. Department of State, Bureau of Consular Affairs, *Visa Bulletin*, Vol. 7, No. 34 (Washington, D.C.: U.S. Department of State, April 1994).

59. *Statistical Yearbook of the Immigration and Naturalization Service, 1992*: 32.

60. Ibid.: 28.

61. Ibid.: 38.

62. Ibid.: 28. Between 1989 and 1991, the proportion of visas going to countries in the Americas increased dramatically to over sixty percent because most legalization applicants came from Latin America, especially Mexico.

63. Harwood, "American Public Opinion": 207–208; Roper Center for Public Opinion Research, "Immigration": 98.

64. Roper Center for Public Opinion Research, Public Opinion Online, Lexis-Nexis (library: news; file: rpoll), June 1990.

65. Roper Center for Public Opinion Research, "The Immigration Story," *Public Perspective* 6:5 (August/September 1995): 11.

Chapter 5

U.S. Immigration Policy in the 1990s: A New Era of Restrictionism?

THE END OF THE AGE OF RIGHTS?

Public opinion polls throughout the 1980s and 1990s have indicated that a majority of Americans would like to impose new restrictions on both legal and illegal immigration to this country.[1] For example, several 1996 Roper polls found that a majority of Americans would favor putting a moratorium on legal immigration for five years.[2] In recent years, this general public sentiment has been given effective political voice as anti-immigration groups like the Federation for American Immigration Reform (FAIR) have become increasingly prominent in the immigration policy debate in this country. Strong and increasingly well-organized public support for new restrictions on both legal and illegal immigration coupled with the Republican victories in both the House and the Senate in 1994 signaled that the immigration policy debate in the United States would likely be entering a new era of restrictionism.

Indeed, within two years, the new Republican Congress pushed through two significant pieces of legislation designed to reduce immigration to the United States. One of the key items in the House Republicans' "Contract with America" was a pledge to cut off many federal benefits for legal permanent residents. In August of 1996, the Republican Congress was able to follow through on this pledge with the passage of welfare reform legislation that denies basic federal benefits to legal as well as illegal immigrants. In addition, the Republican Congress passed restrictive legislation directed at illegal immigration in the fall of 1996. The Illegal Immigration Reform and Responsibility Act of 1996 introduced a variety of new methods designed to deter and punish illegal immigration, including new restrictions on judicial review of I.N.S. decisions, limitations on the ability of immigrants to bring class action suits, and measures designed to minimize document fraud. These new developments in immigration policy suggest that the United States has become serious about reasserting "control" over its borders.

While advocates of restrictive immigration policies may have reason to be optimistic, it is not yet clear that the immigration policy debate in this country can be said to have entered a new era of restrictionism. In the recent past, ostensibly restrictive immigration legislation, including the 1986 Immigration Reform and Control Act and the Immigration Act of 1990, actually has contributed to liberal immigration outcomes. Both of these pieces of legislation contained restrictive elements; however, in order to gain the political support necessary for their passage, they also included provisions that can be characterized as liberal. In each case, the inclusion of liberalizing measures can be attributed to lobbying by a liberal coalition of ethnic groups, churches, civil rights organizations, and employer associations. Although the 1996 welfare reform legislation and illegal immigration legislation are more restrictive in many respects than these earlier efforts, supporters of immigration reform are still faced with many of the same political constraints that hindered earlier efforts at reform.

Therefore, it remains too early to declare that the United States has entered into a new era of restrictionism towards immigration. Despite the demonstrable retrenchment in the influence of liberal norms on developments in U.S. immigration policy in recent years, liberal norms may hinder the effectiveness of new restrictions and may continue to impede the passage of more restrictive measures. The restrictive rhetoric that has dominated the immigration policy debate in recent years is unlikely to be matched by the reality of immigration control. Certainly, the new restrictions are real and cannot be disregarded. However, while current U.S. immigration policy cannot be characterized by the symbol of the "open door," neither is "zero immigration" a realistic goal. Rather, the debate over U.S. immigration policy will continue to be marked by conflict among restrictionist and pro-immigration forces.   The legislative compromises that result from this conflictual debate are not likely to give the U.S. government strong tools for dramatically reducing immigration to this country.

PROPOSITION 187 AND THE POLITICS OF IMMIGRATION POLICY IN THE 1990s

The domestic political factors shaping U.S. immigration policy are not static. As discussed in Chapter 2, widespread nativism early in the twentieth century generated support for immigration restrictions from workers and powerful immigrant groups and mitigated the traditional opposition of business interests to restrictive immigration policies. As a result, Congress created a restrictive and discriminatory national origins system in the 1920s. This national origins system was effective in reducing overall immigration to the United States and, especially, in limiting the immigration of individuals from "undesirable" ethnic groups.   The national origins system was the basic foundation of U.S.

immigration policy in the first half of the twentieth century and represents the peak of nativist influence in the immigration policy debate in this country. The national origins system was eliminated in 1965 as economic prosperity and the civil rights movement swayed the immigration policy debate in favor of pro-immigration forces. Since the 1960s, a coalition of liberal interest groups generally has prevailed in the debate over U.S. immigration policy. However, the prominence of liberal ideas and the influence of humanitarian groups in the immigration policy debate will not necessarily be permanent.

There is evidence that, in the 1990s, anti-immigration forces are growing in strength. At the national level, the Federation for American Immigration Reform (FAIR) continues to be the most visible advocate of restrictive immigration policies. In addition to this national organization, a number of grassroots organizations, including Americans for Immigration Control in Virginia and STOP-IT (Stop the Out-of-control Problems of Immigration Today) in California, have become vocal advocates of restrictive immigration policies. Typically, these groups blame immigrants for a majority of social problems in this country, including unemployment, environmental degradation, drug wars, crime, gang violence, and ethnic tension. Because anti-immigrant organizations view immigrants as the cause of a wide variety of social problems, their opposition to liberal immigration policies is intense. In a fax to the Coalition for Immigrant and Refugee Rights and Services in San Francisco, the California Coalition for Immigration Reform wrote, "It may take some time, but eventually you, the illegal, the devious, the under-handed who hold the laws of this great nation in contempt, will be purged from our midst as will the treacherous elected officials who have betrayed our trust."[3] The proliferation of anti-immigrant organizations and the growing intensity of anti-immigrant sentiment demonstrate that restrictionist forces are attempting to regain some ground in the debate over U.S. immigration policy.

Restrictionist forces also may attain renewed influence in the debate over U.S. immigration policy as a result of a resurgence in the strength of nativism.[4] Anti-immigrant organizations commonly depict immigration as a problem that sets white Americans against ethnic minority immigrants. For example, Betty Hammond, one of the founders of STOP-IT, views illegal immigration, to a significant extent, as a racial problem:

The indomitable American spirit is being awakened. . . . Americans don't like the graffiti in their neighborhoods. They don't like the traffic and overcrowding and the crime. American citizens don't like some of the neighborhoods in Southern California being taken over by illegals. . . . I have to stop our members from taking up weapons. . . . We're out to *stop* the bloodshed. But I'll tell you, I have a feeling the reason there haven't been any more riots in L.A. is because so many people lined up to buy guns. White American citizens got guns to fight back against the illegal aliens and the criminals.[5]

Republican presidential candidate in both 1992 and 1996, Pat Buchanan argued for at least a temporary moratorium on legal immigration by saying, "A non-white majority is envisioned if today's immigration continues."[6] These statements suggest that racial thinking partly underlies political support for immigration restrictions and may indicate that a resurgence in nativism has contributed to a political environment more favorable to restrictionist forces in the debate over U.S. immigration policy.[7]

One of the most visible signs that the debate over U.S. immigration policy might be entering a new era of restrictionism in the 1990s was the passage of Proposition 187 in California in a November 1994 referendum with support from fifty-nine percent of those voting. If fully implemented, Proposition 187 would deny publicly-funded non-emergency medical care, welfare services, and education to illegal immigrants and also would require school officials, welfare agencies, and law enforcement officials to report suspected illegal immigrants to the Immigration and Naturalization Service. Proposition 187 also made the manufacture, sale, or distribution of false documents a felony offense. Proponents of the measure believe that it will deter future illegal immigration flows and will induce undocumented immigrants already residing in the United States to return to their country of origin.

Despite evidence that anti-immigration forces are growing in strength, the status of Proposition 187 in California illustrates the way in which liberal norms and interest groups will continue to limit governmental efforts to restrict illegal immigration. In November 1995, Judge Mariana R. Pfaelzer, arguing that the regulation of immigration falls under the authority of the federal government and that parts of the legislation did not provide due process, ruled in federal court that most sections of Proposition 187 were unconstitutional, with the exception of the provisions on false documents and the section that excludes illegal immigrants from public, postsecondary educational institutions.[8] As a result of recent federal immigration reforms, which will be discussed in greater detail below, supporters of Proposition 187 contend that it is now consistent with federal law and should be implemented. Indeed, Judge Pfaelzer ruled in November 1996 that California could legally deny prenatal care to illegal immigrants. However, in a March 1998 ruling, Judge Pfaelzer struck down the remaining provisions of Proposition 187 as unconstitutional. Thus, in spite of the recent changes to federal immigration policy, Proposition 187 remains in legal limbo, its implementation blocked by the courts.

Even if the courts had not blocked the implementation of Proposition 187, many school officials, welfare agents, and health care workers who provide services to undocumented immigrants had expressed their unwillingness to comply with the measure. Importantly, though Proposition 187 mandates that officials and workers in relevant agencies and institutes cooperate with the Immigration and Naturalization Service in implementing Proposition 187, the proposition did not provide any penalties for failing to cooperate.[9]

Ethnic groups, churches, and civil rights organizations, arguing that the measure, if implemented, would result in discrimination against ethnic minorities, have led the opposition to Proposition 187.[10] Indeed, in spite of the fact that the courts have blocked its full implementation, there is anecdotal evidence that Proposition 187 has already led to an increased incidence of discrimination against ethnic minorities. Reportedly, a school security guard in

Atherton, California, told American-born children of Latin American ethnicity, "We don't have to let Mexicans in here anymore." Other reports of discrimination include pharmacies refusing to fill prescriptions for ethnic minorities and restaurants refusing to serve customers who did not have documentation to prove their legal status.[11] In this way, the political struggle over Proposition 187 in California reflects the same themes that have dominated the debate over illegal immigration in the United States since at least the 1970s. Though nativist and anti-immigration forces may be growing in strength, civil rights considerations and liberal ideas remain central to the debate over U.S. immigration policy.

WELFARE REFORM AND U.S. IMMIGRATION POLICY IN THE 1990s

Although the courts have blocked the full implementation of Proposition 187, proponents of new immigration restrictions have claimed that their goals ultimately triumphed at the federal level, circumventing the need for state-level initiatives. Title IV of the Personal Responsibility, Work Opportunity, and Medicaid Restructuring Act of 1996 (Public Law 104–193), which became law on August 22, 1996, contains a variety of provisions designed to restrict welfare and public benefits for both illegal and legal immigrants. The legislation prohibits illegal immigrants and non-immigrants (immigrants who are legally authorized to be in the country but who are not admitted for permanent residence, for example, temporary workers) from receiving federal public benefits, with limited exceptions for certain benefits, including emergency medical services, certain emergency disaster relief, public health immunizations and treatment of communicable diseases, and housing assistance. It also provides that illegal immigrants are not eligible for state and local benefits programs, again with limited exceptions such as those listed above. In addition to the provisions relating to illegal immigrants, the legislation provides that legal immigrants will not be able to receive specified federal public benefits, including supplemental social security income (SSI), food stamps, temporary assistance for needy families, social services block grants, and Medicaid. Under this legislation, legal immigrants are not eligible for federal means-tested public benefits for the first five years after U.S. entry. Moreover, the legislation provides that the income and resources of a legal immigrant applying for federal means-tested public benefits shall be deemed to include the income and resources of the person's spouse and of an immigrant's sponsor in the case of legal permanent residents. Finally, this legislation allows states, but does not require them, to deny basic state and local benefits to non-citizens who are legally in this country.

One of the fundamental goals of these provisions of the welfare reform legislation was to reduce federal spending on welfare. Evidence is already emerging that welfare reform will not, in practice, be as effective in contributing to this objective as supporters of immigration reform would have liked. After the passage of welfare reform legislation, hundreds of thousands of legal permanent residents rushed to become citizens.[12] Even advocates of immigration restrictions may find this outcome desirable in terms of promoting a stronger civic identity among immigrants. However, it demonstrates that welfare reform's restrictions on the benefits of legal immigrants, who are eligible for naturalization, will not necessarily contribute to significant reductions in welfare spending.

Moreover, most states have continued to provide benefits to legal immigrants. Indeed, only thirteen states have acted on the provision of the 1996 Illegal Immigration Reform and Responsibility Act that enables them to restrict state and local benefits to new legal immigrants. Because the law prohibits the use of federal funds to provide benefits to new immigrants during the first five years of their residency, many states are using state funds to provide benefits to new legal immigrants. In Pennsylvania, one of the states which has adopted legislation restricting the provision of state benefits to non-citizens, a federal judge ruled that states could not discriminate against new legal residents by denying them the same welfare benefits as long-term residents because it would violate the equal protection clause of the Fourteenth Amendment.[13]

Additionally, during the summer of 1997, Congress restored almost $12 billion of the $22 billion immigrant benefits it cut with the 1996 welfare reform legislation in the budget agreement worked out with President Clinton.[14] Specifically, Congress created an exception to the welfare reform law by providing that legal immigrants already in the United States would be allowed to continue receiving SSI after August 22, 1997, the welfare law's cutoff date. Congress also has created an exception to the welfare law's provision that prohibits states from using federal funds to aid legal immigrants by allowing states to purchase federal food stamps for legal immigrants. At least eleven states are providing food stamps to some legal immigrants under this exception. For example, in the state of Washington, all legal immigrants continue to be eligible for food stamps. Notably, the states with the largest immigrant populations continue to provide food stamps to certain categories of legal immigrants. California and New York are purchasing federal food stamps to provide to children, elderly, and disabled legal immigrants. Texas continues to provide these benefits to elderly and disabled legal immigrants.[15]

Critics of welfare reform had said throughout the debate that it was unfair to deny federal benefits to legal immigrants who, in paying taxes, help to provide these benefits. Congressional retrenchment on welfare reform reflects the political pressure that has been brought to bear by immigrant organizations and civil rights groups advocating on behalf of legal immigrants. Republican representatives in states with large immigrant populations have been especially supportive of softening the provisions of the welfare reform legislation dealing with legal immigrants. Concern about this issue among Republicans has become particularly acute as evidence emerges that party registration among important immigrant groups, including Asian-Americans and Latinos, is increasingly Democratic.[16]

Welfare reform legislation was designed not only to reduce federal spending on non-citizens but also to provide some disincentive for legal immigration by placing a higher financial burden on new legal immigrants and their sponsors.

Making immigration slightly more difficult for certain people in financial terms does little to affect the desire to reunify families that fundamentally drives legal immigration to the United States. In the case of legal immigration, what is most notable about immigration reform in 1996 are the proposed restrictions that were not passed. The Commission on Legal Immigration Reform, created by the Immigration Act of 1990, issued a report in September 1994 that recommended several measures designed to reduce legal immigration. The Jordan Commission (so named because it was chaired by former Representative Barbara Jordan of Texas), recommended that overall annual legal admissions should be reduced by one-third; that the preference system should be changed to facilitate the admission of spouses and minor children of legal immigrants (this shift would come at the expense of other family preferences, namely, adult children and parents of citizens and residents as well as siblings of citizens); that the number of annual visas for employment-based immigration be reduced from 140,000 to 100,000; and that the number of refugees should be reduced from 100,000 to 50,000. Though several bills were introduced in Congress after the Jordan Commission issued its report, Congress was unable to act on any of them. For instance, Congress was unable to pass the Immigration in the National Interest Act, which would have eliminated the family preference for siblings and adult children of legal residents and would have reduced annual legal admissions from roughly 800,000 to 595,000 annually, either in 1995 or 1996.

In sum, the 1996 welfare reform legislation does not create any real mechanisms for reducing legal immigration to this country. In this way, it reflects the continuing influence of a liberal coalition of interest groups, including employer associations, ethnic organizations, churches, and civil rights groups, in the immigration policy debate in the United States. Of course, many of these groups, particularly churches, ethnic organizations, and civil rights groups, have expressed their strong opposition to the welfare reform measures which essentially codify discrimination against legal residents. In this way, they are articulating the view that the welfare reform legislation is not fair. However, the codification of unfairness is not the same thing as the adoption of a truly restrictive policy.

Serious efforts to reduce legal immigration to this country would require either significant changes to the current preference system that gives priority to family reunification or, as some advocates of restriction have proposed, a moratorium on legal immigration. A number of bills proposing such changes have been introduced to Congress over the last several years but have gone nowhere. While support for restrictions on legal immigration has grown over the last decade, restrictionists do not have a strong political base in either the Democratic or Republican parties.[17] Liberal advocates of a relatively open immigration policy cross party and ideological lines, making strange political bedfellows out of churches, civil rights proponents, ethnic groups, employers associations, and their representatives in Congress. Interestingly, recent efforts to restrict legal immigration have been opposed not only by this "liberal coalition" of churches, civil rights groups, and employers but also by groups on the political right ranging from Christian fundamentalist groups opposed to restrictions on family reunification to groups opposed to taxes imposed on employers sponsoring foreign workers.[18]   Indeed, pro-family rhetoric has become one of the primary political tools used to defuse arguments for restricting legal immigration to the United States.[19]   In this political context, dramatic change to the system of legal immigrant admissions in the United States is unlikely.

ILLEGAL IMMIGRATION AND U.S. IMMIGRATION POLICY IN THE 1990s

The Illegal Immigration Reform and Immigrant Responsibility Act was passed as part of a large appropriations bill for fiscal year 1997 (Public Law 104–208).[20]   Title I of this legislation provides funding for a variety of border control improvements, including barrier and road improvements, new identifiers for border crossing cards, and, perhaps most importantly, funds for hiring a minimum of 1,000 full-time border patrol agents over the next five fiscal years. It also creates civil penalties for illegal entry into this country and criminal penalties for high-speed flights from immigration checkpoints.   Title I also provides funds for increasing the number of land border inspectors, the creation of pilot projects using automated land border entry, and other measures designed to facilitate legal entry.   Finally, Title I authorizes, for three years, appropriations for 300 additional I.N.S. investigators who are responsible for interior enforcement and the investigation of visa overstayers.

Title II provides for enhanced enforcement against alien smuggling and document fraud, including authorization for I.N.S. wiretaps and undercover operations for these purposes, the expansion of racketeering offenses to the areas of alien smuggling and document fraud, increased criminal penalties for alien smuggling, and increased civil and criminal penalties for document fraud.

Title III provides a variety of new grounds and procedures for exclusion and deportation. Individuals who are in the U.S. illegally for one year or more will be inadmissible as legal immigrants for ten years. Illegal immigrants residing in the United States for at least 180 days will be inadmissible as legal immigrants for three years. Notably, the law also provides for a variety of exemptions from these exclusions, including minors, battered women and children, asylum applicants, and family unity beneficiaries. In addition, there are waivers for spouses and children of citizens and legal permanent residents in cases of "exceptional and extremely unusual hardship." The "incitement of terrorist activity" is designated as a new grounds for exclusion, as is making a false claim of citizenship or renouncing U.S. citizenship in the past for tax purposes. The legislation also establishes a five-year exclusion for student visa violations targeted at students who are authorized to enter to attend a private school but transfer to a public institution.

Among the most important Title III provisions are the new limitations on judicial review which authorize immigration officers to remove aliens whom they determine are inadmissible, without further review in cases in which immigrants arrive with either false documents or no documents and are unable to demonstrate a "credible fear" of persecution that would make them eligible for an asylum hearing. Under these circumstances, individuals will be removed unless they specifically state that they intend to apply for asylum and that they fear persecution. Immigrants will not be told that they may make this claim. For individuals who are able to demonstrate a "credible fear," an asylum hearing before an immigration judge must be provided within a week, but no appeals or judicial review will be possible after this hearing.

Finally, Title III changes the criteria for allowing illegal immigrants of "good moral character" to adjust their status. Prior to this legislation, "suspension of deportation" had been granted to illegal immigrants who could document seven years of continuous residency, good moral character, and that their deportation would cause extreme hardship to them or a relative who is a citizen or legal resident. Under the new process, called "cancellation of removal," illegal immigrants must prove ten years of continuous residency, good moral character, and that their deportation would cause "exceptional and extremely unusual hardship" to a U.S. citizen or resident. This change, which could result in separation of individuals who are not legal residents from their family members who are, led many individuals to try to get arrested by the I.N.S. before the April 1997 implementation deadline in order to be considered under the old rules. [21]

Title IV reduces the number of documents that are acceptable for verifying work eligibility and creates three pilot programs to test the use of an electronic government database to check work eligibility. Employer participation in these pilot programs is voluntary. Title IV also specifies that employers will not be held responsible for violations of paperwork requirements documenting employees' work eligibility if a "good faith attempt" to comply has been made. [22]

Title V echoes the provisions of the 1996 welfare reform legislation that deny federal benefits to illegal immigrants. Interestingly, an exception is made for battered aliens who are no longer living with the batterer and who can demonstrate a connection between the domestic violence and the need for benefits. Title V also amends the earlier welfare reform legislation by specifying that charitable organizations are not required to verify eligibility for means-tested public benefits programs they administer. [23]

The Illegal Immigration Reform and Immigrant Responsibility Act of 1996, which went into effect on April 1, 1997, is a complicated piece of legislation which creates a variety of new restrictions that are likely to create real hardship for many illegal immigrants residing in this country. It is also certain that the newly-expanded I.N.S. authority for summary exclusions will improve its effectiveness in preventing some illegal entries. However, in spite of the fact that policy makers can point to this legislation as an example of their being serious about cracking down on illegal immigration, many experts do not believe it will be effective in reducing the levels of illegal immigration to the United States. Even the I.N.S. signaled that it did not intend to use the legislation in an expansive effort to crack down on illegal immigration. Paul Virtue, executive associate I.N.S. commissioner, said, "We have no intention of having mass sweeps and going out into the community and arresting people."

Rather, the I.N.S. stated its intention to target its efforts at removing criminal illegal immigrants.[24]

This legislation does not make any significant improvements to employer sanctions, even though the post-IRCA record of enforcement indicates that they have not been effective in reducing illegal immigration.[25] Without stepped-up efforts to crack down on the employment of undocumented workers, it is unlikely that the federal government will be able to significantly reduce illegal immigrant flows to this country. Notably, this legislation appropriates far more money towards border control than towards improved enforcement of employer sanctions. On a related point, the Jordan Commission on Immigration Reform called for the creation of a nationwide database of social security numbers that employers would be required to use to check work authorization for prospective employees.   Rather than creating a national program, the 1996 illegal immigration reform legislation only provides for three small pilot programs. Strong political opposition among employer associations, civil rights groups, and ethnic organizations blocked the creation of a national program. Business interests, not surprisingly, have been resistant to any changes that would make employer sanctions more effective. At the same time, civil rights advocates and ethnic groups have argued that a national registry might contribute to discrimination in that ethnic minorities might more likely be scrutinized under this system.

Just as illegal immigration policy reform in the 1990s has done little to improve the enforcement of employer sanctions, it did not appropriate significant resources for interior enforcement in general. While the legislation calls for 1,000 additional border patrol officers annually for the next five years, it only provides for 300 new personnel annually for interior enforcement. The differential funding is based on the assumption that illegal immigrants primarily consist of individuals who enter this country surreptitiously, especially along the U.S.-Mexican border. In reality, a high proportion of illegal immigrants consists of individuals who enter the country legally but who overstay beyond the terms of their visas. Moreover, large numbers enter the country with sophisticated fraudulent documents.   Stronger efforts at interior enforcement would be necessary to address these types of illegal immigration, but Congress has found that providing increased funding to border patrol efforts is more politically feasible.   Civil rights advocates and ethnic organizations lobby against workplace raids and efforts at interior enforcement, which they fear may lead to harassment and discrimination against ethnic minorities who are citizens or who are legally entitled to live and work in the United States. Border control is a highly visible way for Congress to send a signal that it is serious about immigration control that is not as strongly contested among pro-immigration forces.

It also is important to note that many potential migrants with a strong desire to come to the United States will find a way to enter illegally if they cannot enter legally. Fraudulent documents and smuggling techniques have grown more sophisticated as the methods for preventing illegal entry and smuggling have become more advanced. Illegal immigrants have been smuggled into this country inside huge metal containers used to transport cargo across the Atlantic Ocean.[26] Smugglers also have aided the illegal entry of many immigrants by helping "clients" illegally enter Puerto Rico or the Virgin Islands and then having them fly to the U.S. mainland aboard domestic flights, which are not inspected as strictly as international flights. Similarly, smugglers have helped individuals enter the United States illegally via cruise ships from the Caribbean, which do not involve rigid inspection procedures for entry into the United States.[27] As these examples suggest, many individuals with a strong desire to immigrate to the United States are willing to take risks and will find creative methods for entering the country if necessary. Though the 1996 legislation gives the I.N.S. greater discretionary powers in the area of deportation, the I.N.S. would need a substantial increase in its budget to be able to address effectively the various methods of illegal entry. It is not clear that public support for this kind of commitment to the I.N.S. exists in the current political atmosphere, where opposition to "big government" solutions seems as strong as anti-immigration sentiment.

Thus, although the latest effort at illegal immigration policy reform contains many illiberal measures that are likely to affect the lives of immigrants residing illegally in this country, the 1996 legislation will not necessarily lead to a marked reduction in the flow of illegal immigrants to this country. Pro-immigration forces, from business interests to civil rights activists, have blocked the passage of more draconian measures. It is unlikely that the political atmosphere in the future will be any more conducive to serious reform than it has been in the last couple of years. As a result, the federal government simply may be unable to adopt policies that are any more restrictive than those it passed in 1996. As one commentator who follows the immigration policy debate has noted, "In the end, some analysts believe, the illegal immigration issue will become a perennial one like the crime issue—with Washington unable to solve the problem, but unable for political reasons to leave it alone."[28]

CONCLUSIONS

In spite of the fact that restrictionist forces have gained strength in the 1990s, it cannot truly be said that the immigration policy debate in this country has entered a new era of restrictionism. Even though there is widespread public support for immigration restrictions in the abstract and though a variety of groups, like FAIR, are creating significant political pressure for immigration reforms, the political obstacles to serious immigration policy reform are formidable. While the immigration policy reforms passed by Congress in 1996 contain important new restrictions on immigration and immigrant benefits, the restrictive nature of this legislation should not be overestimated. Given that the political atmosphere was highly conducive to reform, proposed restrictions that were not included in the legislation, for instance, a five-year moratorium on legal immigration, are in some respects as notable as those that were adopted. Moreover, as discussed above, serious questions remain about whether the new immigration restrictions that were passed will actually serve to reduce levels of either legal or illegal immigration to this country. The ultimate impact of recent immigration reforms cannot be assessed fully so soon. However, the available evidence to date suggests that interest group politics and liberal ideas will continue to hamper efforts to restrict immigration to this country.

Proponents of restrictionism may run into the opposition of the general public as well as interest groups if they try to go too far in their efforts to restrict immigration. It is true that public opinion polls throughout the 1980s have indicated that a majority of Americans would like to restrict both legal and illegal immigration. Indeed, several 1996 Roper polls indicate that a majority of Americans would favor putting a moratorium on legal immigration for five years. Yet, in response to another poll question, only forty-nine percent of the respondents said immigration levels should be decreased while forty-one percent agreed that immigration should be kept at its present level. Moreover, only twenty-one percent of the respondents in another Roper poll said that they viewed legal immigration as a major problem. As the varied responses to these questions indicate, broad public support for immigration restrictions exists in the abstract. In general, Americans respond less favorably when asked about specific measures for restricting immigration than when asked general questions about whether immigration levels should be reduced. In a 1995 Roper poll, sixty-one percent of the survey respondents disapproved of eliminating the preference for family reunification in U.S. immigration policy.[29] Fifty-six percent of the respondents to a Roper poll conducted after the April 1996 incident in California in which Riverside County sheriffs used force against illegal immigrants involved in a high-speed chase felt that the sheriffs' use of force was unjustified. In sum, even though the American public supports the idea of restricting immigration in the abstract, it is not clear from existing polling data that they would support the kinds of restrictions, such as a broad cutback in allowances for family reunification, even more substantial budgetary increases for the I.N.S., or national identification requirements, which likely would be necessary if the government is serious about reducing immigration flows to this country.

Certainly, in the last couple of years there has been some retrenchment in the influence of liberal norms. However, liberal norms are by no means irrelevant. While current U.S. immigration policy cannot be characterized by the symbol of the "open door," neither is a policy of "zero immigration" a realistic goal. The 1996 changes to U.S. immigration policy dishearten the coalition of interest groups advocating that humanitarian norms and civil rights fundamentally guide U.S. policy. At the same time, anti-immigration groups like the Federation for American Immigration Reform are equally disappointed that Congress has not yet been able to reduce immigration further by limiting family reunification, strengthening employer sanctions, or adopting a national identification requirement. Civil rights considerations and liberal ideas continue to shape the debate over immigration policy reform even in an environment that increasingly has appeared to favor restriction.

Although civil rights considerations fundamentally shape the debate over immigration policy in this country, U.S. immigration policy does not adequately protect immigrant rights. Indeed, one of the perverse effects of the most recent immigration policy reforms is that, although they may not meet the objectives of proponents of immigration restrictions, they have confirmed the deepest fears of many immigrant rights advocates. Since the implementation of the 1996 Illegal Immigration Reform and Immigrant Responsibility Act, the media have documented a variety of cases that raise questions about the fundamental fairness of U.S. immigration policy. As a result of the new provisions in the 1996 legislation on the exclusion of immigrants convicted of crimes, Saeid Aframian, a Persian Jew who was convicted ten years ago of credit card fraud, will be deported back to Iran and separated from his wife and two children, all U.S. citizens, even though he has had a clean record over the last decade. Eramasi Ernesta Attah, a young woman who has been living in the United States since she was four years old, will be deported back to Nigeria where she has no contacts because she has been convicted of shoplifting. Refugio Rubio, a fifty-seven-year-old man who has been living in the United States for decades, was arrested at his recent citizenship interview and will be deported because of a 1972 conviction for marijuana possession with intent to distribute.[30] The I.N.S. also wants to deport Jesus Collado, a restaurant manager in the Bronx, because he was convicted of statutory rape in 1974 at the age of nineteen for having sex with his fifteen-year-old girlfriend. He has a wife and three children, all legal residents, and has spent six months in jail while fighting deportation.[31]

The implementation of the 1996 illegal immigration reform legislation also has confirmed the fears of civil rights advocates that it would contribute to discrimination against U.S. citizens and legal residents who are ethnic minorities. For example, police in Chandler, Arizona, authorized under the 1996 Illegal Immigration Reform and Immigrant Responsibility Act to take actions to enforce immigration law, aided in I.N.S. efforts to round up illegal immigrants in the area. Their efforts included stopping cars and looking for illegal immigrants in churches and restaurants. In their efforts, they detained many U.S. citizens without probable cause, and several of these citizens have now initiated a lawsuit against the police.[32] Evidence is also emerging that the denial of public benefits to legal immigrants under the welfare reform legislation is causing hardship for legal immigrants. Notably, these immigrants do not leave the United States as a result; they simply face a more difficult struggle to get by in this country.[33]

Even though the consequences of the most recent immigration policy reforms have had negative consequences in regard to the protection of basic immigrant rights, the rhetoric of civil rights, nonetheless, integrally shapes the current debate over U.S. immigration policy. In *The Age of Rights*, from which the title of the present work borrows, Louis Henkin claims that universal human rights are the "idea of our time." To the critics who point out that formal acceptance of human rights norms is meaningless given that human rights abuses continue to exist across the globe, Henkin responds that the idea of human rights, even if only recognized by hypocritical governments, remains important: "Even if it be hypocrisy, it is significant—since hypocrisy, we know, is the homage that vice pays to virtue—that human rights is today the single, paramount virtue to which vice pays homage, that governments today do not feel free to preach what they may persist in practicing."[34] In a similar vein, the idea of civil rights remains important in the debate over U.S. immigration policy, even though elements of this policy are unfair and discriminatory.

U.S. immigration policy is being made in an age of rights. Since the 1960s, the U.S. government has not been free to "preach" discrimination or to adopt a policy that was formally discriminatory. In this political context, restrictions on immigration become far more difficult than they would be if explicit discrimination was allowed. While anti-immigrant sentiment has become more intense and well organized in recent years, proposals for restrictive immigration legislation still face significant political opposition. In the current political environment, it is possible that more restrictive legislation will be adopted. However, any new immigration restrictions likely will represent political compromises that also acknowledge the concerns of liberal interest groups, including the protection of basic civil rights and non-discrimination. In addition to demanding immigration policies consistent with civil rights concerns, traditional advocates of liberal immigration policies often support a number of policy alternatives for reducing the pressures for immigration to the United States and addressing its costs. These policy alternatives include investment in major immigrant-sending countries, the enforcement of minimum-wage and labor standards to minimize the exploitation of cheap, illegal labor, immigration taxes, and border crossing fees. Federal reimbursement to states for the costs of undocumented immigrants also has been defended as a way of addressing the costs of illegal immigration without impacting the rights of either illegal immigrants or legal residents.[35] These policy alternatives, in addition to the proposals for a computerized national registry, a national identification card, and stronger border control and enforcement measures, are likely to be significant issues in the perennial debate over U.S. immigration policy. In any event, the U.S. immigration policy debate will continue to be marked by dissension rather than consensus. Liberal ideas and civil rights rhetoric will continue to fundamentally shape this debate in an age of rights.

NOTES

1. James G. Gimpel and James R. Edwards, Jr., *The Congressional Politics of Immigration Reform* (Boston: Allyn and Bacon, 1999): 35–37.

2. Polling data, unless otherwise noted, is from the following source: Roper Center for Public Opinion Research, Public Opinion Online, Lexis-Nexis (library: news; file: rpoll), 1996.

3. Cited in Ruth Conniff, "The War on Aliens: the Right Calls the Shots," *The Progressive* (October 1993): 22–29 reprinted in Robert M. Jackson, ed., *Global Issues 94/95* (Guilford, CT: The Dushkin Publishing Group, Inc. 1994): 53.

4. See, for example, George J. Sánchez, "Face the Nation: Race, Immigration, and the Rise of Nativism in Late Twentieth Century America," *International Migration Review* 31:4 (Winter 1997): 1009–1030.

5. Ibid.

6. Patrick J. Buchanan, "What Will America Be in 2050?" *Los Angeles Times*, 28 October 1994: B11 cited in Leo R. Chavez, "Immigration Reform and Nativism: The

Nationalist Response to the Transnationalist Challenge," in Juan F. Perea, ed., *Immigrants Out! The New Nativism and the Anti-Immigrant Impulse in the United States* (New York: New York University Press, 1997): 63.

7. Certain polling data suggests that the U.S. public's opposition to immigration is focused more on overall numbers than the ethnic origins of immigrants. Edwin Harwood, "The Crisis in Immigration Policy," *Journal of Contemporary Studies* 6:4 (Fall 1983): 46–47; Kenneth K. Lee, *Huddled Masses, Muddled Laws* (Westport, CT: Praeger, 1998): 22–27.

8. Philip L. Martin, "Proposition 187 in California," *International Migration Review* 29:1 (Spring 1995): 256. Pfaelzer cited the 1982 Supreme Court decision in *Plyler v. Doe*, which said that, under the equal protection of the Fourteenth Amendment, children had a right to public education regardless of their immigrant status.

9. Ibid.: 258–261.

10. B. Drummond Ayres, Jr., "Minority Groups Joining in Debate over Immigration," *The New York Times*, 1 November 1994: A1; David Gonzalez, "Bishops Issue a Statement about Aliens," *The New York Times*, 18 November 1994: A12. Importantly, the Mexican government also voiced its opposition to Proposition 187 and established links with Hispanic-American groups in an effort to help organize opposition to the measure. Tim Golden, "Government Joins Attack on Ballot Idea," *The New York Times*, 3 November 1994: A11.

11. Kitty Calavita, "The New Politics of Immigration: 'Balanced-Budget Conservatism' and the Symbolism of Proposition 187," *Social Problems* 43:3 (August 1996): 291.

12. "Editorial Opinion," *The Arizona Republic*, 30 September 1997: B4.

13. Robert Pear, "Judge Rules States Can't Cut Welfare for New Residents," *The New York Times*, 14 October 1997: A1.

14. Jason DeParle, "With the Economy Humming, Welfare Has Its Image Polished," *The New York Times*, 11 September 1997: A1.

15. Linda Feldman, "Rethinking Immigrant Benefits," *The Christian Science Monitor*, 6 January 1998: 1.

16. Dan Carney, "Republicans Feeling the Heat as Policy Becomes Reality," *Congressional Quarterly Weekly Report*, 17 May 1997: 1131; Todd S. Purdom, "California G.O.P. Faces a Crisis as Hispanic Voters Turn Away," *The New York Times*, 9 December 1997: A1.

17. Dan Carney, "Can the U.S. Regain Control of Its Borders?" *Congressional Quarterly Weekly Report*, 5 October 1996: 2815.

18. Christian Joppke, "Why Liberal States Accept Unwanted Immigration," *World Politics* 50 (January 1998): 279.

19. Lee: 128–139.

20. The Illegal Immigration Bill can be found in Division C of this legislation.

21. Patrick J. McDonnell, "Hunting a Way In," *The Los Angeles Times*, 9 March 1997: A3.

22. A detailed discussion of the provisions of this legislation is found in Austin T. Fragomen, Jr., "The Illegal Immigration Reform and Immigrant Responsibility Act of 1996," *International Migration Review* 31:2 (Summer 1997): 438–460.

23. Title VI of this legislation includes a variety of miscellaneous provisions. Two amendments on immigration and refugee policy are especially interesting. First, the definition of refugee is expanded to cover individuals fleeing persecution as a result of resistance to coercive family planning policies. Second, the practice of female genital mutilation is criminalized. Title VI also requires that information regarding the legal status of this practice be distributed to immigrants from countries in which female genital mutilation is practiced.

24. Jim Sprecht, "Panic Spreads as Immigration Deadline Nears," *USA Today*, 31 March 1997: 3A.

25. Carney, "Can the U.S. Regain Control of Its Borders?": 2814.

26. "Eleven Stowaways Use Old Plan in Asylum Bid," *The New York Times*, 9 June 1994: A12.

27. Ashley Dunn, "Smugglers of Chinese Find New Routes to U.S. Shores," *The New York Times*, 1 November 1994: A1; Joel Brinkley, "For Aliens, Cruises Provide Easy U.S. Entry," *The New York Times*, 29 November 1994, Al.

28. Carney, "Can the U.S. Regain Control of Its Borders?": 2815.

29. Roper Center for Public Opinion Research, "The Immigration Story," *Public Perspective* 6:5 (August/ September 1995): 11.

30. Patrick J. McDonnell, "Criminal Past Comes Back to Haunt Some Immigrants," *Los Angeles Times*, 20 January 1997: A1.

31. Mirta Ojito, "New Law Resurrects an Old Crime," *The New York Times*, 15 October 1997: A17.

32. Ruben Navarrette, Jr., "Constitutional Slights; Chandler's I.N.S. Sweep Another Black Mark in Valley's Treatment of Latinos," *The Arizona Republic*, 31 August 1997: H1.

33. Rachel L. Swarns, "Denied Food Stamps, Many Legal Immigrants Scrape for Meals," *The New York Times*, 8 December 1997: A19.

34. Louis Henkin, *The Age of Rights* (New York: Columbia University Press, 1990): x.

35. Sam Howe Verhovek, "Texas Plans to Sue U.S. Over Illegal Alien Costs," *The New York Times*, 27 May 1994: A10.

Appendix A

Major Developments in U.S. Immigration Policy[1]

1793 Executive Statement: President George Washington announced an open-door immigration policy.

1798 Alien and Sedition Acts: The Aliens Act of June 25, 1798, gave the president authorization to deport aliens who threatened the peace and security of the United States. The Alien Enemy Act of July 6, 1798, authorized the president to deport or detain male aliens from enemy countries during wartime.

1819 Steerage Act: This act required the masters of vessels transporting immigrants to submit passenger lists to customs officials, which would later be given to the State Department and Congress. This requirement marked the beginning of official government immigration records. This act also provided safeguards for passengers by limiting ships' carrying capacity and mandating that basic food needs be met. Later acts reaffirmed the requirement for passenger lists and expanded safeguards regulating conditions on passenger ships.

1864 Contract Labor Act: Congress legalized contract labor importation. This act was repealed in 1868.

1875 Immigration Act: This act marked the beginning of direct federal regulation of immigration. The legislation made it a felony to contract to supply "coolie labor" and prohibited the "importation" of Asians without their consent. Convicted felons and prostitutes were defined as excludable aliens.

1882 Chinese Exclusion Act: This act specified that Chinese individuals were not to be eligible for citizenship and prohibited the immigration of both skilled and unskilled laborers from China for ten years. This restriction did not cover government officials or merchants, and an exception was extended to skilled labor in new U.S. industries for which domestic labor was unavailable.

1882 Immigration Act: The first federal head tax, set at fifty cents per immigrant arriving by ship, was established. This act also added "mental defectives" and individuals who would become public charges because they could not take care of themselves to the list of excludable aliens.

1884 Chinese Exclusion Act: This act clarified the 1882 act by stating that it applied to all Chinese individuals, whether or not they were subjects of China.

1885 Alien Contract Labor Act: This act made labor contracts to encourage immigration illegal but exempted various categories, including skilled workers in jobs for which there was not an adequate supply of U.S. workers, domestic servants, and relatives. In an 1887 amendment, the Secretary of the Treasury was authorized to enforce this act by repatriating contract laborers on arrival. An 1888 amendment provided that individuals who had entered in violation of this legislation could be deported within one year after their arrival.

1888 Chinese Exclusion Act: This legislation made it illegal for any Chinese persons, except government officials, teachers, students, merchants, or tourists, to enter the United States.

1891 Immigration Act: This act created the position of Superintendent of Immigration in the Treasury Department, which subsequently established the Bureau of Immigration. Paupers, polygamists, individuals with contagious diseases, and individuals likely to become a public charge were added to the excludable classes. In the 1882 act, the public charge provision had covered individuals who would become public charges because they were unable to care for themselves. This slight modification of language allowed for greater administrative discretion in the application of this exclusion.[2] In addition to the creation of an immigration bureaucracy and expanded grounds for exclusion, this legislation specified that professionals, ministers, and professors were exempt from the Alien Contract Labor Act but removed the exemption for relatives. Finally, the 1891 legislation authorized the deportation of illegal immigrants within one year of arrival.

1892 Chinese Exclusion Act: Congress extended all previous legislation pertaining to Chinese exclusion for ten additional years.

1893 Immigration Act: This act specified that passenger lists had to require additional information, including occupation, marital status, and mental and physical health conditions, in an effort to assist in determining eligibility for immigration.

1902, Act of April 29: Specifying that Chinese exclusion would be in effect unless a new treaty with China covering immigration was negotiated, this act indefinitely renewed previous Chinese exclusion legislation. This act also provided for the application of Chinese exclusions throughout U.S. insular territories, with the exception of Hawaii.

1903, Act of February 14: The Bureau of Immigration was transferred to the Department of Commerce and Labor under this legislation.

1903 Immigration Act: In addition to reaffirming prior immigration laws, this act added beggars, epileptics, the insane, and anarchists to the list of those individuals who could be excluded from legal admission to the United States. Also, the head tax on immigrants was increased to two dollars, though immigrants from Canada, Mexico, Newfoundland, and Cuba were exempted.

1904 Chinese Exclusion Act: Previous Chinese exclusion legislation was reenacted without any time limit.

1907 Gentleman's Agreement: In diplomatic negotiations, the Japanese government agreed not to give laborers passports to the United States unless these individuals had previously resided in the United States or were joining parents, wives, or children in this country.

1907 Immigration Act: The head tax was increased to four dollars, but immigrants from Canada, Mexico, Newfoundland, and Cuba were exempted. More excludable classes were specified, including individuals with tuberculosis, "imbeciles," individuals with other physical or mental defects that might hinder their ability to support themselves, unaccompanied children, and individuals acknowledging that they had committed a crime of "moral turpitude."

1913 Immigration Act: The Bureau of Immigration and Naturalization was placed under the authority of the Department of Labor when the Department of Commerce and Labor was separated into two agencies.

1917 Immigration Act: After years of legislative struggle over the issue, a literacy test, especially designed to restrict immigration from southern and eastern Europe, was passed over President Wilson's veto. Exemptions from the literacy test were designated for the wives, parents, grandparents (fathers and grandfathers over fifty-five), and unmarried daughters of legal aliens or citizens. Additional exemptions were made for refugees from religious persecution and aliens who had resided in the United States continuously for five years. An Asiatic barred zone was created, prohibiting permanent immigration from this region. The head tax was raised to eight dollars, and more excludable classes of immigrants were defined, including chronic alcoholics and vagrants.

1918 Sedition Act: This legislation authorized jail terms for individuals who held disloyal political opinions. Under this act, many German immigrants were detained in internment camps.[3]

1918 Entry and Departure Controls Act: This legislation gave the president the power to deport or exclude immigrants deemed to threaten public safety during war or national emergencies.

1921 Emergency Immigration Restriction Act: Annual quotas were established for every nation, set at three percent of that nationality in the U.S. population according to the 1910 U.S. census. Nations in the Asiatic barred zone were not given an immigration quota. Certain classes of immigrants were exempt from the quotas, among them individuals involved in commerce, tourists, minor children of citizens, and individuals residing in the Western Hemisphere for at least a year. In a 1922 act, this requirement was changed to five years in an effort to deter individuals who were migrating to Mexico and Canada with the intention of eventually immigrating to the United States. Preferences within the quotas were established for family members and aliens who had served honorably in the armed forces. First adopted for one year, the act was extended for two years.

1924 Immigration Act: This legislation established two tools for implementing a permanent quota system. First, national quotas were reduced to two percent of a nationality's 1890 population in the United States, with a minimum quota of 100, until a permanent quota formula could be put into place. The use of 1890 as a base year reduced the overall annual quota from approximately 356,000 to less than 165,000. Second, the national origins system established an overall immigration ceiling of 150,000, and quotas within this ceiling were based on the proportion of each nationality in the overall white population in 1920. Exemptions from the quotas were retained for wives and minor children of citizens, natives of the Western Hemisphere, and specified professionals and students. Up to fifty percent of each country's quota was granted to unmarried minor children, parents, and spouses of citizens, with a secondary preference going to skilled agricultural workers. Originally supposed to go into effect in 1927, the national origins quota formula was not implemented until 1929. A system of consular control over immigration was established by requiring entrants to obtain an immigration visa from an American consulate abroad in order to enter the United States.

1924 Appropriations Act: This legislation appropriated funds for the creation of the U.S. Border Patrol, which was established in 1925.

1940, Act of June 14: The Immigration and Naturalization Service was transferred to the Department of Justice.

1940 Alien Registration Act: All aliens were required to register, and those aliens over fourteen years of age had to be fingerprinted. Aliens convicted of aiding other aliens to enter illegally were added to the excludable classes. Also, the provision authorizing exclusions for members of prohibited organizations (i.e. Communist and subversive groups) was extended to individuals who had been members of such organizations in the past. In an amendment of the 1917 Immigration Act, voluntary departure and suspension of deportation were authorized in certain cases.

1942 Bracero Program: The wartime Bracero Program was initiated through bilateral treaties with various Western Hemisphere countries, including Mexico. This program provided for the importation of temporary agricultural workers. Congress, in the Act of April 29, 1943, gave this program retroactive approval. The legislative oversight of this program ended in 1947. Nevertheless, the Bracero Program, with employers rather than the U.S. government as the contracting agent, continued under bilateral agreements from 1948 to 1951.

New legislation for governmental oversight of the program was passed in 1951. Extended by later legislation, the Bracero Program was operational until 1964.

1943 Naturalization Act: This legislation authorized the naturalization of Chinese individuals and, hence, resulted in the repeal of the Chinese Exclusion Acts.

1946 War Brides Act: This act facilitated the entry of foreign-born spouses and children of military personnel.

1946 Naturalization Act: This legislation made individuals from India and the Philippines eligible for naturalization and established small quotas for these countries.

1948 Displaced Persons Act: This legislation allowed for the immigration of over 200,000 individuals displaced during World War II. These refugees could be charged against future quotas for their country of origin. Previously, displaced persons had been allowed entry within the quotas under executive directives. Initially, this act was authorized for a two-year period, but a 1950 amendment extended it until 1951 and increased refugee allowances to over 400,000.

1950 Internal Security Act: In the emerging ideological atmosphere of the Cold War, this legislation included provisions that expanded the grounds for deportation and exclusion of "political subversives."

1952, Act of March 20: In an amendment to the 1917 Immigration Act, this legislation made it a felony to assist in the illegal entry of an alien or to harbor illegal immigrants; however, employment was not to be considered harboring. In addition, this act gave the Border Patrol the legal right to patrol private land within twenty-five miles of the U.S. border.

1952 Immigration and Nationality Act: Enacted over President Truman's veto, this act maintained the restrictive nature of U.S. immigration policy while including tentative provisions for the removal of racial discrimination in these laws. Quotas for independent, self-governing, and UN trustee areas within the former Asiatic barred zone, now called the Asia-Pacific Triangle, were established, but discrimination remained because these quotas were based on race and not national origin. (Immigrants from any country with one-half or more Asian ancestry were charged to the Asian quota.) In a modification of the 1924 national origins system, this act specified that national quotas were to be set at one-sixth of one percent of the number of individuals originating from that area in the 1920 U.S. population. Children and spouses of citizens as well as natives of the Western Hemisphere were exempt from the quotas. Quota preferences were revised in the following manner: first-preference visas of up to fifty percent of the quota limit were granted to immigrants with special skills needed in the United States; second-preference visas of up to thirty percent of the quota limit plus unused visas from the first category were given to parents of adult U.S. citizens; third-preference visas of up to twenty percent of the quota limit plus unused visas from the first two categories were given to spouses and children of legal aliens; fourth-preference visas of twenty-five percent of unused visas from the previous categories were given to siblings and married children of U.S. citizens; the remainder of unused visas from the previous categories were allotted for immigrants outside of the preference categories. In addition to the amendments of the quota system, this act incorporated provisions of the 1950 Internal Security Act, excluding individuals who were or had been members of prohibited political organizations, generally referring to Communist organizations, but created an exemption from exclusion for individuals whose membership in such organizations was involuntary. In another provision, this legislation repealed the Alien Contract Labor Act of 1885.

1953 Refugee Relief Act: More than 200,000 refugees were authorized to enter outside of the quota limitations.

1957 Refugee-Escapee Act: This act defined refugees as individuals fleeing persecution, or fear of persecution, based on race, religion or political opinion from Communist countries or the Middle East and made "refugee-escapees" eligible for unused visas authorized by the 1953 Refugee Relief Act.

1959, Act of September 22: The preference categories under the 1952 Immigration and Nationality Act were revised primarily to facilitate family reunification. The first preference category allotting fifty percent of each quota to skilled immigrants and their spouses and children remained the same. The second preference category, which received thirty percent of each quota, was extended to cover not only the parents but also the unmarried adult children of U.S. citizens. The language of the third preference was clarified so that twenty percent of each quota was to be allotted to spouses and unmarried children of legal permanent residents. (The 1952 legislation referred only to children of legal permanent residents.) The fourth preference allotting visas to siblings and married children of U.S. citizens was raised from twenty-five to fifty percent and expanded to cover the spouses and children of these individuals.

1960 Fair Share Refugee Act: This legislation authorized a temporary program, ending in 1962, to allow refugees under the mandate of the United Nations High Commissioner for Refugees to enter under the parole authority of the Attorney General. This program was designed to close remaining refugee camps in Europe and primarily covered Western Europe. Under this program, the U.S. government committed to admit twenty-five percent of the total number of refugees accepted by other countries.

1961, Act of September 26: This legislation amended the Immigration and Nationality Act by removing the aggregate ceiling of 2,000 on immigration from the Asia-Pacific Triangle. Small quotas were established for countries that recently had gained independence. The legislation also provided that visa applicants were no longer required to answer questions regarding race and ethnicity on the visa application. This act also authorized a temporary program under which non-quota status was given to specified groups whose visa applications were backlogged under the second and third preference categories.

In 1962, a similar temporary program was created for specified groups applying under the first and fourth preference categories.

1965 Amendments to the Immigration and Nationality Act: The national origins system and racial criteria for immigration were eliminated. An immigration ceiling of 170,000 was established for the Eastern Hemisphere, and per-country limits of 20,000 visas were established for Eastern Hemisphere countries. Within the ceiling for the Eastern Hemisphere, visas were allotted according to the following seven-category preference system: (1) unmarried adult children of U.S. citizens (20%); (2) spouses and unmarried children of resident aliens (20%); (3) exceptional professionals, scientists, and artists (10%); (4) married children of U.S. citizens (10%); (5) siblings of U.S. citizens (24%); (6) skilled and unskilled workers in industries for which the domestic supply of labor was insufficient (10%); and (7) refugees (6%). In addition to the new system for the Eastern Hemisphere, a ceiling for the Western Hemisphere, of 120,000 visas, was created for the first time. The per-country limit and the preference system were not applied to the Western Hemisphere under this legislation, and Cuban parolees who became permanent residents initially were counted in the Western Hemisphere ceiling. Because the preference system was not applicable, Western Hemisphere immigrants needed labor certification and attained visas on a first-come, first-served basis. Regarding labor certification, this legislation required the Secretary of Labor to certify that the domestic supply of labor was insufficient before visas could be granted to immigrant workers, while the 1952 act had authorized the granting of visas unless the Secretary of Labor stated that there was already a sufficient supply of labor.

1976 Amendments to the Immigration and Nationality Act: The 20,000 per-country limit and the preference system were extended to the Western Hemisphere. In addition, the legislation provided that Cuban refugees who became permanent residents were not to be counted under the Western Hemisphere ceiling. This act also specified that visas allotted to exceptional professionals, skilled and unskilled workers, and non-preference immigrants under the 1965 preference system required job offers. This legislation also required that U.S. citizens had to be over twenty-one years old for their siblings to qualify for fifth-preference visas under the 1965 preference system.

1978 Amendments to the Immigration and Nationality Act: The hemispheric ceilings were combined into an overall global ceiling of 290,000. The 20,000 per-country limit and the preference system were maintained. This legislation also created the Select Commission on Immigration and Refugee Policy, which was charged to submit recommendations regarding the admission of refugees and legal immigrants as well as the control of illegal immigration.

1980 Refugee Act: This legislation changed the definition of refugee to cover those fleeing from persecution based on race, religion, or nationality in any country, rather than only Communist or Middle Eastern countries. The preference category for refugees was eliminated from the 1965 preference system. As a result, the overall immigration ceiling, excluding refugees, was reduced to 270,000. In place of the preference category for refugees, Congress set a separate target figure of 50,000 for annual refugee admissions, though the exact number of refugee admissions would be determined annually.

1986 Immigration Reform and Control Act: A major development incorporated into this act was the adoption of employer sanctions, which made the knowing hiring of unauthorized immigrants illegal and provided civil and criminal penalties for employers convicted of this crime. Because critics argued that employer sanctions would result in discrimination against citizens and legal residents who were members of ethnic minority groups, anti-discrimination measures were provided for in the act. The legislation also contained legalization provisions for individuals who had resided illegally in the United States since before 1982. The final major provisions of this legislation expanded the H-2 temporary foreign worker program and established temporary residence for seasonal agricultural workers who had resided in the United States for three years. These seasonal agricultural workers would be eligible for permanent residence after two years of temporary status and would be able to seek jobs outside of agriculture; hence, the act also authorized granting temporary residence to replenishment agricultural workers.

1990 Immigration Act: This legislation increased annual immigration levels to a 675,000 flexible ceiling and continues to govern legal immigrant admissions to the United States. Family immigration is given highest priority within this flexible ceiling, with at least 480,000 visas going to family-related immigrants. There is no limit on the number of visas for immediate relatives of citizens, though they are covered within the ceiling on family immigration for the first time. Other relatives of citizens and resident aliens receive the remaining number of family visas, but this number can be no lower than 226,000; thus, overall family immigration may exceed 480,000 if the demand for immediate relative visas is too great. The next preference category, which receives 140,000 visas annually, covers employment-based immigrants. Preference within the employment category is granted to individuals with special abilities, professionals, and skilled workers. A major change in immigration policy included in this legislation is the creation of a permanent diversity program through which 55,000 preference visas are to be made available annually to individuals from countries that have had very low immigration to the United States since the 1965 amendments were passed and are underrepresented in the U.S. population. Finally, the 1990 act expanded the anti-discrimination provisions of the 1986 Immigration Reform and Control Act regarding employer sanctions.

1996 Personal Responsibility, Work Opportunity, and Medicaid Restructuring Act: The welfare reform legislation passed in August of 1996 prohibits illegal immigrants and non-immigrants from receiving federal public benefits, with limited exceptions for certain benefits, including emergency medical services, certain emergency disaster relief, public health immunizations and treatment of communicable diseases, and housing assistance. It also prohibits illegal immigrants from receiving state and local benefits, with the limited exceptions listed above. Under this legislation, legal immigrants are no longer are eligible for food stamps or social security benefits. They also will be denied other federal benefits, including Medicaid and public housing, during the first five years of their residence in the United States. Additionally, the legislation provides that states may also deny cash welfare and other benefits to legal immigrants. Finally, the legislation provides that the income and resources of a legal immigrant applying for federal means-tested public benefits shall be deemed to include the income and resources of the person's spouse and of an immigrant's sponsor in the case of legal permanent residents.

1996 Illegal Immigration Reform and Immigrant Responsibility Act: The Illegal Immigration Reform and Responsibility Act of 1996 contains a number of provisions designed to target illegal immigration. The most important provisions will be summarized here. Title I provides increased funding for border patrol and increases civil penalties for illegal entry. Title II authorizes I.N.S. wiretaps and undercover operations to enforce laws against alien smuggling and document fraud and increases penalties for these violations. Title III provides a variety of new grounds for exclusion, including the "incitement of terrorist activity" and making a false claim of citizenship. Title III also restricts the ability of residents without legal status to bring class action suits against the I.N.S. For instance, lawyers in federally-financed legal services can no longer bring class action suits against the I.N.S. on behalf of illegal immigrants. Immigrants may still bring individual suits, but most will not have the resources to do so. Moreover, this legislation creates new limitations on judicial review of I.N.S. decisions to exclude individuals at the border and other entry checkpoints, such as airports. Under Title IV, only a social security card, green card, U.S. passport, or I.N.S. employment authorization card will be accepted as proof of work eligibility. Birth certificates, certificates of citizenship, naturalization papers, and foreign passports no longer will be acceptable. This legislation adds new protections for employers who, as a result of employer sanctions, might be accused of discriminating. Under the new law, a potential employee must prove that the employer intended to discriminate in order to file a complaint. According to the legislation, employers also will not be penalized for keeping bad records if they have made a "good faith" attempt to keep accurate records. Title V echoes the provisions of the 1996 welfare reform legislation that deny federal benefits to illegal immigrants.

NOTES

1. Sources for this appendix include Vernon M. Briggs, Jr., *Immigration Policy and the American Labor Force* (Baltimore: The Johns Hopkins University Press, 1984); Kitty Calavita, *U.S. Immigration Law and the Control of Labor: 1820–1924* (London: Academic Press, Inc., 1984); E.P. Hutchinson, *Legislative History of American Immigration Policy: 1798–1965* (Philadelphia: University of Pennsylvania Press, 1981); Michael C. LeMay, *From Open Door to Dutch Door: An Analysis of U.S. Immigration Policy Since 1820* (New York: Praeger, 1987); U.S. Congress, Congressional Research Service, *U.S. Immigration Law and Policy: 1952–1979*, 96th Cong., 1st sess. (Washington: U.S. Government Printing Office, 1979); U.S. Immigration and

Naturalization Service, *Statistical Yearbook of the Immigration and Naturalization Service, 1992* (Washington, D.C.: U.S. Government Printing Office, 1993); and Joyce C. Vialet and Larry M. Eig, "Immigration Act of 1990 (P.L. 101–649)," (Washington, D.C.: Congressional Research Service, Library of Congress).

   2. Hutchinson: 410–414.

   3. Calavita, *US. Immigration Law*: 116.

Appendix B

Major Provisions of the Immigration Reform and Control Act of 1986[1]

Employer Sanctions: Employer sanctions are the fundamental legislative change brought about by the Immigration Reform and Control Act (IRCA), which makes it illegal for all employers, regardless of the size of their business, to knowingly hire, recruit, or refer for a fee immigrants unauthorized to work in the United States.[2] Under IRCA, violators of the employer sanctions law are subject to the following system of graduated civil and criminal penalties: first offense, $250 to $2,000 fine for each undocumented immigrant; second offense, $2,000 to $5,000 fine per violation; third offense, $3,000 to $10,000 fine per violation; fourth offense, criminal penalties up to six months in prison and/or $3,000 fine for pattern or practice of violations. In order to fulfill their obligations under this law, employers are required to examine either a U.S. passport, certificate of citizenship or naturalization, foreign passport authorizing work eligibility, permanent resident card, social security card, or birth certificate *and* another identification, for example, a driver's license or other federal or state identification. Employers must attest in writing that they have examined the appropriate documentation and must retain records for three years after a hire or referral or one year after termination of employment. Employers who violate these verification and record-keeping requirements are subject to civil fines of $100 to $1,000. The record-keeping requirements provide an affirmative defense for employers; in order to comply with the law, employers must only examine the appropriate documents and determine that they reasonably appear to be genuine. In other words, employers are not responsible for identifying fraud.[3] Penalties for employer sanctions did not go into effect immediately and would not be incurred for employees who had been hired prior IRCA's passage. IRCA authorized an education period through May 1987 during which no penalties were to be incurred for violations. The following year, employers would receive a warning citation for a first offense. IRCA also gave employers involved with the Seasonal Agricultural Worker Program a two-year exemption from penalties; this exemption overlaps with an eighteen-month period in which illegal immigrants working in seasonal agriculture were able to apply for a special agricultural legalization program. However, agricultural employers could not recruit new workers outside of the United States during this exemption period. The interests of agricultural employers are also acknowledged in a provision of IRCA that specifies that the I.N.S. cannot inspect an open-field agricultural operation without owner consent or a warrant.[4]

Anti-discrimination Measures: IRCA specifies that employment discrimination based on national origin or citizenship status is illegal.[5] This provision applies to U.S. citizens, permanent residents, refugees, or legalized immigrants intending to become citizens. However, IRCA states that it should not be considered discriminatory when employers hire citizens over permanent residents and other immigrants authorized to work if the applicants are equally qualified. IRCA created the Special Counsel for Immigration-Related Unfair Employment Practices in the Justice Department to receive complaints under this provision. An individual must file a complaint with the Special Counsel within 180 days of a violation in order for the Special Counsel to have the authority to investigate the case. Moreover, an individual must provide evidence that he or she intends to become a citizen in order to register a complaint with the Special Counsel. If the Special Counsel decides the complaint has merit, the complainant receives a hearing before an administrative law judge. If the judge determines that an employer is guilty of discriminating on the basis of national origin or citizenship, s/he may fine the employer up to $1,000 for a first offense and up to $2,000 for later offenses. The judge also may require an employer to provide back pay for up to two years. In addition to civil fines for employment discrimination based on national origin or citizenship status, IRCA required the GAO to conduct annual studies for the first three years after the legislation's implementation to determine the extent to which employer sanctions had led to discrimination. Under this provision, if the GAO found evidence of a widespread pattern of employment discrimination resulting from sanctions, Congress could have repealed the legislation by joint resolution within thirty days. In fact, as stated in a 1990 report, the GAO did find that employer sanctions had led to widespread discrimination, though Congress has not taken any steps to repeal IRCA.[6]

Legalization: Under IRCA, illegal immigrants who had resided continuously in the United States since before January 1, 1982, were eligible to apply for temporary resident status during a twelve-month period beginning no later than May 6, 1987.[7] Undocumented immigrants with felony convictions or three or more misdemeanors as well as individuals who have assisted in persecution on the basis of race, religion, nationality, membership in a particular social group, or political opinion were not eligible for legalization. After eighteen months, individuals who received temporary status under this provision could apply for permanent residence status if they could show basic knowledge of English and U.S. history and government. The "registry date," under which the Attorney General can grant legal status to illegal immigrants residing continuously in the United States, was updated from June 30, 1948, to January 1, 1972, by IRCA. Additionally, Cuban-Haitian entrants, a term used by the Carter and Reagan administrations to describe individuals from Cuba and Haiti who were allowed to enter under emergency procedures, became eligible for permanent legal status if they had resided continuously in the United States since before January 1, 1982. Aliens legalized under this provision did not become eligible for most public assistance, including Aid for Families with Dependent Children, food stamps, and Medicaid, for five years, though the legislation provided exemptions from these restrictions for Cubans and Haitians, the blind, the disabled, and the elderly. Under IRCA, qualified designated entities (QDEs) were given a role in the legalization process. Included in recognition of the fact that many illegal immigrants distrust the I.N.S. and might be more likely to seek help from voluntary organizations, including churches, this provision enabled designated voluntary agencies to process applications and give advice and information to undocumented immigrants. Legalization applications and materials were to be confidential and could not be used for any other purpose, for example, to initiate deportation proceedings.[8]

H-2A Agricultural Workers: In order to expand agricultural employers' access to seasonal workers, a separate H-2 category for agriculture, H-2A, was created.[9] As under H-2, the Department of Labor must certify that no willing and qualified domestic workers are available and that the employment of temporary foreign workers will not adversely affect wages and working conditions of domestic workers before H-2A workers will be authorized to enter. If domestic workers apply for a job before fifty percent of a work period authorizing H-2 workers has expired, the employer must hire the domestic workers.[10] Furthermore, the Department of Labor cannot provide an H-2 certification if the employer is involved in a strike or lockout or if the employer has demonstrated significant violations of previous certification. However, the H-2A category differs from the original H-2 program in that the Secretary of Agriculture has input in the certification decision. Another change in the H-2A program is a facilitated procedure for requesting certification. Employers need to submit a request for H-2A workers only sixty days prior to when they are needed. The Department of Labor must make a certification decision at least twenty days before the date for which the H-2A workers have been requested. While waiting for a certification decision, employers also must attempt to find domestic workers for the job. IRCA also mandates that employers provide housing, subsistence costs, and worker compensation to H-2A workers.[11]

Seasonal Agricultural Workers (SAWs): Under another provision designed to expand agricultural employers' access to temporary labor, immigrants who had worked in seasonal agriculture for at least ninety days in each of three years prior to the legislation's enactment were eligible for temporary legal status. These workers became eligible for permanent legal status after one year.

Congress authorized this SAW program for seven years and specified that no more than 350,000 immigrants were to be admitted under its provisions. Immigrants who had worked in seasonal agriculture for at least ninety days in the year preceding the passage of IRCA also were eligible to apply for temporary status, but these workers would not be eligible for permanent residence for two years. Once admitted, seasonal agricultural workers could leave their employment in agriculture. Thus, Congress also authorized a three-year program for replenishment workers if the Secretary of Labor and the Secretary of Agriculture make a joint determination that a legitimate need for seasonal workers exists. Under this provision, replenishment workers were given temporary resident status for three years and required to perform at least ninety days of seasonal agricultural work in each of those years. Thus, unlike the workers admitted under the SAW provision, replenishment workers could not leave agricultural employment after they received temporary status. Under IRCA, the replenishment agricultural worker program was to operate from 1990 to 1993. In 1990, the maximum number of replenishment workers admitted was to be ninety-five percent of the number of immigrants given temporary status under the SAW provision minus the number of these immigrants who worked in seasonal agriculture in 1989. From 1991 to 1993, the maximum number of replenishment workers was to be ninety percent of the total number of SAWs and replenishment workers minus the number of these immigrants who worked in seasonal agriculture the previous year. Eligible migrant workers could apply for adjustment under the SAW provision through the I.N.S., qualified voluntary organizations, or a consular office. In addition to the creation of the new seasonal worker program, IRCA authorized the creation of a Commission on Agricultural Workers to study the need for foreign workers in U.S. agriculture.[12]

Systematic Alien Verification System: IRCA requires states to verify the legal status of immigrants applying for public benefits, including Aid for Families with Dependent Children, Medicaid, unemployment insurance, food stamps, housing assistance, and higher education programs. However, the legislation states that benefits cannot be delayed or terminated while the legal status of the immigrant is being verified.

Appropriations: In addition to the regular appropriations for the Immigration and Naturalization Service, Congress authorized the appropriation of $422 million in fiscal year 1987 and $419 million in fiscal year 1988 to the I.N.S. for the implementation of sanctions. At least $184 million of these funds were to be used on expanded enforcement and sufficient funds also were to be used to increase the Border Patrol by fifty percent. Additionally, the I.N.S. was supposed to use appropriated funds to improve their service responsibilities and community outreach.[13] IRCA specified that the Employment Standards Administration of the Department of Labor was to receive funds necessary to facilitate the enforcement of wage and hour legislation and other labor standards in order to reduce the economic incentives to hire cheap, illegal labor. Regarding the implementation of the amnesty provision, Congress provided for State Legalization Impact Assistant Grants. Through these grants, Congress authorized the appropriation of $1 billion each year for four fiscal years to reimburse states for the costs of legalization.[14]

NOTES

1. The primary sources for this appendix were Nancy Humel Montweiler, *The Immigration Reform Law of 1986* (Washington, D.C.: The Bureau of National Affairs, Inc., 1987) and Frank D. Bean, Georges Vernez, and Charles B. Keely, *Opening and Closing the Doors: Evaluating Immigration Reform and Control* (Washington, D.C.: The Urban Institute; Santa Monica, CA: The RAND Corporation, 1989): 25–34. This appendix focuses exclusively on the major provisions of IRCA. For an overview of IRCA's other provisions, see Montweiler: 80–87. The text of IRCA also is included in Montweiler: 91–179.

2. The House Judiciary Committee, in its interpretation of the law, specified that this language does not apply to labor unions because they do not refer immigrants for a fee or based on a profit motive. See U.S. Congress, House Judiciary Committee, *Immigration Control and Legalization Amendments Act of 1986*, Rept. 99–682, Part 1, 99th Cong., 2d sess. (Washington, D.C.: U.S. Government Printing Office, 1987): p. 56 cited in Montweiler: 33, 324.

3. The potential for fraudulent documentation was widely addressed in the debate over employer sanctions legislation. Some groups called for a universal identification card as a means of reducing the potential for fraud as well as minimizing the potential for discrimination against ethnic minorities entitled to work. Though no specific legislation was adopted, IRCA called for studies on ways to improve verification of legal status. Potential verification methods identified in IRCA include a telephone verification system and new technology for a counterfeit-proof social security card, including magnetic stripes, holograms, or integrated circuit chips. IRCA called on the president to monitor the verification system and, if necessary, to recommend changes. However, Congress, in recognition of strong opposition to universal identification on civil rights grounds, explicitly stated that the president was not authorized to create a national identification card.

4. Montweiler: 24–25, 31–45.

5. The Civil Rights Act of 1964 already had made it illegal for employers of ten or more individuals to discriminate on the basis of national origin. Under IRCA, employers may not discriminate on the basis of national origin *or* citizenship status, and this prohibition against employment discrimination applies to employers of four or more individuals. Bean, Vernez, and Keely: 27.

6. Montweiler: 25–26, 46–53.

7. Short, casual, or innocent absences are not considered to interrupt continuous residence.

8. Montweiler: 26–27, 64–65.

9. IRCA also created an H-2B category that covers non-agricultural employment and operates under the original H-2 rules. Under the original H-2 program, temporary foreign workers are admitted to perform labor for which the domestic labor supply is insufficient. Prior to IRCA, most H-2 workers were admitted to work in seasonal agriculture in the East and in the hotel and restaurant industry. The changes in the H-2 program were designed primarily to meet the demands of Southwestern growers. Ibid.: 68.

10. House Judiciary Committee: pp. 79–83 cited in Montweiler: 69–73.

11. Montweiler: 27–28, 66–74.

12. Ibid.: 28, 74–79.

13. Ibid.: 42–43.
14. Ibid.: 64–65.

Appendix C

Major Provisions of the Immigration Act of 1990[1]

Numerical Limitations on Permanent Legal Immigration: The Immigration Act of 1990 provided for an overall annual cap of 675,000 on legal admissions for permanent residence beginning in 1995. This cap represents an increase from the previous ceiling of 270,000 on legal immigration, though the new cap applies to the immigration of immediate family members of U.S. citizens. Under the overall cap on legal immigration, there is a flexible cap of 480,000 on family immigration under which the immigration of immediate family members of U.S. citizens continues to be unlimited. The number of visas available for other family members of citizens and permanent residents is determined by subtracting the number of immediate family immigrants in the prior year from 480,000. However, the number of visas available for non-immediate family members of citizens and residents cannot fall below a floor of 226,000 in any given year. Thus, the flexible cap on family immigration *and* the overall ceiling on legal immigration can be pierced if large numbers of immediate relatives of U.S. citizens enter the United States in a particular year. The Immigration Act of 1990 provides for 140,000 visas annually for employment-based immigration. Prior to this legislation, less than 60,000 immigrants could enter the United States annually under occupational preferences. Finally, the Immigration Act of 1990 created a permanent diversity program that beginning in 1995, has provided for 55,000 visas annually for immigrants from countries that have been underrepresented in immigration flows to the United States in recent years. Between 1992 and 1994, the legislation provided for a transitional cap of 700,000 on legal immigration. Under this transitional cap, 465,000 visas were reserved for family immigration while 140,000 were set aside for employment-based immigration. During the transitional period, only 40,000 visas were allocated for diversity immigrants.[2]

Per-country Limits: The Immigration Act of 1990 provides for a modest increase in the per-country limits on immigration visas. Until 1990, the annual per-country limits of 20,000 visas, created in the 1965 amendments to the Immigration and Nationality Act, were still in place. The 1990 legislation sets the per-country limits at seven percent of the total number of visas available for family-preference and employment-based immigration, or seven percent of 366,000 (226,000 family-preference visas and 140,000 occupational-preference visas). Based on this percentage, per-country limits currently are set at 25,620. In addition to increasing the per-country limits, the 1990 Immigration Act specifies that seventy-five percent of the visas for spouses and children of permanent residents are exempt from the per-country limits.[3]

Preference Allocation of Visas: Visas for family immigration subject to numerical limitation, set at a floor of 226,000, are allocated annually according to the following preferences under the Immigration Act of 1990: (1) 23,400 first-preference visas are reserved for the unmarried adult children of U.S. citizens; (2) 114,200 second-preference visas are allocated for the spouses and unmarried children of permanent residents, with seventy-five percent of this number reserved for spouses and *minor* children; (3) 23,400 third-preference visas for married children of U.S. citizens; and (4) 65,000 fourth-preference visas for the siblings of adult U.S. citizens. If more than 226,000 family-preference visas are available in a given year, they are added to the second-preference category for spouses and unmarried children of permanent residents. Unlike earlier legislation governing the admission of legal immigrants, the Immigration Act of 1990 provides for a separate preference system for employment-based immigration. Employment-based immigration visas are allocated under the following preference categories created by the 1990 legislation: (1) 40,000 first-preference visas for immigrants of outstanding ability; (2) 40,000 second-preference visas for professionals with advanced degrees or immigrants with exceptional abilities; (3) 40,000 third-preference visas for skilled workers or unskilled shortage workers; (4) 10,000 fourth-preference visas for special immigrants, including religious workers; and (5) 10,000 fifth-preference visas for investors. The Immigration Act of 1990 specifies that the number of visas allocated to unskilled workers cannot rise above ten percent, and visas issued to individuals in the second and third employment-based preference categories require certification by the Department of Labor that native workers are not available. The preference visas for employment-based immigration cover not only workers but also their families.[4]

Permanent Diversity Program: The Immigration Act of 1990 created a permanent diversity program that makes additional visas available annually to diversify the ethnic composition of immigrants to the United States. Between 1992 and 1994, a transitional diversity program was in place. Under this program, 40,000 visas each year were made available to immigrants from countries that have had a proportionally low number of immigrants to the United

States since 1965. At least forty percent of these visas were set aside for Ireland. Applicants for transitional diversity visas had to have an employment offer in order to be eligible. In 1995, the permanent diversity program went into effect. Under the permanent program, 55,000 visas are available annually to individuals from countries that have had fewer than 50,000 immigrants to the United States during the past five years. No country may receive more than 3,850, or seven percent, of the total number of diversity visas. Applicants for permanent diversity visas must have the equivalent of a high school diploma or two years of experience in an occupation requiring vocational training in order to be eligible.[5]

IRCA-related Provisions: The Immigration Act of 1990 includes a number of provisions that modified the Immigration Reform and Control Act of 1986. First, this legislation authorized the allocation of 55,000 visas between 1992 and 1994 for spouses and minor children of immigrants who had received amnesty under IRCA's legalization programs. The number of visas for the immediate relatives of legalized immigrants could be reduced if necessary to ensure that a minimum of 226,000 family-preference visas would be available under the flexible cap on family immigration. In a modification of IRCA's employer sanctions provisions, the Immigration Act of 1990 specifies that IRCA's requirement that individuals who refer or recruit workers for a fee must verify and keep records of the work eligibility of referred employees only applies to agricultural labor recruiters or contractors. Finally, the Immigration Act of 1990 strengthens IRCA's anti-discrimination measures. The 1990 legislation provides that seasonal agricultural workers and replenishment agricultural workers are covered by the prohibition against discrimination on the basis of citizenship status or national origin. Under the Immigration Act of 1990, individuals no longer have to provide evidence of their intention to become a U.S. citizen in order to file a complaint of discrimination based on citizenship status with the Special Counsel for Immigration-Related Unfair Employment Practices in the Justice Department. The 1990 legislation also subjects individuals found guilty of violating the prohibition against national origin or citizenship status discrimination to the same level of civil penalties as employers found guilty of knowingly hiring undocumented workers.[6]

NOTES

1. The provisions discussed in this appendix focus primarily on the modification of the general system for admitting immigrants to the United States for legal permanent residence. The Immigration Act of 1990 also included a number of provisions related to asylum, non-immigrants, naturalization, and illegal immigration and deportation. See Joyce C. Vialet and Larry M. Eig, "Immigration Act of 1990 (P.L. 101–649)," (Washington, D.C.: Congressional Research Service, Library of Congress) for an overview of these provisions.

2. Vialet and Eig: 2; Michael Fix and Jeffrey S. Passel, *The Door Remains Open: Recent Immigration to the United States and a Preliminary Analysis of the Immigration Act of 1990* (Washington, D.C.: Program for Research on Immigration Policy, The Urban Institute, January 1991): 13–14.

3. Vialet and Eig: 3.
4. Ibid.: 3–5; Fix and Passel: 14–18.
5. Vialet and Eig: 5; Fix and Passel: 15.
6. Vialet and Eig: 3–4, 11–12; Fix and Passel: 18–19

Bibliography

ARTICLES AND BOOKS

Bach, Robert L. "Immigration and U.S. Foreign Policy in Latin America and the Caribbean." In Robert W. Tucker, Charles B. Keely, and Linda Wrigley, eds. *Immigration and U.S. Foreign Policy*. Boulder: Westview Press, 1990: 123–149.

Bach, Robert L. and Doris Meissner. *Employment and Immigration Reform: Employer Sanctions Four Years Later*. Washington, D.C.: Immigration Policy Project of the Carnegie Endowment for International Peace, September 1990.

Baker, Susan González. "The 'Amnesty' Aftermath: Current Policy Issues Stemming from the Legalization Programs of the 1986 Immigration Reform and Control Act." *International Migration Review*. 31:1 (Spring 1997): 5–27.

———. *The Cautious Welcome: The Legalization Programs of the Immigration Reform and Control Act*. Washington, D.C.: The Urban Institute; Santa Monica, CA: The RAND Corporation, 1990.

Bean, Frank D., Barry Edmonston, and Jeffrey S. Passel, eds. *Undocumented Migration to the United States: IRCA and the Experience of the 1980s*. Washington, D.C.: The Urban Institute; Santa Monica, CA: The RAND Corporation, 1990.

Bean, Frank D., Jurgen Schmandt, and Sidney Weintraub, eds. *Mexican and Central American Population and U.S. Immigration Policy*. The Center for Mexican American Studies: University of Texas at Austin, 1989.

Bean, Frank D., Thomas J. Espenshade, Michael J. White, and Robert F. Dymowski. "Post-IRCA Changes in the Volume and Composition of Undocumented Migration to the United States: An Assessment Based on Apprehensions Data." In Bean, Edmonston, and Passel, eds. *Undocumented Migration to the United States: IRCA and the Experience of the 1980s*. Washington, D.C.: The Urban Institute; Santa Monica, CA: The RAND Corporation, 1990: 111–158.

Bean, Frank D. and Michael Fix. "The Significance of Recent Immigration Policy Reforms in the United States." In Gary P. Freeman and James Jupp, eds. *Nations of Immigrants: Australia, the United States, and International Migration*. Oxford: Oxford University Press, 1992: 41–55.

Bean, Frank D., Georges Vernez, and Charles B. Keely. *Opening and Closing the Doors: Evaluating Immigration Reform and Control.* Washington, D.C.: The Urban Institute; Santa Monica, CA: The RAND Corporation, 1989.

Briggs, Vernon M., Jr. "Employer Sanctions and the Question of Discrimination." *International Migration Review.* 24:4 (Winter 1990): 803–815.

———. *Immigration Policy and the American Labor Force.* Baltimore: The Johns Hopkins University Press, 1984.

———. *Mass Immigration and the National Interest.* Armonk, New York: M.E. Sharpe, Inc., 1992.

Bryce-Laporte, Roy Simon. "The New Immigration: Its Origin, Visibility, and Implications for Public Policy." In Winston A. Van Horne, ed. *Ethnicity and Public Policy.* Milwaukee: University of Wisconsin System American Ethnic Studies Coordinating Committee/ Urban Corridor Consortium, 1 (1982): 62–88.

Bustamente, Jorge A. "Undocumented Immigration: Research Findings and Policy Options." In Riordan A. Roett, ed. *Mexico and the United States, Managing the Relationship.* Boulder: Westview Press, 1988: 109–131.

———. "Undocumented Migration from Mexico to the United States: Preliminary Findings of the Zapata Canyon Project." In Bean, Edmonston, and Passel, eds. *Undocumented Migration to the United States: IRCA and the Experience of the 1980s.* Washington, D.C.: The Urban Institute; Santa Monica, CA: The RAND Corporation, 1990: 211–226.

Calavita, Kitty. "California's 'Employer Sanctions' Legislation: Now You See It, Now You Don't." *Politics and Society.* 12:2 (1983): 205–230.

———. "Employer Sanctions Violations: Toward a Dialectical Model of White-Collar Crime." *Law and Society Review.* 24:4 (1990): 1041–1069.

———. "The Immigration Policy Debate: a Critical Analysis and Options for the Future." In Wayne A. Cornelius and Jorge A. Bustamente, eds. *Mexican Migration to the United States.* La Jolla: Center for U.S.-Mexican Studies, University of California, 1989: 151–177.

———. *Inside the State: The Bracero Program, Immigration, and the I.N.S.* New York: Routledge, 1992.

———. "The New Politics of Immigration: 'Balanced-Budget Conservatism' and the Symbolism of Proposition 187." *Social Problems.* 43:3 (August 1996): 284–305.

———. *U.S. Immigration Law and the Control of Labor: 1820–1924.* London: Academic Press, Inc., 1984.

Carlson, A.W. "One Century of Foreign Immigration to the United States: 1880–1979." *International Migration.* 23:3 (September 1985): 309–334.

Carney, Dan. "Can the U.S. Regain Control of Its Borders?" *Congressional Quarterly Weekly Report.* 5 October 1996: 2814–2815.

———. "Republicans Feeling the Heat as Policy Becomes Reality." *Congressional Quarterly Weekly Report.* 17 May 1997: 1131–1136.

Castles, Stephen and Godula Kosack. *Immigrant Workers and Class Structure in Western Europe.* 2d ed. Oxford: Oxford University Press, 1985.

Chavez, Leo R. "Immigration Reform and Nativism: The Nationalist Response to the Transnationalist Challenge." In Juan F. Perea, ed. *Immigrants Out! The New Nativism and the Anti-Immigrant Impulse in the United States.* New York: New York University Press, 1997: 61–77.

Conniff, Ruth. "The War on Aliens: The Right Calls the Shots." *The Progressive,* October 1993: 22–29 reprinted in Robert M. Jackson, ed. *Global Issues 94/95.* Guilford, CT: The Dushkin Publishing Group, Inc., 1994: 51–57.

Cornelius, Wayne A. "Impacts of the 1986 U.S. Immigration Law on Emigration from Rural Mexican Sending Communities." In Bean, Edmonston, and Passel, eds. *Undocumented Migration to the United States: IRCA and the Experience of the 1980s*. Washington, D.C.: The Urban Institute; Santa Monica, CA: The RAND Corporation, 1990: 227–249.

Cornelius, Wayne A., Philip L. Martin, and James F. Hollifield, eds. *Controlling Immigration: A Global Perspective*. Stanford, CA: Stanford University Press, 1994.

Crane, Keith, Beth J. Asch, Joanna Zorn Heilbrunn, and Danielle C. Cullinane. *The Effect of Employer Sanctions on the Flow of Undocumented Immigrants to the United States*. Washington, D.C.: The Urban Institute; Santa Monica, CA: The RAND Corporation, April 1990.

Crewdson, John. *The Tarnished Door*. New York: Times Books, 1983.

Curran, Thomas J. *Xenophobia and Immigration, 1820–1930*. Boston: Twayne Publishers, 1975.

de la Garza, Rodolfo O. "Immigration Reforms: A Mexican-American Perspective." In Gillian Peele, Christopher J. Bailey, and Bruce Cain, eds. *Developments in American Politics*. New York: St. Martin's Press, 1992: 309–322.

Domínguez, Jorge I. "Immigration as Foreign Policy in U.S.-Latin American Relations." In Robert W. Tucker, Charles B. Keely, and Linda Wrigley, eds. *Immigration and U.S. Foreign Policy*. Boulder: Westview Press, 1990: 150–166.

Donato, Katharine M., Jorge Durand, and Douglas S. Massey. "Stemming the Tide? Assessing the Deterrent Effects of the Immigration Reform and Control Act." *Demography*. 29:2 (May 1992): 139–157.

Donato, Katharine M. and Douglas S. Massey. "Effect of the Immigration Reform and Control Act on the Wages of Mexican Migrants." *Social Science Quarterly*. 74:3 (September 1993): 523–541.

Dowty, Alan. *Closed Borders: The Contemporary Assault on Freedom of Movement*. New Haven: Yale University Press, 1987.

Espenshade, Thomas J. "Undocumented Migration to the United States: Evidence from a Repeated Trials Model." In Bean, Edmonston, and Passel, eds. *Undocumented Migration to the United States: IRCA and the Experience of the 1980s*. Washington, D.C.: The Urban Institute; Santa Monica, CA: The RAND Corporation, 1990: 159–181.

Espenshade, Thomas J. and Katherine Hempstead. "Contemporary American Attitudes Toward U.S. Immigration." *International Migration Review*. 30:2 (Summer 1996): 535–570.

Finch, Wilbur A., Jr. "The Immigration Reform and Control Act of 1986: A Preliminary Assessment." *Social Science Review*. June 1990: 244–260.

Fischer, Judith L. "Effects of the Immigration Reform and Control Act on Families." *Marriage and Family Review*. 19:3/4 (1993): 233–239.

Fix, Michael and Paul Hill. *Enforcing Employer Sanctions: Challenges and Strategies*. Washington, D.C.: The Urban Institute; Santa Monica, CA: The RAND Corporation, 1990.

Fix, Michael and Jeffrey S. Passel. *The Door Remains Open: Recent Immigration to the United States and a Preliminary Analysis of the Immigration Act of 1990*. Washington, D.C.: Program for Research on Immigration Policy, The Urban Institute, January 1991.

Fragomen, Austin T., Jr. "The Illegal Immigration Reform and Immigrant Responsibility Act of 1996." *International Migration Review*. 31:2 (Summer 1997): 438–460.

Freeman, Gary P. "Can Liberal States Control Unwanted Migration?" *The Annals of the American Academy of Political and Social Science*. 534 (July 1994): 17–30.

————. "Migration Policy and Politics in the Receiving States." *International Migration Review*. 26:4 (Winter 1992): 1144–1167.

Freeman, Gary P. and Katharine Betts. "The Politics of Interests and Immigration Policymaking in Australia and the United States." In Gary P. Freeman and James Jupp, eds. *Nations of Immigrants: Australia, the United States, and International Migration*. Oxford: Oxford University Press, 1992: 72–88.

Fuchs, Lawrence H. *The American Kaleidoscope: Race, Ethnicity, and the Civic Culture*. Hanover, NH: University Press of New England, 1990.

————. "Immigration, Pluralism, and Public Policy: The Challenge of the *Pluribus* to the *Unum*." In Mary M. Kritz, ed. *U.S. Immigration and Refugee Policy*. Lexington, MA: Lexington Books, 1983: 289–315.

García y Griego, Manuel. "Canada: Flexibility and Control in Immigration and Refugee Policy." In Wayne A. Cornelius, Philip L. Martin, and James F. Hollifield, eds. *Controlling Immigration: A Global Perspective*. Stanford, CA: Stanford University Press, 1994: 119–140.

Garis, Roy L. *Immigration Restriction*. New York: The MacMillan Company, 1927.

Gimpel, James G. and James R. Edwards, Jr. *The Congressional Politics of Immigration Reform*. Boston: Allyn and Bacon, 1999.

Goldin, Claudia. "The Political Economy of Immigration Restriction in the United States, 1890 to 1921." *National Bureau of Economic Research Working Paper Series, Working Paper No. 4345*. Cambridge, MA: National Bureau of Economic Research, April 1993.

Goldstein, Judith and Robert O. Keohane, eds. *Ideas & Foreign Policy: Beliefs, Institutions, and Political Change*. Ithaca, NY: Cornell University Press, 1993.

González de la Rocha, Mercedes and Agustín Escobar Latapí. "The Impact of IRCA on the Migration Patterns of a Community in Los Altos, Jalisco, Mexico." In Sergio Díaz-Briquets and Sidney Weintraub, eds. *The Effects of Receiving Country Policies on Migration Flows*. Boulder: Westview Press, 1991: 205–231.

Hagan, Jacqueline Maria and Susan González Baker. "Implementing the U.S. Legalization Program: The Influence of Immigrant Communities and Local Agencies on Immigration Policy Reform." *International Migration Review*. 27:3 (Fall 1993): 513–536.

Harwood, Edwin. "American Public Opinion and U.S. Immigration Policy." *The Annals of the American Academy of Political and Social Science*. 487 (September 1986): 201–212.

————. "The Crisis in Immigration Policy." *Journal of Contemporary Studies*. 6:4 (Fall 1983): 45–59.

————. *In Liberty's Shadow: Illegal Aliens and Immigration Law Enforcement*. Stanford, CA: Hoover Institution Press, 1986.

Haus, Leah. "Openings in the Wall: Transnational Migrants, Labor Unions, and U.S. Immigration Policy." *International Organization*. 49:2 (Spring 1995): 285–313.

Hawley, Ellis W. "The Politics of the Mexican Labor Issue, 1950–1965." In George C. Kiser and Martha Woody Kiser, eds. *Mexican Workers in the United States*. Albuquerque: University of New Mexico Press, 1979: 97–120.

Heisler, Martin O. "Migration, International Relations and the New Europe: Theoretical Perspectives from Institutional Political Sociology." *International Migration Review*. 26:2 (Summer 1992): 596–621.

Henkin, Louis. *The Age of Rights*. New York: Columbia University Press, 1990.

Higham, John. *Strangers in the Land: Patterns of American Nativism: 1860–1925*. 2d ed. New Brunswick: Rutgers University Press, 1988.

Hoefer, Michael D. "Background of U.S. Immigration Policy Reform." In Francisco L. Rivera-Batiz, Selig L. Sechzer, and Ira N. Gang, eds. *U.S. Immigration Policy Reform in the 1980s: A Preliminary Assessment*. New York: Praeger, 1991: 17–44.

Hollifield, James F. *Immigrants, Markets, and States*. Cambridge: Harvard University Press, 1992.

———. "Immigration and Republicanism in France: The Hidden Consensus." In Wayne A. Cornelius, Philip L. Martin, and James F. Hollifield, eds. *Controlling Immigration: A Global Perspective*. Stanford, CA: Stanford University Press, 1994: 143–175.

Hull, Elizabeth. *Without Justice for All: The Constitutional Rights of Aliens*. Westport, CT: Greenwood Press, 1985.

Hutchinson, E.P. *Legislative History of American Immigration Policy: 1798–1965*. Philadelphia: University of Pennsylvania Press, 1981.

"Immigration Policy and the Rights of Aliens." *Harvard Law Review*. 96 (April 1983): 1286–1465.

Jackson, Jacquelyne Johnson. "Seeking Common Ground for Blacks and Immigrants." In David E. Simcox, ed. *U.S. Immigration in the 1980s: Reappraisal and Reform*. Boulder: Westview Press; Washington, D.C.: Center for Immigration Studies, 1988: 92–115.

Jacobson, David. *Rights Across Borders: Immigration and the Decline of Citizenship*. Baltimore: The Johns Hopkins University Press, 1996.

Joppke, Christian. "Why Liberal States Accept Unwanted Immigration." *World Politics*. 50 (January 1998): 266–293.

Juffras, Jason. *Impact of the Immigration Reform and Control Act on the Immigration and Naturalization Service*. Washington, D.C.: The Urban Institute; Santa Monica, CA: The RAND Corporation, January 1991.

Keohane, Robert O. and Joseph S. Nye, Jr. *Power and Interdependence*. Boston: Little, Brown, 1977.

Konvitz, Milton R. *Civil Rights in Immigration*. Ithaca, NY: Cornell University Press, 1953.

Korey, William. *The Promises We Keep: Human Rights, the Helsinki Process, and American Foreign Policy*. New York: St. Martin's Press in association with the Institute for East West Studies, 1993.

Kossoudji, Sherrie A. "Playing Cat and Mouse at the U.S.-Mexican Border." *Demography*. 29:2 (May 1992): 159–180.

Krasner, Stephen D. "Structural Causes and Regime Consequences: Regimes as Intervening Variables." *International Organization*. 36 (Spring 1982): 185–205.

Lahav, Gallya. "Migration Norms and Constraints in Liberal Democracies: Towards an International Family Reunification Regime." Paper presented at the annual meeting of the International Studies Association, San Diego, CA, April 16–20, 1996.

Lee, Kenneth K. *Huddled Masses, Muddled Laws*. Westport, CT: Praeger, 1998.

Legomsky, Stephen H. *Immigration and the Judiciary: Law and Politics in Britain and America*. Oxford: Clarendon Press, 1987.

———. *Immigration Law and Policy*. Westbury, NY: The Foundation Press, Inc., 1992.

LeMay, Michael C. *From Open Door to Dutch Door: An Analysis of U.S. Immigration Policy Since 1820*. New York: Praeger, 1987.

———. *The Struggle for Influence*. Lanham, MD: University Press of America, 1985.

Loescher, Gil and John A. Scanlan. *Calculated Kindness: Refugees and America's Half-*

Open Door, 1945 to the Present. New York: The Free Press, a Division Of MacMillan, Inc., 1986.

Martin, Philip L. "Good Intentions Gone Awry: IRCA and U.S. Agriculture." *The Annals of the American Academy of Political and Social Science.* 534 (July 1994): 44–57.

———. "Proposition 187 in California." *International Migration Review.* 29:1 (Spring 1995): 255–263.

———. *Trade and Migration: NAFTA and Agriculture.* Washington, D.C.: Institute for International Economics, October 1993.

Massey, Douglas S., Katharine M. Donato, and Zai Liang. "Effects of the Immigration Reform and Control Act of 1986: Preliminary Data from Mexico." In Bean, Edmonston, and Passel, eds. *Undocumented Migration to the United States: IRCA and the Experience of the 1980s.* Washington, D.C.: The Urban Institute; Santa Monica, CA: The RAND Corporation, 1990: 184–210.

Miller, Mark J. *Employer Sanctions in Western Europe: A Report Submitted to the German Marshall Fund of the United States.* New York: Center for Migration Studies, 1987.

———. "Never Ending Story: The U.S. Debate over Illegal Immigration." In Gary P. Freeman and James Jupp, eds. *Nations of Immigrants: Australia, the United States, and International Migration.* Oxford: Oxford University Press, 1992: 56–71.

Montweiler, Nancy Humel. *The Immigration Reform Law of 1986.* Washington, D.C.: The Bureau of National Affairs, Inc., 1987.

Moravcsik, Andrew. "Taking Preferences Seriously: A Liberal Theory of International Politics." *International Organization.* 51:4 (Autumn 1997): 513–553.

Morris, Milton D. *Immigration—The Beleaguered Bureaucracy.* Washington, D.C.: The Brookings Institution, 1985.

North, David S. *Immigration Reform in Its First Year.* Washington, D.C.: Center for Immigration Studies, November 1987.

Nye, Joseph. "Neorealism and Neoliberalism." *World Politics.* 40:2 (1988): 235–251.

Papademetriou, Demetrios G. *Coming Together or Pulling Apart? The European Union's Struggle with Immigration and Asylum.* Washington, D.C.: Carnegie Endowment for International Peace, 1996.

———. "International Migration in North America: Issues, Policies, Implications." In Miroslav Macura and David Coleman, eds. *International Migration: Regional Processes and Responses.* New York and Geneva: United Nations Economic Commission for Europe and United Nations Population Fund, Economic Studies No. 7, 1994: 77–107.

Papademetriou, Demetrios G. and Kimberly A. Hamilton. *Converging Paths to Restriction: French, Italian, and British Responses to Immigration.* Washington, D.C.: Carnegie Endowment for International Peace, 1996.

———. *Managing Uncertainty: Regulating Immigration Flows in Advanced Industrialized Countries.* Washington, D.C.: Carnegie Endowment for International Peace, 1995.

Perotti, Rosanna. "Employer Sanctions and the Limits of Negotiation." *The Annals of the American Academy of Political and Social Science.* 534 (July 1994): 31–43.

Piore, M.J. *Birds of Passage: Migrant Labor and Industrial Societies.* Cambridge: Cambridge University Press, 1979.

Portes, Alejandro. "Of Borders and States: A Skeptical Note on the Legislative Control of Immigration." In Wayne A. Cornelius and Ricardo Anzaldúa Montoya, eds. *America's New Immigration Law: Origins, Rationales, and Potential Consequences.* San Diego: University of California, Center for U.S.-Mexican

Studies, 1983: 17–30.

Proper, Emberson Edward, A.M. *Colonial Immigration Laws.* New York: Columbia University Press, The MacMillan Company, Agents, 1900.

Reimers, David M. *Still the Golden Door: The Third World Comes to America.* 2d ed. New York: Columbia University Press, 1992.

———. "An Unintended Reform: The 1965 Immigration Act and Third World Immigration to the United States." *Journal of American Ethnic History.* 3:1 (Fall 1983): 9–28.

Risse-Kappen, Thomas, ed. *Bringing Transnational Relations Back In.* Cambridge: Cambridge University Press, 1995.

Rolph, Elizabeth S. *Immigration Policies: Legacy from the 1980s and Issues for the 1990s.* Santa Monica, CA: The RAND Corporation, 1992.

Roper Center for Public Opinion Research. "Immigration." *Public Perspective.* 5:2 (January/ February 1994): 97–100.

———. "The Immigration Story." *Public Perspective.* 6:5 (August/ September 1995): 8–17.

Ruggie, John. "International Regimes, Transactions and Change: Embedded Liberalism in the Postwar Economic Order." *International Organization.* 36 (Spring 1982): 379–415.

Sánchez, George J. "Face the Nation: Race, Immigration, and the Rise of Nativism in Late Twentieth Century America." *International Migration Review.* 31:4 (Winter 1997): 1009–1030.

Sassen, Saskia. *Losing Control? Sovereignty in an Age of Globalization.* New York: Columbia University Press, 1996.

Schain, Martin A. "Policy Effectiveness and the Regulation of Immigration in Europe." Paper presented at the annual meeting of the International Studies Association, Chicago, IL, February 21–25, 1995.

Schuck, Peter H. "The Politics of Rapid Legal Change: Immigration Policy in the 1980s." *Studies in American Political Development.* 6 (Spring 1992): 37–92.

———. "The Transformation of Immigration Law." *Columbia Law Review.* 84:1 (January 1984): 1–90.

Schwarz, Carl E. "Employer Sanctions Laws: The State Experience as Compared with Federal Proposals." In Wayne A. Cornelius and Ricardo Anzaldúa Montoya, eds. *America's New Immigration Law: Origins, Rationales, and Potential Consequences.* San Diego: University of California, Center for U.S.-Mexican Studies, 1983: 83–101.

Sikkink, Kathryn. *Ideas and Institutions: Developmentalism in Brazil and Argentina.* Ithaca, NY: Cornell University Press, 1991.

Sorensen, Elaine and Frank D. Bean. "The Immigration Reform and Control Act and the Wages of Mexican Origin Workers: Evidence from Current Population Surveys." *Social Science Quarterly.* 75:1 (March 1994): 1–17.

Vernez, Georges, ed. *Immigration and International Relations: Proceedings of a Conference on the International Effects of the 1986 Immigration Reform and Control Act (IRCA).* Washington, D.C.: The Urban Institute; Santa Monica, CA: The RAND Corporation, May 1990.

Weiner, Myron. "On International Migration and International Relations." *Population and Development Review.* 11:3 (September 1985): 441–455.

Woodrow, Karen A. and Jeffrey S. Passel. "Post-IRCA Undocumented Immigration to the United States: An Assessment Based on the June 1988 CPS." In Bean, Edmonston, and Passel, eds. *Undocumented Migration to the United States: IRCA and the Experience of the 1980s.* Washington, D.C.: The Urban Institute; Santa Monica, CA: The RAND Corporation, 1990: 33–75.

Zolberg, Aristide. "Contemporary Transnational Migrations in Historical Perspective: Patterns and Dilemmas." In Mary M. Kritz, ed. *U.S. Immigration and Refugee Policy*. Lexington, MA: Lexington Books, 1983: 15–51.

———. "International Migrations in Political Perspective." In Mary M. Kritz, Charles B. Keely, and Silvano M. Tomasi, eds. *Global Trends in Migration*. New York: The Center for Migration Studies, 1981: 3–27.

———. "Labour Migration and International Economic Regimes: Bretton Woods and After." In Mary M. Kritz, Lin Lean Lim, and Hania Zlotnik, eds. *International Migration Systems: A Global Approach*. Oxford: Clarendon Press, 1992: 315–334.

———. "The Next Waves: Migration Theory for a Changing World." *International Migration Review*. 23:3 (Fall 1989): 403–430.

GOVERNMENT DOCUMENTS

President's Commission on Immigration and Naturalization. *Whom We Shall Welcome*. Report of the President's Commission on Immigration and Naturalization. Washington, D.C.: U.S. Government Printing Office, 1953.

Select Commission on Immigration and Refugee Policy. *U.S. Immigration Policy and the National Interest*. The Final Report and Recommendations of the Select Commission on Immigration and Refugee Policy to the Congress and President of the United States, March 1, 1981.

U.S. Commission on Civil Rights. *The Tarnished Door: Civil Rights Issues in Immigration*. Washington, D.C.: U.S. Government Printing Office, 1980.

U.S. Congress. Congressional Research Service. *U.S. Immigration Law and Policy: 1952–1979*. 96th Cong., 1st sess. Washington, D.C.: U.S. Government Printing Office, 1979.

———. Congressional Research Service. *Selected Readings on U.S. Immigration Policy and Law*. 96th Cong., 2d sess. Washington, D.C.: U.S. Government Printing Office, October 1980.

———. House Judiciary Committee, *Immigration Control and Legalization Amendments Act of 1986*. Rept. 99–682, Part 1, 99th Cong., 2d sess. Washington, D.C.: U.S. Government Printing Office, 1987.

———. House Subcommittee on Immigration, Citizenship, and International Law. *Hearings on H.R. 982 and Related Bills*. 94th Cong., 1st sess. Washington, D.C.: U.S. Government Printing Office, 1975.

———. House Subcommittee on Immigration and Nationality. *Hearings on H.R. 2580: To Amend the Immigration and Nationality Act*. 89th Cong., 1st sess. Washington, D.C.: U.S. Government Printing Office, 1965.

———. House Subcommittee on Immigration and Nationality. *Hearings on Illegal Aliens*. 92d Cong., 1st and 2d sess. Parts 1–5. Washington, D.C.: U.S. Government Printing Office, 1971, 1972.

———. House Subcommittee on Immigration, Refugees, and International Law. *Hearings on H.R. 1510 (Immigration Reform and Control Act of 1983)*. 98th Cong., 1st sess. Washington, D.C.: U.S. Government Printing Office, 1983.

———. House Subcommittee on Immigration, Refugees, and International Law. *Hearings on the Immigration Act of 1989*. 101st Cong., 1st sess. Washington, D.C.: U.S. Government Printing Office, 1989.

———. House Subcommittee on Immigration, Refugees, and International Law. *Hearings on Immigration Reform*. 97th Cong., 1st sess. Washington, D.C.: U.S. Government Printing Office, 1982.

———. House Subcommittee on Immigration, Refugees, and International Law and Senate Subcommittee on Immigration and Refugee Policy. *Joint Hearings on H.R. 5872 and S. 2222 (Immigration Reform and Control Act of 1982)*. 97th Cong., 2d sess. Washington, D.C.: U.S. Government Printing Office, 1982.

———. Senate Select Committee on Small Business. *Hearings on the Effects of Proposed Legislation Prohibiting the Employment of Illegal Aliens on Small Business*. 94th Cong., 2d sess. Washington, D.C.: U.S. Government Printing Office, 1977.

———. Senate Subcommittee on Immigration and Nationality. *Hearings on S. 500: To Amend the Immigration and Nationality Act*. 89th Cong., 1st sess. Parts 1 and 2. Washington, D.C.: U.S. Government Printing Office, 1965.

———. Senate Subcommittee on Immigration and Naturalization. *Hearings on S. 3074 to Amend the Immigration and Nationality Act and for Other Purposes*. 94th Cong., 2d sess. Washington, D.C.: U.S. Government Printing Office, 1976.

———. Senate Subcommittee on Immigration and Refugee Affairs. *Hearings on Immigration Reform (S. 358 and S. 448)*. 101st Cong., 1st sess. Washington, D.C.: U.S. Government Printing Office, 1990.

———. Senate Subcommittee on Immigration and Refugee Policy. *Hearings on the Knowing Employment of Illegal Immigrants*. 97th Cong., 1st sess. Washington, D.C.: U.S. Government Printing Office, 1982.

U.S. Department of Labor, Bureau of International Labor Affairs. *Developments in International Migration to the United States: 1993*, by Roger G. Kramer. Washington, D.C.: U.S. Department of Labor, 1993.

U.S. Department of State, Bureau of Consular Affairs. *Visa Bulletin*. Vol. 7, No. 34. Washington, D.C.: U.S. Department of State, April 1994.

U.S. Immigration and Naturalization Service. *Statistical Yearbook of the Immigration and Naturalization Service, 1990*. Washington, D.C.: U.S. Government Printing Office, 1991.

———. *Statistical Yearbook of the Immigration and Naturalization Service, 1992*. Washington, D.C.: U.S. Government Printing Office, 1993.

Vialet, Joyce C. and Larry M. Eig. "Immigration Act of 1990 (P.L. 101–649)." Washington, D.C.: Congressional Research Service, Library of Congress, 1990.

Index

About the Author

DEBRA L. DeLAET is Assistant Professor of Political Science at Drake University. Her primary research interests are in the areas of international migration and human rights. She is the co-editor, with Gregory Kelson, of *Gender and Immigration* (1999).

ISBN 0-275-96733-6

90000>

EAN

9 780275 967338

HARDCOVER BAR CODE